Zvia Frankfurt

THE CHALLENGE

Treasure; Heaven; Earth
Creation; Heart; All; Life; Love; Ease; Navigation; Gratitude; Energy

A practical guide
to develop and master
the craftsmanships to live
and thrive in and with sound
happiness, health, love & wealth

Tools and ways
to revive whole hearted joy,
make an A - Z revolution in sets of
beliefs, state of being and mind, thinking patterns.

2nd Edition

Disclaimer:
Zvia Frankfurt offers methodologies and technology as an author, mentor and speaker; certified Universal Energy and Reflexology practitioner and teacher. Zvia is not a licensed health practitioner. The information in this book may not, in any manner or way, substitute any other healing or medicinal usage. It is highly recommended to follow and make use of this book's exercises, methods and/or practices when accompanied and guided by a well experienced, skilled and trained practitioner. Any use of it is at user's own and sole responsibility.

Copyright © Zvia Frankfurt
Health Way Creations
www.zvia-est.com
+972 - 77 - 88 55 216 (land line)
+972 - 50 - 52 15 999 (cellular line)

All rights reserved
Citations in critic and evaluation articles, films, video-clips, internet, radio and TV programmes - including the author's name and the book's title - are welcomed without prior written permission of the author.

All or part of this creation covered by the copyright herein may not - without prior written permission of the author - be reproduced or used in any form or by any means: graphic, electronic or mechanical, including photocopying, recording, taping, or information storage and retrieval systems.

Cover design: Angela Treat Lyon, Zvia Frankfurt
Edit, proofreading: Peg Winecoff, Zvia Frankfurt

ISBN No 978-965-91571-0-5

E & O.E.

TABLE OF CONTENT

Acknowledgements and Credits	xx
Appreciation and Gratitude	xxi
Blessings and Wishes	xxii
Foreword	xxiii
Angela Treat Lyon	xxiii
Brad Yates, C.Ht.	xxiv
Joe Rubino, Dr.	xxvi
Perla Dujouvney-Perez, Dr.	xxvii
About the Author	xxviii
Author's Word	xxix

A

Ability	1
E.S.T. exercise	1
Abortion	4
Abundance	4
Abuse	5
E.S.T. exercise	5
Pre-sent Present Presents	6
H.P.T.	7
Ache	7
Ache relief exercises	8
Ankle ache	9
Back ache	9
Falling, knocking, or striking the head	10
Fingers pain	10
Headache	10
Brain stem / back headache	11
Eyes belt: hoop/ring like ache	11
Forehead	11
Migraines	11
Temples	11
Knee joint ache	11
Additional exercises	11
Pain in the arse/ass	12
Pain in the head	12
Pain in the neck	12
Shoulder pain	12
Stomach ache	13

Additional remedies		14
Addiction	14	
Admonition	15	
Age	16	
Agreement	16	
The Four Agreements		16
Aim	16	
All	17	
Always	17	
Ambiguity	17	
Ambition	17	
Amend-ment - Amendment	17	
Angel	18	
Anger	18	
Anger clearing letter		18
Anxiety	19	
Approach	19	
Argument	19	
Ascension	19	
Attitude	20	
Authenticity	20	
Authority	20	
Awareness	20	
Awe	20	

B

Bad	21	
Balance	21	
Balance cration exercise		21
Beat	21	
Beauty	21	
E.S.T. practice		22
Belief	22	
Best	23	
Betrayal	23	
Betrayer		23
Betterment	25	
Birth	25	
Bite	25	
Bitterness	25	
Frequent anger, bitterness, sourness remedy		25
Gall bladder stones		26
Blindness	26	

Bliss	26	
Blood	26	
Blood pressure		27
Bloom	28	
Blossom	28	
Bread	28	
Breast	28	
Breath	28	
Bride	29	
Bright	29	
Brotherhood	29	
Bruise	29	
Remedies		30
Bud	30	
Burden	30	
Business	30	

C

Cancer	31		
E.S.T. remedies		33	
Emotional, soul and spirit nourishment		34	
An easy and simple exercise		36	
Additional remedies		36	
Foods			37
Herbs			37
Outdoors activities		37	
Indoors activities		37	
Indoors and outdoors activities		37	
Cleansing, purifying		38	
Capillary	39		
Remedies		39	
Care	39		
E.S.T. exercise		39	
Careerism	39		
Caress	40		
Cavity	40		
Cell	40		
Chain	40		
E.S.T. remedy		40	
Chance	41		
Character	41		
Charge	41		
Cheapness	41		
Chest	42		

Child	42	
Choice	47	
Clarity	47	
Clarity creation exercise		48
Remedies		48
Class	48	
Closeness	48	
Coma	49	
Commit-ment - Commitment	49	
Common-sense - Commonsense	49	
Company	49	
Compass-i-on - Compassion	50	
Complaint	50	
Completion	50	
Complex	50	
Compulsion	51	
Concept	51	
Concurrence	51	
Confidence	51	
Connection	51	
Consciousness	52	
Constipation	52	
Remedies		52
Contempt	54	
Contentment	54	
Contusion	55	
Remedies		55
Core	55	
Courage	55	
Cramp	56	
E.S.T. exercise		56
Cream	57	
E.S.T. remedies		57
Nappies rush		58
Apple vinegar compress		58
Creation	58	
Creativity creation exercise		59
Criticism	59	
Cry	59	
Culture	60	
Cure	60	
Curse	60	
E.S.T. exercise, blessing creation		61
Custom	62	
Cynic	62	

Cynicism 62
The Four Agreements 62

D

Dare 64
Darkness 64
Death 65
Decision 65
Deed 65
Delight 66
Depression 66
Desire 66
Despair 66
Destiny 66
    The 2nd Agreement 67
Diarrhea 67
Difference 67
Dignity 68
Diligence 68
Dis-appointment - Disappointment 68
Dis-cover-y - Discovery 68
Dis-ease - Disease 69
Diversity 69
Do 69
Dread 69
    Freeze 70
    Flight 70
    Fight 70
    E.S.T. exercise 70
Dream 72
    Happy dream creation 73
Drink 73
Duty 73
Dwarf 74
Dye 74

E

Ease 75
Effort 75
Ego 75
Embrace 76
E-motion 76
Endeavour 77

Energy	77	
Enthusiasm	77	
Epilepsy	78	
Err-or - Error	79	
E.S.T. exercise to discover a hidden truth		79
Escape	80	
Examination	80	
Ex-pensive-ness - Expensiveness	82	
Experience	82	
Eye	82	

F

Failure	83	
Pre-sent Present Presents		83
Faith	83	
Fake	84	
Fare	84	
Fate	84	
Fault	84	
Fear	85	
Female	86	
Festival	87	
Fight	87	
Fixation	87	
Flight	87	
For(e)-give-ness - Forgiveness	88	
Foul	88	
Foul play		88
Fraction	88	
Fracture		88
Fragment	89	
Fraud	90	
Freedom	90	
Freshness	90	
Fright	90	
Fruition	91	
Frustration	91	
Fun	91	
Fury	91	

G

Gaiety	92	
Gall	92	

Gall bladder stone	92
Gall bladder & liver cleansing	92
Gall bladder stones, severe constipation	93
Game	93
Gastritis	93
Gate	94
Generosity	94
Good	94
Grace	94
Gratification	94
Gratitude	95
Growth	95
Grow into	95
Grow out	95
Grow up	95
Growth & immunity system acceleration	95
Exercise	95
Grudge	96
Guilt	96
Gum	96
Remedies	96
Gum bleeding	97
Gum infection	97
Clove bud infusion	97
Gingival	97

H

Habit	98
Habitat	98
Habitation	98
Happiness	98
Hardness	99
Hard drug	99
Hard-fisted	99
Hard-handed	99
Hard-head	99
Heard-headed	99
Additional exercises	100
Hard-hearted	101
Hard-ship - Hardship	101
Hardihood	102
Harmony	102
Hate	102
Head	102

Health	103	
Heart	103	
Heartache		103
Heartbreak		103
Letting Go fun exercise		105
Heaven	105	
Heaviness	106	
Hell	106	
Hematoma	106	
A Word Keeps The Doctor Away		106
Remedies		108
Here	111	
Hi-story - History	111	
Holiday	111	
Home	112	
Honesty	112	
The customer is right		112
Hope	114	
Host-ility - Hostility	114	
Humility	114	
Hunger	115	
Husband	115	
Practices		115
Hypocrisy	116	
Hypo		116
Hyster-i-a(m) - Hysteria	116	
Hyster		117

I

Ice	118	
Ice cream	118	
I'll-temper - Ill-temper	118	
Ill-us-i-on - Illusion	118	
Illustration	118	
Imagination	119	
Immunity	119	
I'm-possibility - Impossibility	119	
I'm-potency - Impotency	119	
I'm-pulse - Impulse	120	
Infection	120	
Inferiority complex	120	
In-flam(e) (e)-mat(e)i-on - Inflammation	121	
In-flue-nce - Influence	124	
Influenza		124

Initiative	124	
Inspiration	125	
Integrity	125	
Intimacy	125	
Intimidation	126	
Intuition	126	

J

Jail	127	
Jam	127	
Jealousy	127	
Joy	127	
Jubilation	128	
Just-ice - Justice	128	
Just-if-i-ca(tio)n - Justification	128	

K

Keep	129		
Keeping		129	
Kick	129		
Kidney	129		
Kidney stones		129	
Remedies		130	
Indian corn hair infusion			130
Kin	130		
Kindness	131		
Kiss	131		
Know	131		
Know-how		131	
Knowledge		131	
You know		131	

L

Labour/Labor	133	
E.S.T. exercise		133
Pre-sent Present Presents		134
H.P.T.		134
Lamentation(s)	135	
Lash	135	
Laugh	136	
Laughter		136
E.S.T. exercise to create & develop laughter		136
Law	136	

The Law of Attraction	137	
Leave	137	
Length	137	
Letter	138	
Lie	138	
The 2nd Agreement	138	
Life	139	
Light	140	
Limit	140	
Line	140	
Live-r - Liver	140	
Liver cleansing	141	
Aggression clearing letter	141	
More remedies	142	
Herbs		142
Apple vinegar		142
Longing	142	
Loss	143	
Love	143	
Loyalty	145	

M

Mad	146	
Marvel	146	
Maturity	146	
Meditation	146	
Memory	147	
Memory development exercise		147
Happy memory creation		148
Memory absence/loss		149
Mentality	149	
Mercy	149	
Milestone	150	
Mind	150	
Miracle	150	
Miser	152	
Mis-take - Mistake	152	
E.S.T. exercise, discover mis-take is in the eye of the beholder		152
Mood	153	
Morality	153	
Ethics		153
Virtue		153
Mourning	154	

N

Naïveté	155	
Narrow	155	
Narrow-hearted		155
Narrow-mind		155
Nature	155	
Second nature		155
Nausea	156	
Navigation	156	
Necessity	156	
Neck	157	
Nerve	157	
Night-mare - Nightmare	157	
For a child waking up		157
For the child within mature me		158
No	158	
Noise	159	
Nose	159	

O

Occupation	160
Operation	160
Opportunism	160
Opportunity	160
Oppression	161
Order	161
Ore	161
Out	161
Out-rage - Outrage	161

P

Pain	163	
Palpitation	163	
Pancreas	163	
Paradise	164	
Partner	164	
Partnership		164
Pass-i-on - Passion	164	
Peace	165	
Person	166	
Phobia	166	
Pit-y - Pity	166	

Plea-sure - Pleasure	167	
Poison	167	
Poisoning cleansing		168
Poison clearing letter		169
The Four Agreements		169
Possibility	170	
Potency	170	
Poverty	170	
PIGEES Formula		170
Power	171	
Power Of The Word		171
Ho'oponopono		175
Presence	176	
Pre-sent present present		176
Five principles to a pre-sent present presents		176
Prison	177	
Prosperity	177	
Punishment	177	
The Four Agreements		178

Q

Qualification	179	
Quality	179	
Quantity	179	

R

Race	180	
Rage	180	
E.S.T. exercise		180
Rage clearing letter		181
Rape	182	
Rash	182	
Additional remedies		183
Reality	183	
Realization	184	
Reason	184	
Reason and Passion		184
Reception	185	
Recognition	185	
Re-cover-y - Recovery	185	
Reflection	186	
Regret	186	

Rejection	186	
Relationship	189	
Relief	189	
Relish	189	
Remembrance	189	
E.S.T. exercises		190
Remorse	190	
Kidney stones		191
Indian corn hair infusion		191
Re(ap)proach - Reproach	191	
Re-sent-ment - Resentment	192	
Resilience	192	
Resistance	192	
Respect	193	
The Four Agreements		193
Response	193	
Responsibility	194	
Retardation	194	
Riches	194	
Ride	194	
Right	195	
Root	195	
Root canal		195
Rout-in-e - Routine	196	
Ruin	196	
Rush	196	
Remedies		197

S

Sadism	198	
Sadness	198	
E.S.T. exercise		198
Satisfaction	199	
Scar	199	
Scarcity	199	
Scare	199	
Sea	200	
Self	200	
Sensation	201	
Sense		201
Sensibility		201
Sensitivity		201
Sensualism		202
Serenity	202	

Sex	202	
Anal intercourse		202
Oral intercourse		203
Sexual harassment		203
Sexual intercourse		203
Sexuality		204
Shame and shyness: Shame	207	
Shyness		207
Shock	208	
Short	208	
Additional remedies		208
For a child whose height potential is greater than manifested		209
Should-er - Shoulder	209	
Should		209
To give a shoulder		209
Shoulder remedies		210
Side	211	
Sight	212	
Silence	212	
Simplicity	212	
Sincerity	212	
Skill	213	
Slavery	213	
Small	213	
Smell	213	
Smile	214	
Sobriety	214	
E.S.T. exercise		214
Sorrow	214	
Spite	215	
Status	215	
Step	215	
Stone	215	
Gall bladder and liver cleansing		216
Gall bladder stones		216
Kidney stones		216
Indian corn hair infusion		217
Storm	217	
Strength	218	
Stress	218	
I am stress free when I fret not and fuss not		218
Study	222	
Stupidity	222	

Success	222
Sugar	223
Survival	223
Sweet	223
Sympathy	224

T

Target	225
Taste	225
Tear	225
Temper	225
Temperature	226
High temperature remedies	227
Tender	229
Tension	229
Terror	229
Test	231
Thread	231
Throat	232
Remedies	232
Tie	232
Timidity	233
Tongue	233
Tongue cramps	233
Tooth	234
Trait	235
Tranquillity	235
Trauma	236
Treat	236
Trial	236
Trust	237
Truth	237
The Four Agreements	237
Turn	238

U

Ugly	239
Under	239
Up	239

V

Vacancy	240
Value	240

Veil	240
Vibration	240
Vict-I'm - Victim	241
Vigour/Vigor	241
Villain	241
Violence	241
Vocation	243

W

War	244	
In the raw		244
Waste	245	
Water	245	
Way	245	
Wealth	246	
Weapon	246	
The Four Agreements		246
Weep	247	
Well	247	
Whip	247	
Whip-lash		248
Whole	248	
Wife	248	
Wild	248	
E.S.T. exercise		248
Will	249	
Will and Have		249
Wind	250	
Wisdom	250	
Wish	251	
Woe	252	
Word	252	
Ho'oponopono		252
Work	253	
Worry	253	
Wound	254	
Wrath	254	
Wreck	254	
Wretch	254	
Wrong	255	

X

Xerography	256

X-ray	256

Y

Yawn	257
Yearning	257
Yell	257
Yelp	257
Yes	258
Yield	258
Young	258
The 2nd Agreement	258
Youth	259

Z

Zap	260
Zeal	260
Zenith	260
Zephyr	260
Zero	260
Zest	261
Zigzag	261
Zing	261
Zombie	261

Epilogue

Drawings

Tapping Points chart	6, 71, 134, 181
Liver, Spleen, Thymus Glands	35
Thymus gland	36, 96, 209
Pre-sent presents present	176

Web-site Links

Willie Skratter's laughing baby	38, 136, 199
Larry Crane, youtube video clips	167, 222
Brad Yates, youtube video clips	219

Acknowledgements and credits

[1] Karen Bishop, 2006, www.whatsuponplanetearth.com, www.gamabooks.com "create heaven in your heart, starlight in your soul,…miracles in your life," pp. xxiii, xxx.

[2] Zvia Frankfurt, www.zvia-est.com
EST charts, Tapping points pp. 6, 71, 134, 181
Liver, Spleen Thymus points   pp. 35, 36, 96, 209

[3] Dean Shrock, Dr, 2010, www.deanshrock.com, "I am one with all there is," pp. 6, 83, 134

[4] Rebecca Marina, 2007, www.celebrationhealing.com, H.P.T., 7, 134

[5] Gino (disarmuwithasmile, netgammon), 2010, Pastis (French), pp. 14

[6] Ruiz, Miguel, 1998, Los cuatro acuerdos "Un libro de sabiduría tolteca." Ediciones Urano. México D.F., México. ISBN 848623253X, The Four Agreements, pp. 16, 62, 67, 138, 169, 178, 193, 237, 246, 258

[7] Donna Eden, 2010, www.innersource.net, Balance exercise, pp. 21

[8] Louise L. Hay, You Can Heal Your Life book, Beauty, pp. 22

[9] Willie Skratter, Laughing baby video clip, pp. 38, 136, 199

[10] Gwen Bonnel, 2005, www.tapintoheaven.com, pp. 48, pp. 190

[11] Gabriel Strassman, 1982, "The customer is right… sometimes," Ma'ariv, pp. 112

[12] Angela Treat Lyon, 2005, www.PIGEES.com, PIGEES pp. 170

[13] Ihaleakala Hew Len, Ph.D.
www.zero-wise.com, Ho'opnopono, pp. 175, 252

[14] Eyar Zuckerman, 2007, May 8, pp. 176

[15] Gibran Kahlil Gibran, 1923, The Prophet, Reason and passion, pp. 184

[16] Mordechi Katz, 2012, katmor@012.net.il, https//sites.google.com/site/katzspa, Gin/Vodka, pp. 228, Eucalyptus globules, pp. 232

Peg Winecoff, bonitabelle@windstream.net, Brain-storming, counseling, editing, proofreading

Ezra Narkis, www.narkisbooks.co.il, Interior pages face image and settings ideas

Appreciation and Gratitude

TO YOU reader,

Avram (b.h.m.) my father for his whole hearted love, sharing, support and will "if there is a chance that you shall be happy there than leave."
Pesia (b.h.m.) my mother whom I transformed from an enemy to a loving mother, soul's friend, spiritual-mate, supporting partner, and more; her infinite belief, confidence, faith, love and wisdom that enabled me to publish this book after she summed-up our last conversation with "dreams come true."
My ever encouraging, generous, inspiring, loving, noble, surprising, supportive and wonderful family in Israel, Mexico, U.K., Uruguay, and USA.

Sandi Weisfeld 'Chanukah', Larry Costanzo, Panayiota Petridou 'tats', 'Phivos', Sylvia Larson from the Shesh-besh (backgammon), Jack Lovell, John Battye, Sigahl Silvera for being a brain storming partners.

Special gratitude to Rachel Tal, Angel-A Treat Lyon, and Peg Winecoff - for their cheering, generosity, guidance, inspiration and presents.

Jose (pepe) Castelazo y J. Alicia Saldaña, Mexico, George Abu-Jarour, The Dominican Republic, Christopher Barton, United Kingdom, Burton A. Amernick, Washington DC, Glen P. Trudel, Delaware, U.S.A.; Gerard Ben Guigui, Paris, France, Mathew West and Baba Elefante CA, U.S.A. and others whose interest in my creation encouraged and nourished me to create in English.

Blessings and Wishes

TO YOU dear reader,

May you find among this book's stories and values health, pre-sent present presents manifestation and realization; emotional, mental and spiritual intelligence greatness and genius results and rewards.

May you find useful exercises and practices to succeed in challenging old and young into youthfulness. Cheerfully delve, delightfully explore, improve and reach new conditions, customs, habits, manners, patterns, perceptions, sets, views and ways, easily overcome barriers, straits, vast planes and prairies, enthusiastically break through way's breaks, enjoy and rejoice accomplishment, appreciation, authenticity, brilliance, comfort, confidence, courage, faith, fulfillment, fun, happiness, honesty, integrity, greatness, magnificence, peace, pure whole hearted cry and laughter, satisfaction, serenity, sincerity, tranquillity, wellness and wealth. May the knowledge and the technology in this book lead and fill your life with sheer bliss, jubilation, love and simplicity of will-powered reality, inspiration, intention, creativity, awareness, attention and action.

Foreword

In The Challenge, you shall find a new world of words, where you can turn things upside down in a new way, every day. Break the rules and break through: discover unique exercises, practices and stories from Author Zvia Frankfurt's own life that help you solve your own challenges, too.

If you desire change, to add more creativity to your life or to follow your heart and make your dreams come true, The Challenge gives you a way to transform your state of mind and thinking patterns from A to Z.

Break out of conventional thought! Discover and delve into new inner realms! You will be entranced as you create new realities, play with esoteric knowledge, create joy, health, love and wealth within fascinating new horizons.

You shall love how The Challenge reveals hidden blessings in times of crisis and recession. If you enjoy word play, where age is one letter short of rage, anger is one letter short of danger...
...then you will love how The Challenge brings you fascinating ways to create, evolve and experience your heart's desire and passion in a pre-sent present presents reality.

May The Challenge challenge you to choose, compose and create heaven in your heart, starlight in your soul, daily miracles in your life[1], abundant love, laughter, passion and wisdom's fruits all around you, all the time!

Angela Treat Lyon
www.AngelaTreatLyon.com
www.eftineveryhome.com
www.pigees.com/abouts.html
808-261-0941

From the moment I first took a look at Zvia Frankfurt's "The Challenge," it was apparent that the book was aptly named. It certainly challenged my expectations, and at first I wasn't sure what to make of it.

And what I came to realize is that this is the genius of the book you are now reading.

There is great truth in the well-worn saying that "If you always do what you've always done, you'll always get what you've always gotten." Since our actions are caused by our thoughts, then it is also true that if we always think what we have always thought, we are going to always do what we have always done.

If we want things to be different, we are going to need to do different things - and that will require us to think differently. Ms. Frankfurt is here to challenge us to do just that.

It is a necessary part of life that we learn to take certain things for granted, so that we do not need to relearn everything each day. We are secure in the knowledge that when we get up in the morning, our feet will go to the floor, rather than float up to the ceiling. We are secure in the knowledge of where our clothes are, where the bathroom is, and a multitude of other bits of information that will be required for getting through the day ahead.

Resting 'secure' in too much knowledge leaves us little freedom to think differently, though. As we stop considering ideas and just accept them as given, we also allow them to control us. We are triggered by words and events at a sub-conscious level, and then think and feel certain things in a habitual way, whether it is for our highest good or not. Much of what we take for granted needs to be challenged. Many dependable - but limiting - concepts need to be taken apart and reexamined to see if they are really working for us.

"The Challenge" is a reference guide - a book to pick up and digest in no particular order, except the one that feels right for you. On each page of this book, you will have the opportunity to look at terms you may have thought you understood - 'secure in your knowledge' about what they meant - and then see them taken apart. In the process, the old programming is interrupted and loses
its ability to limit you.

Through stories and prescriptions for various remedies, Ms. Frankfurt offers a path forward out of the past upsets that certain concepts may have caused. And you may find some of these challenging as well. Again, this is exactly what the doctor ordered. Without being challenged, we stay stuck. And if staying stuck were your goal, you wouldn't have picked this book up in the first place. Notice any resistance, and remember that thinking what you've always thought and doing what you've always done got you what you've always gotten - and you deserve better.

Perhaps you have a snow globe from some souvenir shop. As it sits on the shelf, you get used to it looking the way it does, and take it for granted. But to appreciate it for what it truly can be, you need to shake it up. "The Challenge" will help you shake things up, so that you can break out of the rut of what seemed to be a given - and you can more fully experience life for what it truly can be. You deserve that.

Be Magnificent!

Brad

Brad Yates, C.Ht.
916-729-0348
brad@bradyates.net
www.bradyates.net

Our lives are comprised of a multitude of experiences, emotions, interpretations, and judgments. To fully appreciate the good, we must have had access to the bad. To know happiness is impossible without realizing what it's like to be sad. Life is filled with these dichotomies and ironies. We can't have up without down, front without back, enlightenment without darkness. We want only the good and fear and resent the bad. Our relationship to problems is typically weak or detrimental at best... we try to avoid them at all costs out of an assumption that they are always bad. We fail to recognize that our greatest growth comes as a result of our most challenging issues.

Furthermore, all of these experiences involve judgments and interpretations. All challenges contain within them the gifts that can lead to our evolvement, enlightenment, education, and soul growth. Whether we come away from a complexed or painful situation embittered, resigned, and down on life, or with new insights that can lead to the expansion of possibilities and the enhancement of our lives is a function of how we see the situation and the interpretations we apply to the challenges we experience. All too often, we remain stuck in a vicious drama cycle that feeds our reactive state to life giving us plenty of reason to be angry, sad, or afraid. We choose interpretations that allow us to be right, make another person wrong, keep the status quo in place, or somehow avoid taking responsibility for all aspects of our lives. We struggle, suffer, and fail - forgetting that these reactions are always optional. We forget to live with gratitude for all of our challenging experiences, not realizing the blessings that they can be to our lives. We forgo empathy and choose self-righteousness instead, forgetting that we have the least tolerance in others for those qualities we detest in ourselves. We too often decide not to forgive those who make mistakes while taking pleasure in the dark emotions of anger, hatred, and domination whenever we choose to believe that we are better than others.

We all are inherently magnificent. And there are many paths to discovering and encouraging our internal brilliance. Enlightenment can come in a multitude of ways. The definitions, memories, exercises, stories, and insights you'll find in the following chapters can provide you with the tools, breakthroughs, and gifts that you require to go from wherever you are in life to the next level. I challenge and encourage you to keep an open mind, suspend judgment, and allow yourself the luxury of experiencing the insights that are to follow. By all means, have fun, expect breakthroughs, and enjoy the process.

Wishing you magnificence,

Dr. Joe Rubino

Founder,
Creator,

CenterForPersonalReinvention.com
TheSelfEsteemBook.com

Dear Zvia,

I read the book which expresses you. Your creativity, honesty, emotional and mental richness.

This is a very original book. An autobiography, written very originally. Each and every word is part of deep experience. The healing practices are very personal and cannot be debated.

Yes, there is a lot of love and this is the most important message; The love, the hope, the faith in human spirit and soul - and in this, maybe unintentionally, manifests Erich Fromm's humane philosophy, appointing love as source for the human happiness and health - with whom as a professional I sympathize.

The beauty of the book is in the lightness in which it can be read and the free association streaming through it.

I loved the children counseling very much. I accept this approach very much.

A friendly book, expressing the author herself.

Perla Dujouvney-Perez,
D.M.D. Cl., Psych. M.A.

About the Author

Zvia Frankfurt came out from the maternity ward to live in boarding houses and boarding schools. She absorbed ideals, theories and values of the Hashomer Ha'zair youth movement.
Aharon Yoel Hazan (Hacohen), a Rabbi and an author, was one of her great-grandfathers. The grandparents she knew were a Hasidic (Lubavicher) man and a medicine and business woman; her parents were homestead pioneers.

She healed from Asthma in her childhood, from Epilepsy (Petit-Mal) in her youth. Essential and important components in her healing were moves she made from Ma'anit socially pressure-cooking life-style to Tel Aviv and Hod Hasharon workaholic one.

In 1973, a year after she finished high school, life called her to the teacher's podium, she lectured on kibbutz life to Canadian and U.S.A. College students. In 1976 she did it in Yale University. In 1977 life called her to the leader's podium, she became in charge of 120 volunteers from all over the world, and when volunteers from Great Britain and Ireland asked her to teach them Hebrew, she made their dream come true.

In 1997 she embarked Health Way Creations to transform her black (See: Courage, pp. 55) and broken heart to a joyful, open, peaceful, protected, trusting and vivacious one. She made an agreement with her-self to spread goodness, fill and realize her life's calling, inspire, motivate, teach and vivify people to every day create and live dreams come true, enjoy angels and miracles in her and their lives in a heaven on earth reality.

In 2006 she was Israel Reflexology Association chair woman and in 2010 following her free-bird heart and spirit she moved on to north Israel where she is living more dreams come true, her heart sings and her soul and spirit freely and naturally fly.

She is an author, mentor and speaker in her pre-sent present life.

Author's Word

*To
every human
there is a birth right and
open pathways to challenge
hyster-i('m)a to hi-story; to
choose, compose and create
her/his book of life and living,
as pleases her/his spirit,
rights her/his soul,
and suits her/his
heart.*

It is recommend to randomly open this book, let your e-motion, inspiration and intuition guide you into an eye opening idea, reveal or unveil an aspect, detail, perception, perspective or remedy.

To breakthrough conventions into the immediate core, the heart of the matter, I intuitively created abbreviations from words. Complexity creation, putting together, taking apart is challenging, easy, exciting, fun, interesting, serving and simple than perplexity.

The repetitions in this book originate in the dawn of infancy when we intuitively, naturally and successfully found ways to delve, explore and pass reality and trial tests. The baby's cry expressed need and opened a way to attract attention, supply and support. The first standing on our feet and step, every time anew, opened new ways to delve and explore new worlds, founded and stabilized conditions, customs, habits, patterns, perceptions, sets, views and ways. In perceptions such as: 'What is seen from here is unseen from there'; 'What I was unable to do then or see there, I am able to do here, see now'; that each and every change, condition, habit, manner, pattern, perception, stance, stand, set, view-point and way transformation originated in the ability to act, clarify, commit, dedicate, decide, delve, determine, develop, devote, integrate, love, persist, take responsibility, think, and trust e-motion, inspiration and intuition intelligence and mental skills. A change, re-formation or trans-formation of approach, attitude, behaviour, belief, concept, custom, habit, manner, pattern, perception, stance, stand, set, thought, view, way, or word is creation's secret, the matter of every matter's root.

I gathered the courage to dare expose and share with you, trusting you can benefit, better, experience and live your way, follow your heart, realize your dreams and live your passions through the creation and maintenance of healthy connections between and with the bodies constructing you - the human - as one complete and whole universe: Spirit, Soul, Physics - blood and flesh, E-motions (energy-motion).

My hi-stories are told with humour, in a matter-of fact manner. Few are short, others are long and may seem tedious to you, yet to me they manifest living miracles and dreams come true. Within them you shall come to know-how, prescriptions and techniques that allow and enable me to dare experience the art of creation, craftsmanship development and mastering of dormant gifts, skills and talents that here and now turn

Impossible to I'm-possible
child's cry - the vict-I'm
to the mature chant - vict-Or
joy and jubilation.

May this book challenge, drive, inspire, motivate and serve you to realize the blessings within the c(o)urse, create heaven in your heart, starlight in your soul, and daily miracles in your life[1].

Know enough sadness to know mature for(e)-give-ness,
Know enough sorrow to know youthful living grace,
happiness, love, passion and wisdom's fruits.

Note: The Challenge Vol. 1 Kindle book differs from this edition and www.zvia-est.com e-shop edition.
I am perfect in my imperfection may show in settings and text. Please be free and feel welcomed to write me of any mis-take you find and it's location. I thank you in advance for doing so.

A

Ability: power to do something, skill or talent.

Awareness; **B**est; **I**ntuition; **L**ove; **I**nitiative; **T**reasure; **Y**es

E.S.T. (*) **exercise to ability, awareness, confidence, diligence, esteem, flexibility and posture development**

♦ It is recommended to practice this exercise along a sea shore, country road, lawn, with bare feet or wearing socks.
Important!
When practicing the exercise:
1.   Listen to your breath.
2.   Hum or sing "It is possible, each and everyway is open, I am always at the right place on the right time, my life is divinely orchestrated, as long as I sing." You may add phrases like: "I am ability," "I am brilliance," "I am capability," "I am elastic and flexible," "I am happiness," "I am potency," "I am success," "I act on inspiration," "All is in divine and in perfect orchestration, order and timing…"
3.   Concentrate and focus on relaxing and posture, in every part of your body. When you feel your self tense up, stop, take several deep breaths, let your self relax.
4.   It is essential to make this exercise fun and joyful. Humour, whole hearted smile and laughter are great components.

Stage 1
♦ Estimate or measure the course length along which you choose to practice this exercise.
♦ For the first times select a course that is a few metres/yards long.
♦ To the experienced hikers among us it is recommended to choose a course a few tens of metres/yards long.
♦ Divide the course, in your mind, to equally short distances, help yourself to using mile stones/signs along the course, a slightly differing distance between them is of minor importance.

Part 1:
♦ Walk with both feet straight forward.

Part 2:
♦ Walk on your tip toes, with both feet straight forward.

Part 3:

(*) E.S.T.: Esteem Self Transformation

♦ Walk with both feet pointing outward, Charlie Chaplin style.

Part 4:
♦ Walk on your heels, with both feet straight forward.

Part 5:
♦ Walk with both feet pointing inwards.

Part 6:
♦ Walk backwards, with both feet straight forward, along a few metres/yards only.

Part 7:
♦ Walk sideways, <u>right shoulder</u> leading the way, head looking straight forward (not in direction of progress), along a few metres/yards only.

Part 8:
♦ Walk sideways, <u>left shoulder</u> leading the way, head looking straight forward (not in direction of progress), along a few metres/yards only.

Proceed to stage 2 after this stage feels easy and fun.

Stage 2
♦ Gradually increase the length of each part in stage 1 to a few tens of metres/yards, and a total course of a few hundreds of metres/yards.

Proceed to stage 3 after this part feels easy and fun.

Stage 3 - Part 1:
♦ Walk with both feet straight forward along approximately 50 metres/54-55 yards.

Part 2:
♦ Walk on your tip toes, with both feet straight forward, along approximately 50 metres/54-55 yards.

Part 3:
♦ Place your weight <u>on the outside</u> of your feet, toes <u>pointing outward</u>, and walk along a couple of metres/a few yards at most.

Part 4:
♦ Walk on your heels, along approximately 50 metres/54-55 yards.

Part 5:
♦ Place your weight <u>on the inside</u> of your feet, toes <u>pointing inwards</u>, and walk along a couple of metres/a few yards at most.

Part 6:
♦ Walk backwards, with both feet pointing straight ahead, along 10 metres/10-11 yards only.

Part 7:
♦ Walk sideways, <u>right shoulder leading</u> the way, head looking straight forward (not in direction of progress), along 10 metres/10-11 yards only.

Part 8:
♦ Walk sideways, <u>left shoulder leading</u> the way, head looking straight forward (not in direction of progress), along 10 metres/10-11

yards only.

Proceed to the next stage after this stage feels easy and fun.

Stage 4:
♦ Gradually increase the distances to tens and hundreds of metres/yards courses, making the complete whole course a few kilometers/miles long.

Stage 5 - part 1:
♦ Walk with both feet straight forward, so long that it feels comfortable.

Part 2:
♦ Walk <u>on your tip toes with both feet straight forward</u>, along a few metres/yards course only.

Part 3:
♦ Walk <u>on your tip toes with both feet directed outward and heels inwards</u>, along a few metres/yards course only.

Part 4:
♦ Walk <u>on your tip toes, with both feet directed inwards and heels outwards</u>, along a few metres/yards course only.

Part 5:
♦ Walk <u>on the outside of your feet, toes pointing straight forward</u>, for as long as it feels easy.

Part 6:
♦ Walk <u>on the outside of your feet, toes directed outward</u>, for as long as it feels nice.

Part 7:
♦ Walk <u>on the outside of your feet, toes directed inward</u>, for as long as it feels pleasant.

Part 8:
♦ Walk <u>on your heels, with feet directed straight forward</u>, for as long as it feels right.

Part 9:
♦ Walk <u>on your heels, with feet pointing outward</u>, along a few metres/yards course only.

Part 10:
♦ Walk <u>on your heels, with feet pointing inwards</u>, along a few metres/yards course only.

Part 11:
♦ Walk with your weight placed on the inside of your feet, <u>toes pointing forward</u>, for as long as you feel like it.

Part 12:
♦ Walk with your weight placed on the inside of your feet, <u>toes pointing outward</u>, for as long as it pleases you.

Part 13:
♦ Walk with your weight placed on the inside of your feet, <u>toes pointing inward</u>, for as long as it feels right to you.

Part 14:
♦ Walk backwards with both feet directed straight forward until you are filled with cheerfulness and are satisfied with your progress.
Part 15:
♦ Walk sideways, <u>right side shoulder leading</u>, looking straight forward (not sideways to see where you are heading to) until you fill with "Yes I made it," delight and enthusiasm.
Part 16:
♦ Walk sideways, <u>left side shoulder leading</u>, looking straight forward (not sideways to see where you are heading to).

Freely play with different combinations of the above parts, paying attention to your breath, heart, soul and spirit.

Aim, concentrate and focus on big, far-fetched, uplifting goals, ideas, targets, thoughts and words.

As a baby, I lifted up my head, turned from side to side, crawled, sat, stood and only then did I take my first step, practicing each stage until it became comfortable, natural, stable, sure, and turned into a custom.

When I began with a small, simple and short distance, and gradually enlarged and expanded the distance and the time frames, I gained the ability and skill to master the aches, anguish, anxiety, pains, stress and become tension free.

Abortion: the stopping of an illness, infection, etc., at a very early stage. Anything that fails to develop, progress, or mature, as a design or project. Miscarriage, abortive attempt, misfire, failure. Biol. The arrested development of an organ or an embryo at a more or less early stage. Any malformed or monstrous person, thing, etc. The expulsion of a human fetus within the first twelve weeks of pregnancy, before it is viable.

Affection; **B**irth; **O**asis; **R**ejuvenation;
Time; **I**mmunity; **O**rchestration; **N**ewborn
Awareness; **B**lessing; **O**rientation;
Refinement; **T**reasure; **I**nner self; **O**pening; **N**ext

E.S.T. Exercise - see: pp. 5

Abundance: an extremely plentiful or over sufficient quantity or supply. Affluence; wealth.

Ability; **B**reath; **U**nity; **N**eatness;
Dance; **d**are; **A**ction; **a**ttitude; **N**ow; **C**larity; **E**ducation

See: Wisdom, pp. 250

Abuse: wrong or improper use; misuse. Harshly or coarsely insulting language. Bad or improper treatment; maltreatment. A corrupt or improper practice or custom. Obs. Deception; misrepresentation.

Affection; **B**rilliance; **U**nity; **S**implicity; **E**ntity

See: Foul play, pp. 88

E.S.T. exercise[*]

1. Find a place and a time in which you feel comfortable, free and safe to practice emotional and spiritual transformation. You may practice while walking, sitting or lying down. Sit with your back straight, head up, both your feet firmly on the floor/ground. Lie down with your legs, back and head straight on a mattress, floor or ground (i.e. all body parts are within mattress frame, no bent knees, nape or neck). Use a pillow to ease stress and tension in knees, or rolled towel under the nape (back and head resting on mattress). You are here to experience change, be open to awareness, listen to your e-motions.

2. Set the jug and glass within easy reach, the paper, pen or pencil on a desk or a firm surface on which you are comfortable to write. On the paper draw a 10 - 0 e-motion scale, 10 = strongest e - motion, 0 = zero e- motion.

3. Write down words and/or phrases that came up while you were listening to your inner self. These words and phrases are your key-phrases and key-words to insert in the following sentences:
Although I…[*] I completely and deeply love myself.
Although I…[*] I whole heartedly honour myself.
I deeply and fully for-e-give and accept myself although…[*].

4. Start gentle tapping with one hand's fingers tips on the outer-side of your other hand (The Karate chop point), or gently massaging - in a clockwise-direction - your sore-chest points (marked **S** in the chart). While gently tapping with your finger tips on the Karate chop point or massaging the sore-chest points start saying, out loud, the

---
[*] E.S.T. is also known as Tapping, E.F.T. (Emotional Freedom Technique) and M.T.T. (Meridian Tapping Technique).
[*] fill with key-words, key-phrases

phrases and words you wrote down in stage 3 above.

Let words flow freely and refrain from corrections.

Repeat this step until you feel ready for the next stage.

5. Move to repeat, saying out loud, the key-phrases and/or key-words you wrote in stage 3 above while gently tapping with your finger tips, on the following points:

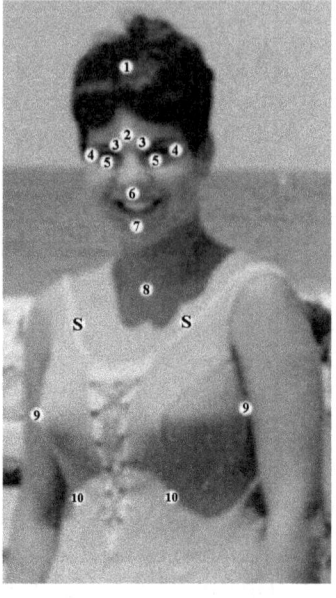

1 Top of the head (Chakra 7)
2 Depression above eyebrows/nose ridge (Chakra 6)
3 Eye brow inner side rim
4 Eye out side rim
5 Eye lower rim
6 Under the nose (depression)
7 Chin (depression)
8 Clavicle bone (v shape - Chakra 5)
9 Under the armpit (man: nipple line, woman: bra strip line)
10 Ribs 7-8 (L: over spleen, R: over liver)

6. Take a deep breath, close your eyes and listen to your emotional body. What emotional level are you in now on the e- motion scale you drew-up in stage 2 above? Write it down.

Repeat stages 4, 5 & 6 until you feel relieved or ZERO e-motion.

Should a new emotional/ideology wave well up, flow through stages 3, 4, 5, & 6 with the new key-phrases and key-words it brought up.

Pre-sent present presents

1. Find a place and a time where you feel protected and safe.
2. Lie down, sit or stand with your back and head in a straight line.
3. Gently shake your arms and legs loose to clear stress.
4. Take a deep breath, calmly exhale, let all negativity and tension leave.
5. Take another deep breath and say out loud, "I am one with all there is"[3], calmly exhale.
6. Take 2-3 deep breaths, calmly exhaling, while listening to your body language, to what it reveals to you.
7. Take a deep breath and say out loud, "I now connect with my soul and spirit energy and feel it."
8. Take another deep breath. Calmly exhale and begin to return to sense your surroundings and say out loud, "I feel calm, love, peace

and success."
9. Open your eyes. Welcome back. Nurture that feeling of divine ease, love, peace and success.

H.P.T.[4]

Heart Point Technique

Find a place and a time where you feel at peace and protected.

Lie down, sit or stand with your back and head in a straight line.

1. Raise an arm up to the sky, straight up and to its full length. Close your eyes, focus on your breathing. Unite with the universe until you feel it's enough or sense energy streams, heat waves, gentle bites at your finger tips or spontaneous, involuntary, or unconscious movement of the raised hand.

2. Lower your hand, gently and tenderly cap the top of your head with it. Ask for divine light to shed its rays on the cause, reason or story behind the scene. Let it flow, run the film, watch each frame.

3. Lower your hand to gently touch the depression point above your eyebrows/nose ridge (Chakra 6). Ask for divine assistance and guidance in transforming the cause/reason/story to one that brings you joy and fills your heart with peace.

4. Lower your hand to gently, lovingly, softly and tenderly cap your heart. Express appreciation, forgiveness, gratitude and thankfulness to both old and new. Let those feelings rise to a climax and your heart fill with joy, peace and tranquillity.

5. Raise your hand to gently, lovingly and tenderly cap the consolidation point. (Upper neck, where the spine meets the skull. It is called the consolidation point because it symbolizes the point where spirit/thought consolidates with action/matter). Run both films, starting with the cause/reason/story one, then continue to run the one that brings you joy, fills your heart with peace.

Ache: hurt, pain.
A manifestation when being in a state of anger, compassion, fear, pity, sympathy, sorrow, and their like.

Advancement; **C**onfidence;

Hear no evil, see no evil, speak no evil; **E**legance
Approach; **C**uteness, **c**uddle; **H**eart; **E**levation, **e**njoyment

ACE is one letter short of ACHE

ACHE is one letter short of CHEAP and CHEAT

Hello hidden, inner, mysterious me
What are you now revealing to me?
A time to make a choice?
A time to take a stand?
What is my truth?
Who do you belong to?
Cheap custom, cheat habit, compulsive manner, manipulative pattern, set or way?
Or
Ace's happiness, joy?

In 7th grade, one day my mother welcomed me with, "Go hang yourself on the first tree on the road." That week she welcomed me in this way more times. On Saturday I stayed in my bed till my father came and said, "It's not enough that your mother ran away? Are you running away too?" I then happily jumped out of bed, dressed, joined my father and enjoyed the rest of the day. When I walked to the bus station that evening, and on days thereafter, I saw my mother standing on the porch of her temporary one room flat. On Thursday I walked to the porch where she stood and I recall I said, "Father wants you back home. I couldn't care less if you never come back." On Saturday I came home and found my mother there.

E.S.T. Exercise - see: pp. 5
Pre-sent present presents - see: pp. 6
H.P.T. - see: pp. 7

Ache relief exercises

Important!
Please listen to the ache. Honour, own and respect it. Don't fear it, push, strain or stress. Pain feels unbearable? Give yourself a break, a chance and the time of day to rest, focus on your breathing, to connect with your inner harmony and peace. Remember, you can at any time you choose and decide to, begin anew to realize you can feel your breath freely and naturally flowing along, bringing you onward from one stage to the next.

♦ Resting between each stage is allowed and recommended.
♦ In every exercise place foremost attention and focus on your breathing.

Should your breath feel constricted, flat, heavy or short, go back to the 1st step in the stage, take a deep and peaceful breath, start anew.

♦ Feeling fear? Stress? Tension? Tightness?
Take three deep and peaceful breaths and repeat the step.
♦ Feeling unbearable pain?
Stop exercising, rest for three to four hours, then begin exercising anew.

Ankle ache: Sit on a chair with a straight back.
♦ Put both feet together firmly touching the floor.
♦ Straighten your back against the chair back. Lift your chin up. Fix your gaze at an imaginary or real point straight ahead.
♦ Place your hands on your thighs and gently lift one leg up from the floor. Begin to gently and slowly create circles, with the uplifted foot, focusing on as large and round as possible circle. Three times outward, three times inwards. Place your foot on the floor, let it rest.

Raise your leg, foot pointing forward. Gently and slowly stretch the foot three times upward and three times downwards. Place your foot on the floor, let it rest.

While sitting or standing, gently jerk and shake your ankles and feet to clear remaining strain, stress or tension.

Back ache: It is best to practice the following exercise as soon as you feel or imagine the pain is about to begin. If your back muscles are cramped already, repeat this exercise every four hours, until the last pain leaves. **Important**: Stop as soon as you feel pain. Take time to rest, three to four hours. Start with step 1, proceed to step 2 and to step 3. When you have succeeded in completing a stage, then and only then, proceed to the next one. Remember you are here to heal, not to win a competition or race.

Lie down on your back. Focus on your calm deep breathing throughout the following three stages:

1. Inhale a calm and deep breath. Exhale gently while you reach out with your hands to hold your femur or knee.

Once you hold your femur/knee, inhale again, and when exhaling pull your femur/knee one notch closer to your body. Hold it there to inhale.

Repeat 5 times, each time bringing your knee one notch closer to your body.

Repeat it with your other leg.

2. Spread your arms wide open, setting them at shoulder height in a straight line on the bed.

Verify both arms are straight with shoulder line.
Place both your legs straight on the bed.
Verify both legs are straight on the bed.

Turn your face to one side. Lightly bend and gently lift the leg (on the same side that your head is turned to). Cross it over the other leg that is lying straight. Let it rest on the straight leg while you take three calm deep breaths letting the tension ease.

Gently lift it up and bring it back to a straight position.
Repeat three times with each leg.

3. Bend down one leg; place its foot on the bed. Bend the other leg, gently lift it up and cross it over the bent leg. With both hands hold the bent femur/knee of the leg that is resting on the bed. Proceed as described in stage 1 above.

Falling, knocking, or striking the head backward: a block? Resistance? To a need and a way to break through, let go, clear, or set free a limiting belief, e-motion, perception, stance, stand-point, state of mind or view-point.

Falling, knocking, or striking the head forward: fear stricken block in a time to move forward? My feet are frozen and paralyzed in fear? Fear of change, development, expansion, growth, progress, success?

Fingers and fingers joint pain:

Exercise 1:
♦ Join your hands together, fingers integrated, and place them (palms flat open) on your chest.
♦ Attentively, gently and intentionally begin to turn your palms outward while keeping your fingers integrated. Straighten your arms and elbows to full stretch ability, keeping your arms straight at chest height.

Feel the pressure in your fingers, forearms and arms muscles as they stretch.

Repeat this exercise three times. Freely jerk and shake loose your arms from shoulders to fingers to clear remaining strain, stretch or tension.

Exercise 2:
♦ Repeatedly bend your fingers, in different and various directions. Imagine and visualize that now you are breaking, crashing, disintegrating to pieces, kneading, massaging, playing the guitar, flute or piano.

Repeat this exercise three-five times, freely jerk and shake arms and fingers to clear strain, stress or tension.

Exercise 3:
♦ Bend your elbows, press your palms together, keeping fingers as wide apart as you can, fingers pointing downward toward the floor.
♦ Begin turning them, pressed against each other, upwards to your chest. Feel the stretching tension in your palms sides, fingers, wrists, forearms and arms muscles as you rotate your hands up and down.

Repeat this exercise three-five times. Freely jerk and shake arms and fingers to clear strain, stress or tension.

Headache: First and foremost take time to ask yourself:
♦ When did I last drink a glass of filtered fresh water?
♦ Is this my thirst call?

♦ Am I dying of thirst?

If it is thirst, take 2-3 sips of lukewarm fresh filtered water, chew and mix them attentively and intentionally with saliva, gently swallow each sip, rest some, repeat. You want to finish the entire glass over a period of one hour. You don't want to strain or stress your kidneys.

♦ When did I last eat?
♦ Is this my hunger call?
♦ What am I hungry for? Physical food? Is this E-motion, perhaps Soul or Spirit craving?
♦ What did I eat?

If it is physical food allow yourself to eat at peace, attentively and intentionally chew each mouthful until it is mixed with saliva into a watery mash.

Otherwise, reflect instead of reproach. Wonder instead of thinking you know:

♦ Where is its origin? Its end? How do they connect? What is it revealing to me? What is it telling me?

♦ Ask yourself what is stressing you? Check where in your upper body, throat, sinus, nose, gums, eyes, ears you are in-flame; blood pressure? (See: Blood, pp. 26)

Brain stem / back headache: High blood pressure? Time to let hard-headedness leave for now?

Eyes belt (hoop/ring like pain): Inside eyes high pressure; narrow mind, narrow vision, short sight, small mind.

Forehead: Low blood pressure? Fear to move forward?

Forehead belt (Hoop/ring like ache): A limiting belief, condition, custom, habit, manner, pattern, perception, stance, stand-point, set or way. Is it time to replace one with a new one that feels good, serves and suits this stage and time best?

Migraine: Arrested nerve, captivated sadness, an imprisoned sorrow, miserable me, poor me, this is too much for me.

Temples: Low blood pressure?

Knee joint ache: Take the time to ask:
♦ What is this ache telling me?
♦ Wanting me to be aware of? Realize?
Disproportion? Fear of? Lack of ability, confidence, firmness, ground, stability, steadfastness, sureness to cope, handle complexity or move forward to the next phase?
♦ Is it here to remind me it is easy, natural and simple to create and take one piece and one step at a time in forming my life's roadmap?

E.S.T. Exercise - see: pp. 5

Additional exercises

Exercise 1:
- Sit on a chair with a straight back.
- Feel both your feet firmly, flatly and safely touching the floor.
- Let your back calmly rest on the chair's back, lift your chin up, straighten your back and head, fix your gaze at an imaginary or real point in the horizon.
- Place hands on your thigh. Lift healthy leg up until you feel stretch tension in the biceps muscle, and/or knee and thigh muscles. Keep your leg in a straight line with the knee.
- Let it stay in this position for a peaceful count of 1-2-3.
- Let it down, gently bending the knee. Place the foot on the floor and shake it loose to clear remaining ache, strain, stress or tension.

Repeat this exercise three times with each leg. Stand up, gently jerk and shake legs from hip to toes, alternately.

Pain in the arse/ass: Being, feeling, inner-self sensing a bottom of an abyss, fear of shift, fear to shift, rigidity. An inner-self perception that I am a pain in the arse or perceiving another as one. The arse vertebrae is one of two outward spine structures, parallel to the Thorax (chest).

Pain in the head: Beginning, genesis wake up call to a limiting belief, time to change a belief's/state of mind 'modus automatus'.

Pain in the neck: Being, feeling, sensing hard-headed me, rigid me, stiff me, stubborn me, stuck in my past me; weak me, holding with all my force, might and power on to the past, being captivated in the past, stress filling the gap between my desire and my ability, my dream and my reality. An inner-self perception that I am a pain in the neck or perceiving another as one. The neck vertebrae is one of the two inward spine structures, parallel to the Lumbar (abdomen).

Shoulder pain, frozen/stiff shoulder:
Exercise 1:
- Stand or sit. Lift your chin up, straighten your back and head.
- Bend one of your elbows and place fingers tips on shoulder joint cavity of this arm.
- Turn your face towards this arm, fix your look at the elbow's edge.
- Begin to turn your arm and shoulder joint forward while:
1. Your gaze is fixed at elbow's edge.
2. You focus your attention and concentration on drawing a flowing circular movement with your elbow. Your aim and target are to create and reach as large, round and perfect circle as you possibly can to your best ability.

Feel and listen to your shoulder and neck muscles e-motion and story.

Repeat three times before you proceed to do it with your other arm.

Proceed to do the above backwards.

Exercise 2:
♦ With your back straight, chin and head up, gaze straight forward. Attentively and intentionally turn your head to one side as far as you possibly can ache, pain, stress, strain or tension free. Feel and sense every muscle in your chest, shoulders and neck.
Remain in this position for a peaceful count of 1-2-3.
Turn your head back, with the same attention, focus and intention, until you are looking straight ahead.
Repeat three times.
Proceed to do the above to the other side.
♦ With your back straight, chin and head up, gaze fixed straight forward, attentively and intentionally lower your head backwards in as round an arch-like angle and as far back as you possibly can ache, pain, stress, strain or tension free. Feel and sense every muscle in your chest, shoulders and neck.
Remain in this position for a peaceful count of 1-2-3.
Raise your head upward with same attention, focus and intention, until you are looking straight ahead.
Repeat three times.
Proceed to do the above forward, in as round an arch-like angle as you possibly can, all the way for the chin to touch the neck.
Exercise 3:
♦ Exercise 1 above, with straight arm.
Exercise 4:
♦ Clip laundry clips to the tissue between each finger, let each clip remain until you feel pain relief or pains becomes too much to bear.
Exercise 5:
♦ Sit or stand with your back straight, looking straight ahead at an imaginary or real point. Jerk and shake your shoulders to clear tension, letting them hang free and loose by your side.
♦ With a free and loose shoulder, arm gently touching your side, fingers pointing towards the floor, raise your elbow up to 90° (like an 'L'), fingers pointing forward. Attentively and intentionally rotate the forearm 90° or more sideways, fingers pointing to the side away from body. Once you reach the limit of your ability, open and straighten the elbow, fingers pointing to the floor, (keeping your upper arm gently touching the side of your body) feeling and sensing the arm and upper back muscles strain and stretch sensation.
Repeat three times with each arm, alternately.
Stomach-ache: Spiritual and emotional birth giving, state of being, turmoil, book-keeping, fear, unfinished affair it's time to attend to, heal, let go and out of my system, resolve?
Which food, ingredient, perhaps nutrient is my body telling me is making me feel sick? What am I giving birth to this time? Perhaps my body reveals a limiting belief, nerve racking fear? Acid,

bitter, gall, sour me? A condition, custom, habit, manner, pattern, perception, set, or way that it's time I replace with a new one?

E.S.T. Exercise - see: pp. 5
Pre-sent present presents - see: pp. 6

Additional remedies

Anise, Chamomile flowers, Cinnamon bark, Ginger root, Oregano oil, Rosemary leaves.

Gently massage stomach, in a clock wise direction, with either: 1.8 acid ratio olive oil mixed with 1-2 drops of any of the following pure essential oils: Chamomile, Casia, Cinnamon, Ginger, Rosemary, Star of Anise, or with some Arak (Lebanese), Ouzo (Greek), Pastis (French)[5].

Addiction: the state of being addicted, esp. to a habit-forming drug, to such an extent that cessation causes severe trauma.

Awareness; **D**are, **d**edication; **D**elight, **d**rive;
Intelligence; **C**hange; **T**ruth; **I**nspiration; **O**ption; **N**erve[*]

E.S.T. Exercise - see: pp. 5

Sometime between my 18th and 21st year I found a packet of Kool cigarettes a Canadian volunteer left on the table. After a few days curios me took a cigarette out, lit a match to the cigarette, and inhaled. I filled with amusement and wonder. What's going on here? What's happening? A cool sensation filled me. Coughing? None. I began smoking.

Between 1978 and 1984 I was an export/import clerk in a factory for gas heaters. At the end of one winter season I quit smoking. "Hey, I quit smoking," "Until when?" "Until further notice." Autumn came and I returned to smoking. It continued so along two more years. The third time I returned to smoking I continued smoking for several more years. In 1989 I stopped once more. Once again I was asked, "Until when?" And once again I said "Until further notice." This time it lasted approximately a year and a half. The day the Gulf War ended friends lit cigarettes after dinner, I thought to myself, take one. I took one, smoked it and in the following day I was back to smoking nearly 20 cigarettes a day.

---
[*] Strength, vigour, or energy

One Friday in May 1997 I arrived to a Huna lesson and slept through it, later to drive to my Shabbat shopping: food, flowers, cigarettes. I felt drowsy and tired along the way. When I arrived at the shopping place I did a U turn with the car, having decided to leave it all, and drove straight home. I came home and went to sleep. Sometime after I woke up I wanted a cigarette and remembered I have none. "Shall I go buy some? No, not on Friday evening, I never bought cigarettes on a Friday evening," I thought. The following day I wanted to smoke a cigarette and remembered that since yesterday I have none. "Should I go buy some? No, I never bought cigarettes on a Shabbat," I thought. On Saturday evening I answered my unasked question, "Tomorrow you shall buy some on your way to the office." When I arrived at the office I remembered that… once again I did not buy cigarettes. "All is well, you shall buy them on your way home," I thought to myself. I arrived at my home and… ops, "Once more you did not stop to buy." On Monday I started to read the writing on the wall - I can do without. "Friday - Saturday passed without them, then Sunday's office and home hours. Monday too, here, see? You can" I said to myself. My innermost truth behind this time was that all along my smoking years I declared out loud that I am not an addict I can quit anytime I choose. Morning phlegm? Never existed, Cough? When I caught a chill or cold. In the years before the last 'quit' I decided to cut down the daily quantity and succeeded. I don't remember that I ever smoked "for the fun of it." I always hated the smoke smell in my clothes and hair. The last 'quit' came after I got angry at myself for not standing up to and walking my word. This time I did not waver, when asked, "Until when?" I replied, "It's for good." When asked by a guest "May I smoke here?" my answer was "You can smoke outside." The expression "I can do without" came to mean ability, empowerment and inner strength for a new habit to settle in.

Admonition: the act of admonishing. Counsel, advice or caution. A gentle reproof or warning.

Affection; **D**ear; **M**agic; **O**ption; **N**ow;
Intuition; **T**rust; **I**nsight; **O**h; **N**ew me

Age: the length of time during which a being or thing has existed.

Awareness; **G**ratitude; **E**nergy
Affluence; **G**enuineness; **E**-motion

AGE is one letter short of **RAGE**

Agreement: the act of agreeing or of coming to a mutual arrangement. The state of being in accord.

Amiability; **G**ratefulness; **R**emedy; **E**nergy;
Esteem; **M**erriness; **E**ssence; **N**ascence; **T**angibility

The Four Agreements[6]

1. Never assume, opine, postulate, suppose or take for granted.
   When in doubt, clear, inquire, investigate, verify.
   When unsure, ask, clarify, make clear and make sure.
   Assumptions, inferences and suppositions create fictitious films or scenarios.
2. Be true to your word, honour it, respect it, stand up to it and walk it.
   One's words are state of being and state of mind reflection and perception.
   Be truthful, sincere, honest, genuine, and authentic.
   Honouring, respecting, standing up to and walking my/your word is honouring and respecting, standing up to my/yourself. Be coherent; mean and speak your idea, intention, opinion then act on it and walk it.
   A word is a belief energy that create e-motions and reality.
   Declaration is an arrow to destination; A destiny creator.
3. Acknowledge and walk the truth: that at each and every moment you are doing the best; that in the doing new ideas can come up and that acting on these new ideas and following a new idea is a way to do better, excel and succeed.
4. Maintain a non-participant observatory approach and attitude remembering to never take things personally. Words express and reflect their speaker's perception; stance-stand-set-view point, state of being and state of mind.

Aim: act of aiming or directing a thing at or towards a particular point or target.

Ardour; **I**ntention; **M**erriness

All: everything, all matter, the universe.

Air; **L**ife; **L**ove
Abundance; **L**ivelihood; **L**uxury

Always: continually.

ALWAYS?
ALL WAYS?
ALL THE WAYS.

Ambiguity: doubtfulness or uncertainty in meaning or intention. The condition of admitting more than one means.

Authenticity; **M**atch; **B**eing; **I**dentity;
Gratitude; **U**p; **I**ntegrity; **T**ruthfulness; **Y**es

Ambition: an earnest desire for some type of achievement or distinction, as power, fame, wealth.

Ability; **M**astery; **B**est; **I** am; **T**rust; **I**ntuition; **O**neness; **N**obility

Amend-ment - **Amendment**: the act of amending. The state of being amended. An alteration of or addition to a bill, constitution, etc. A change made by correction, addition, or deletion.

Art; **M**ind; **E**volution; **N**orm;
Definition; **M**ake; **E**ffect; **N**est; **T**reasure

A time to say amen?
A time to amend (a) ment(al) state?

Angel: a person whose actions and thoughts are undeviatingly virtuous. One of a class of spiritual beings. A celestial attendant of the Holy Spirit. An attendant or guardian spirit. A person who performs acts of great kindness.

All; **N**ature; **G**ratitude; **E**xpansion; **L**ove
Attitude; **N**est; **G**enius; **g**enuine, **g**reatness; **E**xultation; **L**everage

Anger: a strong feeling of dis-pleasure and belligerence aroused by a perceived or sensed wrong.

Anecdote; **N**ascence; **G**ratitude; **E**ase; **R**eset

> Life is too short a road to anger along.
> Wave anger away, for(e)give and live
> graceful gratitude, happiness and joy
> of pre-sent present presents.

ANGER is one letter short of **DANGER**

Too long an age or rage range

ONE minute of anger is SIXTY joyless seconds

E.S.T. Exercise - see: pp. 5

Anger clearing letter

1. Find a time and a place where you feel comfortable, free and safe.
2. It is important to keep a free and intuitive flow, do not stop to correct or read what you write, else you stop to think, "what more do I want to let go and out of my system."
3. Take a pen and paper, sit down and start writing in the following format:
To (reason, person, situation)
free intuitive flow…
Signature
Date
4. Tear your letter to pieces.
   Burn the pieces (optional).
   Throw pieces and/or ash to waste bin.

5. Discard, when going out, into the trash can.
   Repeat this procedure three days in a row.
   On days 2 and/or 3, should nothing come out, write
To (reason, person, situation)
your signature and the date
   and follow steps 4, 5.

Anxiety: distress or uneasiness caused by imaginary danger or perceived misfortune. *Psychiatry*: a state of apprehension and a psychic tension found in most forms of mental disorder. Syn. Fear, worry, disquiet. apprehension.

Awareness; **N**ow; **X**erox; **I**nfinite; **E**ase; **T**hanksgiving; **Y**ield

> E.S.T. Exercise - see: pp. 5,
> Anger clearing - see: pp. 18

Approach: any means of access, as a road, ramp etc. The method used or steps taken in setting about a task, problem, issue etc. The course followed in landing or in joining a traffic pattern.

Attitude; **P**eace; **P**leasure;
Resilience; **O**ngoing; **A**ffection; **C**reativity; **H**eaven

Argument: disagreement; verbal opposition or contention; alteration: a violent argument. A discussion involving differing points of view: debate. Syn. Controversy, dispute.

Awareness; **R**esonance; **G**enuine;
Usefulness; **M**iracle; **E**ssence; **N**ew; **T**reasure

Ascension: the act of ascending; ascent.

Affection; **S**hift; **C**ourtesy; **E**nvironment;
Nourishment; **S**uccess; **I**nnovation; **O**asis; **N**obility

Attitude: manner, disposition, feeling, position etc. toward a person or thing.

Astounding; **T**alent; **T**reasure;
Intuition; **T**enderness; **U**sher; **D**elight; **E**cstasy

Authenticity: the quality of being authentic; genuineness.

Ardour; **U**nity; **T**hanksgiving; **H**eaven; **E**arth;
Navigation; **T**ruth; **I**dentity; **C**reativity; **I**ntegrity; **T**ime; **Y**outh

Authority: a power or right delegated or given. An accepted source of information, advice, etc. An expert on a subject. Mastery in execution or performance, as a work of art or literature, piece of music, etc.

Autonomy; **U**tterance; **T**reasure;
Hear no evil, see no evil, speak no evil;
Observance; **R**oyalty, **r**elief, **r**esilience; **I**ntention; **T**aste; **Y**ield

Awareness: mindful, knowledgeable, conscious, informed.

Allowance; **W**holeness; **A**rt;
Revelation; **E**ducation; **N**ascence; **E**levation; **S**tream; **S**weetness

Awe: an overwhelming feeling of reverence, admiration, fear, etc. produced by that which is grand, sublime, extremely powerful, or the like.

All is well; **W**holeness; **E**cstasy
Aspect; **W**ellbeing; **E**ase
Assembly; **W**isdom; **E**xpression

B

Bad: not good in any manner or degree; lacking or characterized by a lack of moral qualities; suffering from ill health, pain or injury; caused or characterized by uneasiness, or annoyance; cross, irritable or surly; regretful, contrite, dejected, or upset.

Beauty; **A**ttitude; **D**ance
Behavior; **A**dvancement; **D**are
Ball; **A**greeability; **D**o

E.S.T. Exercise - see: pp. 5

Balance: A state of stability, as of the body or the e-motions. A state of harmony, as among the elements of an artistic composition. A state of dominance or authority over others. An instrument for determining weight, esp. by the equilibrium of weights suspended from opposite ends of a bar having a fulcrum as its centre. A state of equilibrium as among weights or forces.

Bliss; **A**ffection; **L**oyalty;
Ascension; **N**est; **C**reativity; **E**ndowment

Balance[7] **creation exercise**
Say, out loud, two-three times, "balance," while boxing or tapping on each of these energy centres: V shape in your clavicle (collar) bone; chest centre; heart.

Beat: a stroke or blow. A throb or pulsation.

Beam; **E**volution; **A**ureate ness; **T**ime

Beauty: a quality that is present in a thing or person giving intense aesthetic pleasure or deep satisfaction to the sense or the mind.

Bliss; **E**nergy; **A**ffection; **U**nity; **T**ransformation; **Y**ield

E.S.T. practice to awaken and empower beauty[8]

Every day go and stand before a mirror. Carefully, evaluate, examine, observe and study your face and neck, skin complex, forehead, eye-brows, eyes, nose, cheeks, mouth, chin, wrinkles, pimples. Look at your face in the mirror and say out-loud, "I am beautiful, I am beautiful, I am beautiful." Repeat three days in a row, and whenever you feel like it.

Belief: something believed; an opinion or conviction. Confidence in the truth or existence of something not immediately susceptible to rigorous proof: a statement unworthy of belief. Confidence, faith, or trust: a child's belief in his parent.

Brotherhood; **E**xpansion; **L**egitimacy; **I**nnermost; **E**ssence; **F**ruit

On my 13th year I fell in love for the first time. I ached and cried. In my early twenties I once more fell in love, with John, an English volunteer. John moved in with me. We lived like a couple in every meaning and sense. After one of the times he refused to marry me, I swallowed sleeping pills. He called my father to drive me to the ER where my stomach was pumped. My fear separated us. Our separation made John drink till he lost control. I concluded I no longer wanted to create or see such sorrow. Thus with my own mind, I imprisoned myself in a golden cage at the tower's top. Destructive, devastating belief such as: to such a cruel and vicious world who wants to bring children to and limiting belief such as: I no longer want to create or see such sorrow created and filled my reality till I reached the age of intelligence (40s) and decided I do not want to grow up to be bitter, or continue walking along the full with good intentions straight road to hell - others walk.

> I replaced a prejudice with a new belief
> and a new reality emerged

♦ Reality is the result of one's set of beliefs, perception, prejudice, thought, stance, stand-point, view-point - conscious and sub-conscious.

♦ A belief opens a way for me to believe, first and foremost, in myself, in who I am, what I want to become and grow into, my abilities, my blessing, brilliance, genuine genius ness, gifts, skills, talents and treasures.

Best: most agreeable emotional state, highest degree of competence, or the like, wishes or kindest regards. The highest quality.

Bestowal; **E**ndowment; **S**elf; **T**reasure

Betrayal: a breach or failure of trust. Disclosure: divulgence, divulgement, divulgation, give away, blabbing, tattling. Treachery: improbity: double cross, sell out, Judas kiss. Seduction: unchastity: violation, abuse, debauchment, defloration, deflowering, defilement, ravishment, ravage, despoilment, rape, stupration.

Bridge; **E**xpansion; **T**ruth;
Revival; **A**dventure; **Y**oung; **A**rdour; **L**istening

Betrayer: Informer: snitch, tattler, tattletale, talebearer, blab. Traitor: deceiver: traitor, treasonist, quisling, rat, snake in the grass, double-crosser, double-dealer, turn-coat, archtraitor, Judas, Judas Iscariot, Benedict Arnold, Quisling, Brutus. Seducer: unchastity: deceiver, debaucher, ravisher, ravager, violator, despoiler, defiler, raper, rapist.

Shortly after my 56th birthday I answered the telephone and heard, "I told you I want to help you pay the mortgage… when you die your apartment will be my children's…" I went ballistic. A female friend I shared the conversation with encouraged me to see how generous this offer is. However, men friends thought differently. I honestly, sincerely and truthfully wanted to see it as such, so I dared call and ask, "Where is this coming from? What is the truth?" I shared my fears. "You should not be afraid, I am following mother's verbal will…" I walked the words I heard, called a lawyer, and asked him to draft a document to set the verbal agreement in writing. I sent the draft to the offering party, and heard, "This is not what I meant, it's not what I had in mind, I am taking a step backwards and time to reconsider." I put down the telephone, and felt my back muscles cramp from bottom to top. I called up a reflexology practitioner to see me 'now'. She apologized it's her time with her son and that when evening comes all she wants is to go to sleep. I drove home hoping rest would bring relief. The pain started paralyzing me so I called up another practitioner. She said she's with her son. It then came to me that perhaps I am to get out of this situation all by myself. So I busied myself with playing games on the computer and internet and reading e-mails to have my attention drawn to 'betrayal'. I tapped on betrayal, treachery and deceit for a whole week, gaining some pain relief, yet the mood deteriorated. So on Thursday I called up Nira Hartman and asked if we could move forward our scheduled homeopathy spiritual counseling meeting, Nira agreed, and in our meeting when betrayal did not yield, she asked me for synonyms. Deceit and treachery did not yield either. When I arrived home I opened Roget's International Thesaurus to discover that betrayal is also connected with seduce: violate, abuse, rape, force. I tapped on these and went to sleep, later waking up to answer the cellular telephone. I heard an apologetic female voice say, "We are five minutes from you, may we come now instead of at midday?" "Yes," was my reply. When I opened the door I met a young man and woman, who were looking for an apartment to let. Before they left I heard, "We think it would be fair for you to send us the contract." I did so. On Saturday night they called me to clarify and verify this clause or another and I heard, "We thought that is what it means, we can sign the contract anytime you like. Tomorrow during day time we are busy, perhaps then in the evening?" Two weeks later I moved to Nahariya to live more dreams come true.

E.S.T. Exercise - see: pp. 5

Key-phrases/words: *Preliminary rounds*: abused, angered, betrayed, boiled, broken, completely and utterly heartbroken, cross, crossed, deceived, defiance, defied, devastated, dis-appointed, dis-appointment, dis-honest, dis-loyal, dis-respected, dis-trust, double-crossed, failed, failure, fear of bankruptcy, fear of dis-appointment, fear of falling, fear of failing, fear of failure, frustrated, fucked-up, guilt stricken, guilty, humiliated, harmed, hurt, hypocrite, insincere, lied to, miser-able, raging mad, raped, raving mad, screwed-up, shameful, shameless, shuttered, stupid, twisted, twist-minded, un-faithful, un-truthful, violated... *Positive affirmations rounds*: authentic, faithful, healing this aching and painful wound, honest, letting go, letting out, loyal, clearing this condition, custom, habit, manner, pattern, perception, set, stand-point, view and way, respected, seeking relief, sincere, truthful, trust, trust-worthy...

Betterment: the act or process of bettering something; improvement. That which is made or becomes better.

Belief; **E**ase; **T**aste; **T**ouch;
Excellence; **R**ecognition; **M**eaning; **E**lasticity; **N**avigation; **T**alent

Birth: any coming into existence. A fact or act of being born. Act of bearing offspring; childbirth. Lineage, extraction, or descent. High or noble lineage.

Being; **I**n; **R**evelation; **T**ransformation; **H**appiness

Bite: act of biting. Wound made by biting. Mouthful of food. Light meal. Slightly bitter or sour taste. Sharp feeling of coldness.

Bliss; **I**sland; **T**enderness; **E**xpansion

E.S.T. Exercise - see: pp. 5

Bitterness: one of the basic four taste sensations, not sweet, sour or salt. Piercing, stinging. Sarcastic or cutting.

Breeze; **I**ntegrity; **T**enderness;
Trust; **E**steem; **R**ejuvenation; **N**ew; **E**xistence; **S**tamina; **S**tage

E.S.T. Exercise - see: pp. 5

Key-phrases/words: *Preliminary rounds*: angry, bitter, defied, depressed, harmed, helpless, hopeless, hurt, melancholic, pained, powerless, sore, sour, wounded... *Positive affirmations rounds*: balance, expand, heal, hopeful, joy, love, relief...

Frequent anger, bitterness, sourness remedy

Ingredients:
Citrus juice squeezer
Crystal glass
Fresh ripe yellow lemon
Olive Oil (cold pressed, acidity value up to 1.8)

21 days procedure:
Women in fertility cycle are to begin procedure on cycle's 7th day.

Every day, half an hour before your first drink or meal, squeeze fresh lemon juice, mix it with the olive oil to a homogenous mixture, drink to health.

Begin with 1 table spoon each, proceed to 2 table spoons each.

Gall bladder stones

Ingredients:
Citrus juice squeezer
Crystal glass
Large size strainer
Mellow, ripe and yellow lemons
Olive Oil (cold pressed, acidity value up to 1.8)

3 days procedure:
Women in fertility cycle are to follow this procedure between cycle's 7th-28th day.

Place strainer near the toilet seat.

Every night, two and a half hours after your last drink or meal, squeeze fresh lemon juice, fill half of the crystal glass with the freshly squeezed lemon juice and half with the olive oil. Mix the lemon juice and olive oil to a homogenous mixture, drink to your health and lie down. Mentally prepare yourself to liquidity feces. When time comes, place the strainer under your rump, and when done, look for the stones in it.

Blindness: state of being blind. Lack of sight.

Brightness; **L**ight; **I**nsight;
Niceness; **D**are; **N**ew; **E**steem; **S**unshine; **S**phere

Bliss: extreme happiness; ecstasy. Spiritual joy.

Blessing; **L**ove; **I**ntegrity; **S**implicity; **S**tate of being and mind

Blood: red fluid connective tissue that circulates through the cardiovascular system to transport substances throughout the body. Juice of a plant. Family descent. Temperament. Pure breed animal.

Dandy.

Breath; **L**ife; **O**asis; **O**pening; **D**elight

On a summer holiday before a boy started his 1st grade class in Primary school his parents gave him mathematics workbooks for 2nd grade pupils. The boy asked me to come up with the answers, I - in return - demanded he read the exercise out loud for me to hear, and encouraged him to come up with his own answer. Not having or getting his way with me, he turned to his nieces. I asked them to stay out of it and if they want to know why. "No" was the adolescent answer. The adolescent niece then picked up the telephone, called her uncle and told him what I had said to her and her younger sister. Later that day that boy's father (her uncle) fired me.
In this case the father gave 1st priority to his 2nd grade blood related niece rather than to his 1st grade blood related son.

Blood relations and "It's in the blood" is an excuse

Blood pressure: is a state of being and beliefs expression. High blood pressure expresses high stress and at times mal kidney function, or to ensure blood supply through blocked/clogged arteries. Low blood pressure expresses low vitality force, grief.
High blood pressure manifests in bleeding from the nostrils, "drill" like noise in the head, headache (See: Headache, pp. 10), cheeks and/or nose covered with protrusive capillaries.
High/low blood pressure manifest as pain in various locations in the head (brain-stem, forehead, temples).
Low blood pressure manifests in cold/frozen hands, fingers, feet; and is also known as poor circulation.

Before jumping to conclusions or rushing to take the doctor's prescribed pills, you may want to ask your doctor to refer you to a Doppler Ultrasound which defines blood flow = arteries' clogged/open level; follow the following exercises and remedies:

E.S.T. Exercise - see: pp. 5
Key-phrases/words: ***High blood pressure***: *Preliminary rounds:* I am in an atomic stress, horrible tension, like a pressure cooker, pressed as a tampon, restless, stressed out, tensed up, my high blood pressure scares/ trouble s me... *Positive affirmation rounds*: I give myself permission to calm down, I let the stress leave, I calm down now, I am calm, I am rested, I am peaceful, my blood pressure is 120/ 80 now. ***Low blood pressure***: I am free to raise my life power, I am

vibrant health, my vitality force, my blood pressure now rises to 120/80 levels. My blood pressure is within 120/80 bracket...

> Pre-sent present presents - see: pp. 6

Drink fresh filtered water, lukewarm or at room-temperature. Walks in nature, or along a colourful flowers blooming and green grass. ***High blood pressure***: Hawthorn flowers and leaves with Mistletoe leaves, Tilia (Linden, Basswood) flowers and European Olive leaves infusion: pour eight glasses of boiling hot water on 5 grams of each, let it cool for 20 minutes, drink to health. Infusion from 5-6 Olive leaves per glass, Sage leaves. Chinese Blood Pressure Herb Tea. ***Low blood pressure***: power walk, bitter chocolate cubes, a small cup of Turkish coffee or a small glass of sweet red wine.

Bloom: period of greatest productivity. Beauty and freshness.

Brilliance; **L**ove; **O**ngoing; **O**asis; **M**iracle

Blossom: state or time of flowering. Period of maximum development or greatest productivity.

Breeze; **L**ightness; **O**utlet; **S**erenity; **S**oul; **O**ffering; **M**otion

Bread: a food made of baked dough or batter. Such a food as symbol of one's livelihood; sustenance. *Slang*, Money.

Blessing; **R**efreshment; **E**lation; **A**ffluence; **D**eluxe

Breast: front part of the body from the neck to the abdomen; chest. Either of two milk-secreting glandular organs on a woman's chest. Source of nourishment. Any front part or surface.

Brightness; **b**ed; **R**eflection; **E**lation; **A**ffection; **S**unshine; **T**ruth

Breath: act or process of breathing. Vitality. Gentle wind.

Bravo; Respect; Existence;
Authenticity, authority; Thanks; Heaven

Bride: a woman recently married or about to be married.

Bliss; Renaissance; Integrity; Development; Essence
Brotherhood; Relationship; Intuition; Dream; Everything
Beauty; Riddle; Inner-self; Desire; Enigma
Bestowment; Revelation; Inspiration; Dearness; Esteem
Bridge; Re-form; Insight; Dedication; Enthusiasm
Breath; Resilience; I ; Devotion; Ease
Brightness; Right; I am; Delight; Elasticity
Beloved; Road; Innovation; Daylight; Expression
Best; Rhyme; Inside; Delicacy; Era

Bright: brightness, splendor.

Beam; Relaxation; Insight; Gratitude; Heart; Thankfulness

Brotherhood: state or relationship of being brothers. Fellowship. Association of men united for common purposes. All the members of a profession or trade.

Blossom; Relationship; Oasis; Treat; Home;
Esteem; Reason; Hear no evil, see no evil,
speak no evil, harmony; Order; Ongoing; Dedication
Beauty; Resilience; Option; Trust; Heaven;
Expansion; Ripple; Harbour; Oneness; Overture; Delight

Bruise: an under the skin haemorrhage from a blow, contusion, fall, injury, pressure or stroke.

Bridge over troubled water;
Rejuvenation; Up: Innovation; Stimulus; Exuberance

> See: Contusion, pp. 55
> Hematoma, pp.106

Remedies

Rest time with one or more of the following:

> E.S.T. Exercise - see: pp. 5

♦ Ice cold compress.
♦ Haematoma pure essential oil synergy.
♦ Homeopathy: Arnica rich cream and/or Arnica globules/drops.
Apply as soon as possible, repeat until you are pain free.

Bud: an immature or undeveloped person or thing. A small axillary or terminal protuberance on a plant, containing rudimentary foliage (leaf bud), the rudimentary inflorescence (flower bud), or both (mixed bud). An undeveloped or rudimentary stem or branch of a plant. In certain animals of low organization, a prominence that develops into a new individual; gemma.

Bliss; **U**sher; **D**estination
Being; **U**tterance; **D**elight

Burden: a heavy load. Duty; responsibility. Something difficult or worrying.

Bitterness; **U**ltimate ness;
Rage; **D**evastation; **E**go; **N**arrowness
Beauty; **U**niqueness; **R**adiance; **D**evotion; **E**steem; **N**ascence

> E.S.T. Exercise - see: pp. 5

Key-phrases/words: *Preliminary rounds*: burden, concerned, heavy, loaded, overwhelmed, stressed, sick of, tired of, worried… *Positive affirmation rounds*: ease is my default state, easy going, happy, freely flowing, light, taking it easy…

Business: an occupation, profession, or trade. That with which one is mainly and principally concerned. Affair, situation.

Bestowal; **U**nity; **S**anity; **I**ntegrity;
New; **E**volution; **S**unshine; **S**ureness

C

Cancer: a malignant and invasive fungus growth or tumor, esp. one originating in epithelium, tending to recur after excision and to metastasize to other sites. Any evil condition or thing that spreads destructively. The fourth sign of the zodiac, between June 21 and July 22.

Call; **A**ffection; **N**est; **C**alm; **E**ase; **R**ealization
Caress; **A**mazement; **N**ext; **C**hance; **E**ndowment; **R**elief
Choice; **A**musement; **N**ew; **C**ommitment; **E**volution; **R**emedy
Composition; **A**nswer; **N**iche; **C**onfidence; **E**xcellence; **R**evival
Comfort; **A**pproach; **N**orm; **C**orrection; **E**xpression; **R**evolution
Creativity; **A**ttitude; **N**ovice; **C**uddle; **E**xuberance; **R**oad
Cure; **A**uthority; **N**urture; **C**uriosity; **E**xultation; **R**ipple

A dream (See: Dream, 72) awakened the following memories: One Friday, in spring 1987, I came to my parents home for the weekend. My father told me that this week he had a routine ultra-sound and the technician said he had seen something and suggested he urgently see the Doctor. In that conversation and in others to come, it was Holy-spirit forbid we call the child by its name. In that conversation I heard, **"That's it, I am going to die."** Two days later he was hospitalized and was operated. The operation that was supposed to last 45 minutes lasted longer. When the Doctor came out of the operating room he told me that the operation turned out to be more complicated because of the tumor's size (in the left kidney) and that they had to cut two of my father's ribs. My father arranged for his colleagues to come and drive him home from the hospital. When I saw them, I warned my mother to shut up. If dad wants to go to the cotton gin plantation to meet his friends and see his office, let him. He did. We followed after him and drove home together.

He lived five more years, during which time he devotedly maintained his daily routine.

In July 1992, the family gathered for a Saturday lunch. It was the 1st family reunion in which I did not hear nor see him rush my mom to hurry up and drive back home. I did not then know it was also his last weekend alive. The following Wednesday, after the 7th radiation treatment, he called me up and asked me to come over to the hospital. I left the office early and drove to the hospital to meet him and mom at the Emergency room. He instructed me to go make sure with his colleagues that business goes on as scheduled. I made the telephone calls and later that day - with my mom - I drove to my apartment. The following night, at approximately 23:15 hrs I felt a blow hit my heart. I sat up in bed and heard my inner voice say "drive to dad." I looked at my mother, peacefully sleeping and stayed with her. When day came, I rushed my mother to get up and hurry up to go to dad. We arrived at the hospital and saw the door to his room was closed. We were asked to wait until the bathing routine ends and to meet with the Shift Manager Doctor. In that meeting I heard that when my father's condition started deteriorating (the time I felt the blow hit my heart) the staff called his home instead of calling one of his children. In the middle of our meeting with the Shift Manager Doctor she rushed out of the office. We waited and then I suggested that in the meantime, we should go see dad. Seeing the door was closed, we stood beside it waiting. When it opened, the Shift Manager Doctor came out holding the A.C.G. paper slip in her hands. I saw the straight line on it and then heard her say, "Forgive me, I am so sorry..., but please give us a few minutes and then you can walk in and bid him your goodbye." His colleagues told me that they knew nothing. His death hit them like a lightening bolt on a midsummer's day. Years later my mother told me how happy they both were when, six months after the operation, they started enjoying intimacy anew and that the last couple of months they lived together were hell on earth.

In August 1998, shortly before I left Israel to attend a seminar in Holland and later travel with a friend from Marseille, France, to Barcelona, Spain, my mother offered to baby-sit Pizki (my dog). She asked me to come visit her when I returned from my trip. Pizki ran to his death the same week. When I came back from my trip, at the beginning of October, I went to visit my mom and heard that in August she started bleeding. The Doctor wanted to rush to operate on her. She refused and set the date to the end of October. In the hospital I found out that the bleeding was a symptom of cancer. The day she walked out of the hospital, on our way to the car, she said, "**I don't have the power nor the time for this**." Sometime later, she told me that when she came home from the hospital, she and Ronit (one of her counselors) had mutually decided, "**There is no room for crab** (in Hebrew crab and cancer is the same word), **we now let it go, out to its habitat.**"

In mom's first meeting with the Oncology Doctor she answered the Doctor's Chemotherapy offer with, "Now my shoulder is in pain and **I don't have the energy for anything else**." My mother healed herself, by drinking Lemon grass and Verbena infusions, with the aid of good and loving people along the way that treated her with Universal Energy, and nutritional supplements, free from chemotherapy, radiation treatments or any other oncology medicines or therapies.

Years later we cried and raged together through the humiliation, sadness and sorrow on her healthy way to death. With time this dream allowed me to tap (See: E.S.T. exercise, pp. 5) to clear the anger, frustration, guilt and sorrow I held within from my father's death. I was accused, blamed and censured, by my own self, for not following my heart the night it called me to be 'dad's girl' for the last time in our life. The tears washed the agony and sadness to reveal, "Great, I know what I want of life, but what is it that life wants from me?"

I saw the light in wholeness greatness. What life wanted from me was to do what 'mother's daughter' could, should, was to do, and did, and 'dad's girl' couldn't and did not do. The power of anger and rage, sorrow and will motivated me to create profound impressions and memories with my mother that to me are miracles and wonders. A renewed appreciation, gratitude and value for life surfaced for once more a door opened for me to enrich and mature - into being 'mom's daughter'. It reminded me that every minute and every second I am at liberty to make a choice and question: "Am I holding on to the four corners of the altar, my belief system, a prejudice, stance, thoughts patterns, my chain, handcuffs, and prison cell, or do I now choose to come out, free, liberated, to a new amazingly challenging, fascinating, gratifying and wonder-full new horizon, and land on a new rewarding rung?"

E.S.T. Remedies

Whole hearted happiness and laughter boost and empower our immune system. Our beliefs, mood and state of mind nourish it. Willingness and an open-minded approach and attitude to change spiritual, physical, mental, and emotional nourishment customs,

habits, manners, and pattern, are essential components to boost and empower our immune system, and to healing.
Connect with:
♦ Alone time: Let your body dance, move or wiggle freely, expressing its emotional and spiritual state of being. Marvel at a flower's beauty, colour or fragrance, a child brilliance, cheerfulness, creativity and genius, clouds colour and shape, the sea colours, music or waves, walking along the beach, forest, green fields, meadow, park, vast planes.

> See: Anger, pp. 18
> Creation, pp. 58
> Err-or, pp. 79
> Laugh, pp. 136
> Smile, pp. 214

♦ Acquire new heart empowering and inspiring beliefs. Let go of limiting beliefs, harmful prejudice, hurt programming.
♦ Listen to joyous and peaceful music, songs that revive whole hearted blissful and cheerful laughter and smiles.
♦ Replace acid rich diet with alkaline diet.
Disconnect from:
♦ Acid-full, humiliation-full, hurt-full, gossip, narrow-mindedness, small talk.
♦ Listening to economics, informative, news, reality, or talk programmes, which empower panic and terror, nurture fear, stress and tension.
♦ Reading drama, spy, tragedy, war articles or books, daily news papers, magazines.
♦ Watching drama, horror, reality, talk, tragedy films and TV programmes, series and shows that brain wash the belief system and feeds acidity, anxiety, bitterness, hyster-ia, panic, soreness, stressful or terror driven expressions and perceptions .

Emotional, soul and spirit nourishment

It is recommended to practice the following exercise outside, once a day, up-to 1¼ minutes for each stage, 5 minutes total.
1.   Stand with your knees slightly bent, relax your arms and legs. Straighten your back and head, and raise your chin up. Gaze at a fixed dot (imaginary or real) on the horizon.
2.   Clench your fists and begin to box on the depression marked **1** in the chart on pp. 35. Use the Left fist to box on the right side depression, the Right fist to box on the left side depression.
While boxing with your fists on the depressions begin to move your eye to create a ∞ shape. Choose the easy one from the following possibilities: from right to left, from left to right, from down to up,

from up to down. When you feel your eyes are getting tired from creating the ∞ shape in one direction proceed to another one. Target: developing and mastering the ∞ shape in all four directions.

3. While your gaze is still fixed at the point (imaginary or real) in the horizon, begin to box/tap with your fists on the centre of the chest (over the thymus gland[*] - marked **2** in the following chart). Begin with easy, gentle and soft boxing/tapping, and gradually progress to a more powerful and vigorous boxing that will shake and create vibrations in your whole chest and rib cage. Should stress well up, combine with dancing, jerking and jumping, roaring, screaming, shouting or yelling in a wild animal like ecstatic enthusiasm or pain.

4. While your gaze is still fixed at the point (imaginary or real) in the horizon move to box on ribs 7-8 (marked **3** in the chart - left fist boxing on left side: over spleen, right fist boxing on right side: over liver) and in a clear and loud voice recite or sing the following, two times:

"I am gratitude. I look and move forward with faith, courage, confidence and clarity. I assimilate every change in my life with ease, love, peace and simplicity."

♦ Turn 90° (clockwise, to the right), continue boxing, while fixing your gaze at an imaginary or real point in the horizon. Repeat reciting/singing the above phrase.

♦ Turn 90° (clockwise, to the right), continue boxing, while fixing your gaze at an imaginary or real point in the horizon. Repeat reciting/singing the above phrase.

♦ Turn 90° (clockwise, to the right), continue boxing, while fixing your gaze at an imaginary or real point in the horizon. Repeat reciting/singing the above phrase.

Once this phrase becomes customary, change its words to ones that are cheering, pleasing and uplifting to your heart, soul and spirit.

---

[*] The thymus is a specialized organ in the immune system. The functions of the thymus are the production of T-lymphocytes (T cells), which are critical cells of the adaptive immune system, and the production and secretion of thymosins, hormones which control T-lymphocyte activities and various other aspects of the immune system. One of its most important roles is the induction of central tolerance.

The turn of 90° is to face and front all four winds.

E.S.T. Exercise - see: pp. 1

Clearing e-motional, mental and spiritual debris opens me up to happiness, health, love, success and wealth

E.S.T. Exercise - see: pp. 5

Key-phrases/words: *Preliminary rounds*: abuse, anger, bitterness, boil, criticism, depression, frustration, grief, guilt, harm, hesitation, hurt, lack, pain, rage, rejection, repression, reproach, resentment, sadness, scarcity, shame, sorrow... *Positive affirmations rounds*: calm, cheerfulness, confidence, courage, faith, following my heart, forgiveness, happiness, hearty laughter, honesty, integrity, love is my true nature, passion, peace, relief, respect, success, value, worthiness...

An easy and simple exercise to practice any place and time

Box or tap, two-three times daily, for one to three minutes, on the centre of the chest (the ribs protecting the thymus gland^(*)).

Whole hearted laughter and love to happiness and health

Additional remedies

♦ Believe miracles and wonders do happen.
♦ Trust that spontaneous healing is a way to heal yourself and your life. Now is a time to re-form and trans-form. Let the anger, evil and frustration leave, open to and welcome whole hearted gratitude, happiness, love, peace, and relief. Let them fill you and your life, settle in your heart, expand and grow as your new customs, habits, manners, patterns, stance, stand-points and state of being and state of mind.
♦ Take time to rest as much as you feel like it, busy yourself with activities that bring and vibrate wholehearted cheerfulness, happiness, joy, inspiration merriness and peace.

---

^(*) The thymus is a specialized organ in the immune system. The functions of the thymus are the production of T-lymphocytes (T cells), which are critical cells of the adaptive immune system, and the production and secretion of thymosins, hormones which control T-lymphocyte activities and various other aspects of the immune system. One of its most important roles is the induction of central tolerance.

Foods: Replace fish, meat and western indulgences with beans, chia, fruits, grains, legumes, lentils, vegetables. Follow protocols for sodium bicarbonate with molasses and tap water, or with pure maple syrup to raise your PH.
Herbs: Calendula, Cow-parsnip leaves, Horsetail, Lemongrass, Melissa, Plantain leaves, Tinging Nettle, Swedish Bitter, Verbena, Wakame seaweed, Wood Sorrel juice, Almonds (wild with bitter flavour); Apricot, peaches, plums pips.

Outdoors activities

♦ Begin enjoying a daily activity in nature, be it a calm, peaceful and relaxed sitting on a bench watching nature, passers-by or reading; a leisure walk along a sea-side, field, meadow or the neighbourhood park; swimming in the lake, river or the sea, letting your inner wild-child splash water and be as wild as he/she feels and likes.
Start with 10 minutes a day and gradually increase it up to an hour a day. Once an hour a day becomes easy and natural, you may change your activity schedule to include longer times every other day.
♦ Play with the sea waves, river or the swimming-pool water. Jump head long straight into the water or wave. Let out a cry or shout as you dive deep, jerk and shake your arms and legs under the water, kicking the water with all your might and passion, letting all the anger and hell break loose and come out.

Indoors activities

♦ Start enjoying a 10-15 minutes daily relaxation in a bath tub at 37° Celsius (99° Fahrenheit) water temperature, with 1 kg (2.2 lbs.) salt and 6-8 drops of pure essential oil, or taking a shower at your leisure, as many times a day as you feel like it.
♦ Every day find a time and a place to listen and surrender yourself to cheerful, happy, joyful and peaceful music and songs. Watch as many cartoons, comedies, musicals, dance shows and music concerts as you can or feel like.
When listening to music or while watching musicals and music concerts, listen to your heart and follow its way. Let your heart open and pour out its joy and laugher, abuse, acid, anger, bitter sadness or sorrow.
Exhibit and express all of them through dancing, drawing, drumming, exercising, jumping, laughing, singing, sketching, painting, tapping, writing, as often as you feel like it.

Indoors and outdoors activities

Reading: Cartoons, fairy tales and stories such as Alice In Wonderland, The Little Prince, etc., jokes books and magazines.
Laughing: Along the years you may have forgotten what a good whole hearted laughter feels and sounds like. Now is a good a time to

claim and revive this laughter anew.

Please note that at the beginning of the process all you may feel and sense is an artificial and forced laughter coming out. Then may come a gentle shy-some smile spreading over your face or lips. These are natural stages along the way.

Begin with artificially forced laughter sounds. Please do not allow its sound or voice to deter or stop you. Please remember it's the 1st step you are taking to claiming and getting your natural whole hearted laugh. Repeat daily, as many times as you feel like it, all the way up to the time that you hear your whole hearted laugh is filled with joy.

♦ Find a time and a place to stand in front of a mirror. Attentively, diligently and intentionally look at your face, from the top down. Appreciate, observe and study each and every detail.

When you have appreciated, observed and studied your face, neck and chest, straighten your posture and look in the mirror. It may feel odd to you at the beginning.

When your posture is as straight as it can be look in the mirror again, and think, "I can laugh, I want to laugh, I am laughing." Then let your laughter come out. Should you feel like making faces to encourage laughter - do so.

Internet surfers are welcome to watch Willie Skratter's[9] laughing baby video-clip and join in with its laughter. It's another way to begin a day with hearty laughter and bring back a cheerful, happy, joyful, merry laughter.

See: Anger pp. 18
Creation, pp. 58
Laugh, pp. 136
Smile, pp. 214

Cleansing and purifying

Begin your day drinking a glass of freshly filtered lukewarm water, taking two-three sips at a time, attentively and intentionally chewing each one and swallowing, before consuming food or other liquids. Along the day prepare and drink freshly made: Verbena, Melissa, Lemon-grass, or Chamomile (raw-material) infusions. Take as many showers as you like, each and every day, give in to letting the water cleanse and wash your body, mind, soul and spirit, surrendering to its comforting, easing and soothing touch and vibration.

Lie down to rest or sleep whenever you feel like it and for as long as your body feels like it and wants to. During rest and sleep time our systems cleanse and attend to the matters that survival mode prevent it from.

Capillary: *Anat.* One of the minute blood vessels between the terminations of the arteries and the beginning of the veins.

Comfort; Advantage; Peace;
Inner-flow, Life, Love, Ardour; Realization; Yarn

Remedies

Guji berries: 1 flat tablespoon per day, rinse with hot water, soak in a crystal glass with filtered fresh water, for 45 minutes and more. Drink the juice. For better results add the berries to your breakfast Budwig protocol. You can also eat them as your breakfast 1st course.
Important Note: Do not eat Guji berries if you consume any blood diluting medicine.
Wakame sea-weed: cut a part of a leaf, soak the cut part in filtered fresh water water, in a crystal glass then cut it to small pieces, mix the cut wakame and the water with a vegetable salad, cooked dishes - before serving.
Sea Kelp.
Chia seeds: mix 2 spoons, per day, in your vegetables dish or salad.

Care: worry, anxiety, concern. A cause or object of concern, worry, anxiety, distress, etc. Sincere attention, solicitude, caution. Protection: charge or temporary keeping.

Choice; Awareness; Right; Enough is enough

Care Out.	NURTURE & NOURISHMENT IN
Worry Out.	PLEA-SURE & PLEASURE IN
Anxiety Out.	CALM, EASE & RELIEF IN
Concern Out.	SERENITY & SINCERITY IN

E.S.T. exercise

Every time you hear "care," "concern," or "worry" say in your heart, or out loud, "Delete, dispersed, ... (and the alternate word[*])."

Repeat three and more months straight, until the alternate word naturally comes out loud of your mouth.

Careerism: devotion to a successful career, often at the

---
[*] alternate word: all is well, gratitude, love, peace…

expense of one's personal life, ethics etc.

Comfort; **A**ffluence; **R**esilience; **E**steem;
Equilibrium; **R**elief; **I**ntegrity; **S**elf; **M**ake

> On a second thought: is it one of slavery manifestations? A hide away? A safe place? Perhaps a shelter?

Caress
: an act or gesture expressing affection, as a gentle stroking, a kiss or embrace. To touch or stroke gently with or as with affection. To treat with favour, kindness, etc.

Cuddle; **A**ffection; **R**ebirth; **E**ssence; **S**elf; **S**uavity

Cavity
: any hollow place; a cavity in the earth. *Anat.* A hollow space within the body, an organ, a bone, etc. *Dentistry*, a hollow place in a tooth structure, commonly caused by decay.

Cause; **A**dmittance; **V**oid; **I**nteraction; **T**urned-flow; **Y**ield

Cell
: a small room, as in a convent or prison. Any of various small compartments or bounded areas forming part or a whole. A small group acting as a unit within a larger organization.

Centre; **E**arth; **L**ife; **L**ove

Chain
: a series of metal rings passing through one another, used either for hauling, supporting, or confining, or as an ornament. Something that bonds or restrains.

Cheerfulness; **H**eart; **A**bility; **I**ncarnation; **N**est

E.S.T. Remedy
Every time you hear or read the word "chain" think and visualize a bicycle's chain, for example. Recall and remember chain is made of

rings. A ring is breakable, changeable and replaceable be it part of a bicycle's chain, a DNA chain, genealogy, or other.

See or visualize yourself changing, repairing, replacing or taking a part the broken/ill/infected ring with a healthy, complete and whole one.

Chance: the unpredictable and unwilled element in occurrence. Luck or fortune. A possibility or probability of anything happening. An opportunity.

Choice; **H**armony; **A**miability; **N**ascence; **C**hannel; **E**nthusiasm

Character: the aggregate of features and traits that form the individual nature of some person or thing. One such feature or trait. Moral or ethic quality. Qualities of honesty, courage, or the like; integrity. Reputation. Good repute.

Confidence; **H**eaven; **A**wareness; **R**ecognition;
Aroma; **C**hemistry; **T**enderness; **E**mergence; **R**eality

What Ace? Ache? Act? Arch? Are, Art?
Which Cat? Chart? Charter? Cheat? Each? Every?
Hat? Heart? Race? Rat? Rate? Tar? Tea? Tear? Trace?

Charge: the quantity of anything that an apparatus is fitted to hold at one time. A duty or responsibility laid upon or entrusted to one. Care, custody, or superintendence. Anything or anybody committed to one's care or management.

Creation; **H**eart; **A**ffection; **R**elief; **G**ift; **E**xistence

Cheapness: vulgarity, commonness, immorality, embarrassment, sheepishness, stinginess.

Choice; **H**ear no evil, see no evil, speak no evil;
Earth; **A**miability; **P**eace; **N**ew; **E**ase; **S**election; **S**upport

Chest: the trunk of the body from the neck to the abdomen, thorax. A box, closet or cabinet for storage, safekeeping of valuables, etc.

Confidence; **H**armony; **E**steem; **S**urprise; **T**reasure

Child: a baby, infant or young. A boy or girl. A daughter or son.

Cheerfulness; **H**eart; **I**nnocence; **L**ife; **D**efinition
Clarity; **H**eaven here and now; **I**ntuition; **L**ove; **D**elight
Creator; **H**uman-being with merits and values;
Inspiration, integrity; **L**ivelihood; **D**escription

Being a child is a life-time role. It is a roll which allows and enables me/you to cheerfully delve, develop, expand, grow into, grow-out, grow-up, learn, thrive, be and feel valuable, worthy and youth-full, die young at an advanced age. It also challenges an adolescent to ask "what is my way with the child within me (that I am) and my child?" Am I castrating, educating, respecting, swooning, taming, her/him? How do I really and truly perceive and treat my child and the child within me? as a deserving and worthy human being, or? For educating is completely and entirely different. Educating is allowing, encouraging and supporting a child to freely and naturally express her/himself, giving the child freedom and space, honouring and respecting a child's brilliance, expression, space, timing, uniqueness and way.

A child is a human-being equal to me/you, with an authentic, healthy and natural desire and dignity to develop, progress, thrive; an open mind, lack of experience. A child comes to this world for joy and to be in joy, for love and to love in and with peace, to please and to be pleased, to correct, grow, reflect and right. Thanks to my child I have plenty of chances and several opportunities to do things I did not do, amongst them to enjoy activities and ideas I did not before, to check myself, to correct my way, grow and reflect on myself and my way with my child and others, to right myself. For what triggers me to accuse, anger, despair and reproach are my invalidated, negated and repressed - for too long an age - e-motions, qualities and values. I shall do right with my child to ask my child, ask myself and find it within me and myself to correct/right wrong, quit mal-treating my child - the child that I am and the child I parent. My child is not my competitor, enemy, property nor saviour, nor is he/she here to anger, fight, threaten, or wrong.

Please nurture, pamper and treat the child within you and your child with affection, attention, awareness, considerate and kind approach (instead of reproach), loving attitude - smile and touch too, respect and sense of responsibility - a mature enjoys; rather than recycle/walk your ancestor's way and word of abuse, accuse, blame, criticize, harm, hurl, hurt, rape, press, push, repress, reprimand, scold, scorn, stress, terrorize or violate the child. Give her/him/yourself a break and the time of day to go about delving, experiencing, exploring and living life, walking her/his/your way and word with her/his/your authenticity, creativity, curiosity, freedom and free-will, intelligence, knowledge, know-how, planning, timing, wisdom and desire to develop, grow, progress, succeed and thrive. **A child is born with** authenticity; blessings, clarity, creativity, dignity, honesty, gifts, innocence, intelligence, integrity, open-mind, respect, simplicity, sincerity, skills, talents and wisdom - often a time exceeding mine/yours - the adult, **and is here to** experience, live, manifest, reflect and realize honesty, joy, justice, love, peace, respect truth and wisdom. **Did you know that a child smiles over 400 times a day? How many times a day do you smile? There is no** bad child, a brat, combinator, criminal, devil, disrespectful, evil, faker, liar, manipulator, murderer, robber, Satan, spiteful, spoiled rotten, thief, vicious, or violent child. **There is a child EXPERIENCING, FEELING and LIVING** abuse, anger, degradation, depression, deprivation, despise, discourage, fear, frustration, harm, hell, helplessness, hopelessness, humiliation, hunger, hurt, hyster-ia, invalidity, insecurity, loneliness, miser-y, negation, oppression, rejection, resentment, resistance, sorrow, starvation, strait, violation, unworthiness and other powerful e-motions. **There is a child that acts** on words, experiences, feels, lives, minds and senses their primitive and true meaning and message be them hidden, non-verbal or verbal, outspoken or unspoken, taking words at their face value.

Please let the child within you, the child you are, and your child feel, know and sense he/she is dear and important to you, matters to you and that you love and respect her/him and is here to nourish and support her/him. Please caress, cheer, comfort, embrace, encourage, hug, love, morally and spiritually nurture, pamper and support the child within you and your child - approach and treat your child the way that makes you feel desired, honoured, loved, respected and worthy - the way you want to be approached and treated. Communicate - ask instead of order or reproach, converse, share and talk like you do with a confidant, friend and soul mate, have a conversation and a dialogue with your inner-child and your child like you want to be conversed with and talked to - with authenticity, clarity, dignity and respect. Practice authenticity, creativity, clarity, integrity, love, peace, simplicity, sincerity, tenderness and truthfulness with your child and yourself. Attentively listen to what your child says, speaks and tells - your child is your best and most loving guide, mirror, reflection and teacher. Honour, love, nourish, nurture and respect the child you are and your child. Let the child within you and your child know that grown-up me/you allows, guards, lets, permits, protects, supports and welcomes he/she to safely manifest and practice her/his authenticity, brilliance, dignity, genius, gifts, goodness, greatness, kindness, skills, talents and wisdom with sheer delight, happiness, joy, love and success. Statistic shows a child hears **ONE YES to every TWELVE** nos. My/your challenge and goal is to achieve **TWELVE YES's TO ONE** no. How do I/you create this change? We create it by being more attentive, mindful and respectful to our own selves, space and timing, our child and her/his space and timing, optimistic, positive, emphasizing, radiating and voicing inner clarity, confidence, generosity, kindness and single-meaning - i.e. a no is a no, a yes is a yes, a promise is a word come true, and by walking our intention and word. By giving and showing our child means, technology, tools and ways to express, live and manifest her/his brilliant and genuine true self rather than programme her/him to fear life and living, perceive life and the world as being too dangerous to freely and wholeheartedly make best of riding and surfing their waves.

> In 2003 I applied to a baby-sitter job, knowing not it will end up as being a seven years career with children borne to career oriented parents; and upgrade me to becoming an authority. "…when I am out from home you listen to Zvia and do what she says, Zvia is your mother;…" made me into the authority a mother is given, observed and perceived as, entrusted and trusted with, by her children. During my hours with the children I also gave and showed them means, technologies, tools and ways to express, handle, live, manage, manifest and walk their gifts and true-selves, come out through the strait straight into a new plane.

How did I do that?
What did I do and say?

> "Zvia come," I heard the approximately 4 years old said when I washed dishes. I asked him for a moment - to take the towel and dry my hands - and saw he walked straight out to the front door porch. When I came to the front door porch I saw him in mid-air, in a jump from the porch, approximately 60-

70 cm/2 feet high, to the parking lot. He safely landed a few cm/inches from my car's bumper, pavement's curb-stone and a sewer pipe. Enjoying his tremendous success he came running from the parking lot, up the stairs back to the porch and excitedly asked me if I saw that - intending and planning to do the same one more time. I asked him for a moment of his time, and then I asked him if he sees the prospective obstacles, directed and drew his attention and eyes by pointing each one of them out verbally and with arm movement, observed his body language and listened to his answers. I then asked: would you like to bump into any one of them? What would it feel like to bump into each one of them? Will you feel good or hurt? The lesson ended with my suggestion that he should always take time to consider, study and test a course before following and walking it, and questions for him to come up and to find out the answer to: what would you choose to be the course of events to safely reach the destination, in one complete and sound piece? Check, consider, study and test the way beforehand and along it - or bump into an obstacle? He then jumped a 2nd time and this time safely landed in a greater (safer) distance from any of the obstacles. Having now succeeded even more he repeated the action until he was satisfied.

"Zvia come," I heard his voice come from the backyard garden. I walked out and saw him standing on a surface, approximately 1.20-1.40 metres / 4-5 feet high. It came to me that his plan was to jump from this surface to the lawn. I told him that because of my fear I give him permission to do that while holding on to my hand. He held my hand, jumped and safely landed on the lawn. Enjoying his success he repeated it until his mother came over and in a fear stricken raised voice said "It's dangerous, it is prohibited."

I walked with him to meet his sister in the gymnasium. When we neared a T junction, my eyes saw him running off the pavement straight into the middle of the junction. My heart fell into my panties, I looked to all three directions to see there were no cars coming along and in two steps made it to where he stopped and stood, picked him from the ground up to my bosom, hugged and kissed his face; **me**: I got terribly scared, please do not do this again; **him** (crying):I ask forgiveness, I did not mean. Lesson time came after we were back on the pavement and calmed down. We stood there, conversed, discussed and looked at pavement being the route for people to safely walk on, road the route for driving cars, stopping and taking time to look in all directions, making sure no car is nearing or in sight before going from the pavement to the road, what would it feel like to bump with a car, what are prospective results of bumping with a car (getting hurt, wounded - no danger brainwashing, fear, guilt or reproach programming nor mention of drama/horror/ hysteria/terror/tragedy customs creators and founders, such as: bone breaking, do you know how dangerous this was? tearing a limb off, going to a hospital, seeing a doctor, what were you thinking when you did that? You nearly got yourself killed and their likes), and of having better and more chances, opportunities and time to see and sense obstacles when walking as opposed to running. He never again ran from the pavement to a junction or a road when being with me.

At the end of one lunch, the 7 years old took her plate and cutlery from the dining table to the kitchen. I reminded her to clear the leftovers from the plate into the waste bin. She casually reached to open the closet door while giving me the 'who do you think you are to tell me what to do' look. When I suggested it is easier to take the waste bin out and put it on the floor I saw in her face that despair well up and then that the leftovers she cleared out and off the plate landed all around the waste bin, on the floor and the closet bottom. I asked her to mind and see what she was doing and saw she annoyed and upset more. She then asked me to come and clean after her, **me**: do you know why I demand? **She**: why? **Me**: because I mind how you shall cope, handle, and manage situations when you are 40 years old. I saw that her face light up; she happily progressed to clean the place up. I joined forces with her to never again see her being careless, a slob and sloppy when I was around.

In one of our lunch times together I talked of the beauty I see and the love that I have to Bougainvillea and heard that she too loves it, a few times asked her mother to teach her how to say it and that to date she fails to succeed in pronouncing it. What then happened made me dis-cover and realize that a child takes words at face value. **Me (a metaphor)**: We can do it when you take my hand and walk my word. **She** stopped eating and reached out to take my hand. I took her hand, and while holding her hand got out of the chair, stood up, and we started walking. During our hand in hand walk in circles around the living room I asked her to repeat what I say. In our 2nd round I found out that the way to success lies in cutting the ever so complexed word to short and small phonetic syllables (Bo - gen - vi - le - a), progress to longer phonetic syllables (bogen - vi - lea, bogen - vilea) to end it with Bougainvillea. In the 3rd round she succeeded in getting it right. We walked the word along two more circles before she reached the stage of being and feeling happily content and satisfied with her new success. To teach her younger brother a complicated word I used the same technique. It worked with him just as well; and yielded: **mother**: I wonder from whom did he learn this word, he loves it so much he keeps repeating it all the time; then in a mused tone she continued with "And I went with him to twelve sessions with a speech therapist;" **and inside me**: 'If only you knew, saw and were aware of the gifts in your home - you would know it was me and my doing' broke my heart and contributed to my resigning.

To bring into, out and up and to create acceptance, confidence, for(e)-give-ness, joy, love, peace, success, wealth and more you may choose and decide to allow yourself to check your hi-story, yourself, your ways, reflect on them, how did I feel when my parent... what did I feel in same/similar situation, what is my model, what a model am I to my child? Changing an approach and attitude can save you and your child from pain killers, psychology and other therapies sessions - **See**:

> Beauty, pp. 21
> Foul play, pp. 88
> Growth, pp. 95
> Rejection pp. 186
> Right, pp. 195
> Violence, pp. 241

Choice: the act or instance of choosing; selection. The right or opportunity to choose. An alternative.

Consciousness;

Hear no evil, see no evil, speak no evil;

Order; Island; Creation; Eden

Clarity: the state or quality of being clear or transparent to the eye. Clearness or lucidity as to perception or understanding, freedom from ambiguity.

Cuddle; **L**ove; **A**wareness; **R**eality; **I**nner; **T**ruth; **Y**outh

Clarity creation exercise[10]

Find a place and a time where you shall feel at peace and protected.

1. Stand with both knees slightly bent and flexible, or sit on a chair with a straight back and no arms, both of your arms freely and loosely hanging on your sides.

2. From beginning to end of this exercise focus on breathing (inhaling, deeply, through your nostrils; exhaling, peacefully, through your mouth).

3. While you create with one arm (elbow locked straight) as round and as wide a circle as you possibly can (bottom, up backward and down forward), lift the opposite leg straight up. Close the circle with a tender touch of your finger tips on the straight uplifted knee.

Repeat with each arm and leg alternately.

Stop this exercise the moment you notice constricted, heavy or quick breathing, you are holding your breath, or when 60 seconds have passed by.

This exercise is also beneficial and useful to come out of addiction, to balance inner forces, clear stress, feel relief.

Reconsider practicing it before bedtime when sleep wonders away, after exercising this exercise.

Remedies

Abundant rest, day and night, light and sound free, sleep.
Day sleep: **adult** and **child**: as much as body asks for.
Night sleep: **adult**: 9 and more hrs, **child**: 8 and more hrs.
Babies, sick and tired people are to sleep as much as and whenever they feel like it.

Class: a number of persons or things regarded as forming a group by reason of common attributes, characteristics, qualities, or traits. A group of students meeting regularly to study a subject under the guidance of a teacher. The system of dividing society. Any of several grades.

Creation; **L**esson; **A**ngel; **S**election; **S**implicity

Closeness: being close, near to one another, together. Bringing together parts of.

Coast; Love; Ocean; Self; Esteem;
Nobility; Endurance; Stability; Strength

Coma: a state of prolonged unconsciousness.

Caress; Observance; Meaning; Affection
Cradle; Obeisance; Miracle; Assurance
Cuddle; Opportunity; Mirth; Authority

Life is here for me to freely choose,
whole heartedly experience and live
my dreams come true with
gratitude, joy, passion, peace and pleasure.

All is in divine and perfect
orchestration, order and timing.

Commit-ment - **Commitment**: the act of committing, pledging, or engaging oneself. The state of being committed.

Creation; Oasis; Mind; Majesty; Intuition;
Truth; Make; Endowment; Nest; Treasure

Common-sense - **Commonsense**: a sound practical judgment that is independent of specialized knowledge, training, or the like. A normal native intelligence.

Creativity; Origin; Mastery; Make; Offspring;
Nascence; Serenity; Ease; Newness; Simplicity; Esteem

Company: a number of individuals assembled or associated together. Companionship or fellowship. Society taken collectively.

Companionship; Opportunity;
Mentality; Potency; Affection; Nearness; Yield

Compass-i-on
Compassion: a feeling of deep sympathy and sorrow for another's suffering or misfortune, accompanied by a desire to alleviate the pain or remove its cause.

Cold-mind; **O**ffer; **M**astery; **P**eace;
Ability; **S**elf; **S**ignificance; **I**sland; **O**therness; **N**eatness

COMPASS TURN
OUT com-passion, misfortune, sorrow, suffering, sympathy's ache & pain
IN intuition, love and sense

Complaint
an expression of discontent, pain, censure, grief, or the like. A cause of discontent, pain, censure, grief, or the like.

Cheer; **O**bservation; **M**erriness;
Plea-sure; **L**aughter; **A**wareness; **I**nsurance; **N**ewness; **T**ip

E.S.T. Exercise - see: pp. 5

Completion
the act of completing. The state of being completed. Conclusion, fulfillment.

Comfort; **O**ngoing; **M**irth; **P**leasure; **L**uxury;
Endowment; **T**ruth; **I**ntuition; **O**ffspring; **N**est

Complex
composed of interconnected parts; compound; composite. Characterized by a very complicated or involved arrangement of parts, units, etc.

Connection; **O**asis; **M**asterpiece;
Present; **L**eisure; **E**xistence; **X**erox

E.S.T. Exercise - see: pp. 5

Key-phrases/words: *Preliminary rounds*: complexity, bewilderment, confusion, loss, from too many trees the forest is lost... *Positive affirmations rounds*: clarity, confidence, ease, simplicity, step by step from one stage to the next stage...

Compulsion: the act of compelling; constraint; coercion. The state or condition of being compelled. A strong, usually irresistible impulse to perform an act that is contrary to the will of the subject.

Competence; **O**ption; **M**ind; **P**reference; **U**nity;
Leisure; **S**implicity; **I**ndependence; **O**penness; **N**iceness

E.S.T. Exercise - see: pp. 5

Concept: a general notion or idea. An idea of something formed by mentality combining all its characters or particulars; a construct.

Creativity; **O**mnipresence; **N**et; **C**radle; **E**cstasy; **P**urity; **T**ruth

Concurrence: Accordance in opinion; agreement. Co-operation, as of agents or causes; combined action or effort. Simultaneous occurrence; coincidence.

Caress; **O**ccasion; **N**ow; **C**uddle; **U**nity;
Revelation; **R**ipple; **E**ntity; **N**est; **C**uriosity; **E**xploration

Confidence: full trust; belief in the reliability of a person or thing. Self-reliance, assurance, or boldness. Certitude.

Choice; **O**pportunity; **N**ascence; **F**reedom;
Independence; **D**ear; **E**ase; **N**iceness; **C**ertitude; **E**steem

Connection: the act of connecting. The state of being connected. Link, bond, association, relationship.

Call; **O**h; **N**earness; **N**ow; **E**lasticity;

Closeness; **T**enderness; **I**ntegrity; **O**ption; **N**iche

Consciousness: the state of being conscious; awareness.
The thought and feelings, collectively, of an individual or of an aggregate of people. Full activity of the mind and senses.

Conductivity; **O**neness; **N**urture; **S**implicity;
Clarity; **I**ndependence; **O**ffspring; **U**nity;
Sanity; **N**ow; **E**nsemble; **S**erenity; **S**acredness

Constipation: a condition of the bowels in which the feces are dry and hardened and evacuation is infrequent and stressful.

Casualness; **O**pportunity; **N**avigation; **S**tream; **T**urn; **I**nnovation; **P**eace; **A**ttitude; **T**hankfulness; **I**ntegrity; **O**utlet; **N**ext

♦ An emotional, mental or spiritual constipation manifests in physical constipation.
♦ Anxiety, awe, dread, fear, fright, horror, oppression, panic, repression, terror, scare, or worry block, dehydrate, prevent or stop free flow activity, digestion, emission, inspiration, cleansing or clearing. They may also manifest as diarrhea.
♦ Physical, mental and emotional debris are poison and toxin to our being, body, mind, soul and spirit health and wellness.
♦ Alcoholic drinks, artificial flavours and food ingredients, beverages, cigarettes smoking, milk chocolate, coffee, drugs, tea, processed foods, salt, soft drinks, sugars dehydrate and thicken the blood. Processed foods such as white flour, white sugar, white rice also act as glue in our stomach and intestine, and increase acidity. You may want to consider replacing them with fresh filtered water, organically grown fruits and vegetables, home cooked, made and prepared drinks and foods, raw foods such as a whole wheat flour, whole rice, whole sugar and fiber rich foods.
♦ Lying down and sitting during the better part of a day lowers metabolism rhythm, builds up pressure and stress. Results manifest in poor/slow bowel movements, blood clotting, muscle cramps and pains, numbness, sclerosis, temporary paralysis, and more.

Remedies

E.S.T. Exercise - see: pp. 1

E.S.T. Exercise - see: pp. 5

Key-phrases/words: *Preliminary rounds*: anxious, blocked, fear stricken, frozen to death, introverted, oppressed, paralyzed, repressed, scared, terrorized, worried… *Positive affirmation rounds*: I choose to be easy, to be free, to feel calm, to flow, to relax and let go, to take it easy, let out, clear, I am out of danger, I am protected, I am safe…

♦ Find a place and a time where you shall feel at ease, and safe.
Sit or stand straight. Take a deep breath, close your eyes.
Focus on your breath and let your imagination begin a ride on a magic and wonderful tour in which you ask your body to tell you what is the block? What am I holding onto? Allow your body to relax, to feel safe, to let go, cleanse and clear. When you see black, let your heart calm. Say to yourself, "I am protected and safe. I now give my body permission to calm, clean and clear, I love flowing freely and naturally, I love harmony. I feel great when my body lets out and my bowl movement gently and peacefully pushes forward and lets out all that serves me no more. I love the sensation that follows an easy, gentle, peaceful and relaxed evacuation flow."
Sit on the toilet, close your eyes, focus on your breath, let your body relax, feel the urge to let out gently and peacefully move feces forward and out. Look at it, its colour, it's texture, open your eyes and tap on the key-phrases/words that came up while you were focusing on your breath and visualizing the process (E.S.T. exercise - see: pp. 5).

♦ Take a vigorous walk, cellular telephone, mp3, mp4, and their likes free. Begin with 10 minutes per day. You want to develop attention, awareness and consciousness to learn to hear and listen to your body and inner-self language. Focus on your breath, e-motions, feelings, mood, sensations, senses, temper and thoughts patterns.
Walk along and amid bush, a forest, lake, meadow, pasture, sea shore, streets rich with natural plants and trees, gardens or parks. When after 10 minutes you feel easy and light, increase to 15-20 minutes, then 20-30 minutes until you reach 45 minutes to an hour. After 45 minutes to an hour feel easy, begin creating different walking manners and playing with them (E.S.T. Exercise - see: pp. 1). Take the time to relax, before you proceed to the next issue on your agenda.

♦ Drink fresh filtered water, warm, lukewarm or at room temperature. Chew 2-3 sips at a time, every 10-15 minutes.

♦ Drink, on an empty stomach (half an hour before your breakfast or first drink, or two and a half hours after your last meal or drink, other than water, and before you go to sleep), a homogenous mixture made from Olive oil (cold pressed, under 1.8 acidity rate) with freshly squeezed lemon juice, mixture ratio: 1 x 1; up to 1/3 glass. In extreme cases up to 1 glass.

♦ Eat (per day), 3-5 dates, 2-3 figs, 2-3 raw Brazil nuts, a handful of raw cashew, hazel, pecan, pine, walnuts and their likes. Sea kelp. Chew each mouthful until saliva makes mixture feels like a watery paste.

♦ Eat one crystal glass of freshly made melon, tomatoes or watermelon puree with 1 tablespoon of Olive oil (cold pressed, under 1.8 acidity rate). Chew each mouthful until saliva makes mixture feels like a watery paste.

♦ Eat vegetables cooked in water then mixed with Olive oil (cold pressed, under 1.8 acidity rate). Orange coloured vegetables (carrot, sweet potato, pumpkin, etc.). Chew each mouthful until saliva makes mixture feels like a watery paste.

♦ Wearing bright, fresh, hot, rich, young green, orange, red, turquoise, yellow coloured clothes and underwear stimulates the metabolism, uplifts mood and spirit. Dark coloured clothes, black, bottle-dark-green, dark-blue, dark-brown, dark-purple run and slow down the metabolism and mood.

♦ Eat 1 tablespoon of freshly grounded coriander seeds, mixed with some freshly grounded cardamom seeds before your breakfast, coffee or tea and drink plent of fresh filtered water.

♦ Guji berries (See: Remedies, pp. 39)

Contempt: the feeling with which a person regards anything considered mean, or worthless; disdain; scorn. The state of being despised; dishonour; disgrace.

Confidence; Orchard; Now; Treat;
Essence; Matter of fact; Paradise; Time

E.S.T. Exercise - see: pp. 5

Key-phrases/words: *Preliminary rounds*: contempt, disgust, repulsive, frustration... *Positive affirmation rounds*: content, grateful, happy, satisfied...

Contentment: the state of being contented, satisfaction, ease of mind.

Casualness; Openness; Nature; Trust; Existence;
Nest; Treat; Mainspring; Entity; Newness; Treasure

Contusion: an injury in which the subsurface tissue is injured but the skin is not broken; bruise.

Cease fire, Operation, New, Time,
Uniformity, Season, I am, Openness, Newborn

A bruise may create internal haemorrhage, swelling, or a haematoma. Healing time range is from few days to a month.

Remedies

Rest time with one or more of the following:

E.S.T. Exercise - see: pp. 5

♦ Ice cold compress.
♦ Haematoma pure essential oil synergy.
♦ Homeopathy: Arnica rich cream and/or Arnica globules/drops.
Apply as soon as possible, repeat until you are pain free.

See: Hematoma, pp. 106

Core: the central, innermost, or most essential part of anything. The central part of a fleshy fruit, containing the seeds.

Concreteness; Oh; Reality; Endowment

Courage: the quality of mind or spirit that enables a person to face… with firmness and without fear; bravery, dare.

Cuddle; Objectivity; Ultra; Realism; Ability; Gain; Experience

In July 1997, I shared my desire to leave the company with its accounts and tax consultant. He told me he'd let me do that only if I go meet a medium and hear what he has to say. I heard this medium met with his father and later with him also and that what he told them within a couple of years came true. "How much will this cost me?" I asked. "150 NIS," he replied. We made the appointment. In the meeting

I saw how attentively and mindfully the medium studied the coffee glass and then the crystal ball. I heard him say, "I see black, all black, I see nothing." "Should I resign?" I asked. He answered, "What are you doing there still?" "How long before I leave?" I asked. "Within two months you will be out of there," was his reply. Two months later I flew over to Johns wedding (See: Belief, pp. 22) knowing that when I come back from my holiday I will be learning Reflexology, and what's after that? Grand is Holy-spirit. Years later, in one of my meetings with the accounts and tax consultant, I heard he said, "You have los pelotos de un buey" (balls of a bull).

Cramp: a sudden, involuntary, persistent contraction of a muscle or group of muscles, esp. of the extremities, sometimes associated with severe pain. A piercing pain in the abdomen. An intermittent, painful contraction of structures of a wall containing involuntary muscle, as in biliary colic or in the uterine contractions of menstruation or of labour. E-motion, soul or spirit labour pain.

Co-existence; Relief; Acceptance; Mirth; Peace

Night time, pre-menstruation, menstruation and rest time ramps: please remember cramps are a way to let you know that your body is now busy with moving on perhaps moving out? Take a moment to look back, check what did you eat before it started? Did I over ate? Did I strain? Did I over-work? What is my body now moving out of it's system? Certain medicines, e-motional, mental, sentimental and spiritual poisoning, excessive consumption of sweets may also result in cramps, create acidity and deficiency in calcium, magnesium and vitamin D. Take action to change the cause, sometimes to stop is the medicine, you may also want to consider to enrich your diet with calcium, magnesium and vitamin D nutritional supplement before you retire to nights sleep together with 10 minutes daily exposure to the sun during sunrise or sunset hours.
Cold/ice compress.

E.S.T. exercise

1. Find a place and a time where you feel at ease and safe.
2. Get fresh filtered water. Take a sip, chew and mix it with saliva, gently and peacefully swallow.
3. Stand or sit with your back straight and head up, or lie down. Clear neck, shoulders, hands and legs from stress. Focus on your

breath and in your heart say: "I am grateful for my elastic, flexible, healthy, powerful and strong muscles."

Repeat this phrase until you feel at ease.

Repeat this exercise once and more daily, every day, for three straight months. In addition, once a week, practice muscles stretch, appreciate, check, diagnose, evaluate, examine, observe, and test the difference, bless, cherish and nurture it.

Cream: the part of whole milk that is rich in butterfat.

Crest; **R**espect; **E**lation; **A**bility; **M**anna
Closeness; **R**e-form; **E**steem; **A**ffection; **M**astery

CREAM is one letter short of **SCREAM**

> No more ice cream I scream

Butterfat, cream or any other fat serves to preserve existing condition, to resist change. Fat is a conservative.

The skin is part of our respiratory system. Its tissue enables cleansing, clearing and letting out emotional, medicinal, physical, sentimental and spiritual rubbish or refuse.

Itching, rushes, sweat are expressions and manifestations of emotional, medicinal, physical, sentimental and spiritual excessive heat, poisoning and stress. Sweat also serves as cleansing, sedative, and soothing vehicle.

Cream application on the skin is like cream icing on a cake. A cream coating applied to the skin to supposedly cure itching, rushes, or for sweat prevention causes stress-related expressions and manifestations, poisoning and toxicity.

E.S.T. remedies

Find a place and a time where you feel comfortable, free and safe. Sit with your back and head straight up, both feet solid and steady on the ground, i.e. ankles and knees at 90°, or lie down with your back, head, legs and neck straight (no pillow, preferable) on the ground, floor or a solid mattress.

Take one breath, inhale calmly (through your nostrils) as deeply as your inner-self lets you, exhale slowly (through your mouth).

Close your eyes, take one more such breath, relax, and continue with normal breathing while taking time to reflect, think, sense and visualize yourself as a cake covered with icing cream.

How does it feel?

What do I feel? Maybe sense?
When I cream rather than scream what am I preserving?
Which change am I preventing from occurring?

Drink lots of fresh filtered water at room temperature or lukewarm.

Take showers with lukewarm or at room temperature water.

Nappies rush
Fill a bottle (glass, preferable) with 500 cc (2½ glasses) fresh filtered water. Add 3-4 drops of Lavender pure essential oil, shake a little. Soak a cotton or linen cloth in the solution, and wipe secretions clean.

5% Apple vinegar compress:
Ingredients:
A glass bowl
5% Austrian, British, Dutch, German or Swiss made Apple vinegar
Cannabis/Cotton/Linen cloth
Cannabis/Cotton/Linen socks
Water, at room temperature or lukewarm
Dosage:
Babies: ¼ glass 5% Apple vinegar + ¾ glass fresh filtered water.
Children: ⅓ glass 5% Apple vinegar + ⅔ glass fresh filtered water.
Teens: ½ glass 5% Apple vinegar + ½ glass fresh filtered water.
Adults: pure vinegar.
Procedure:
Pour the vinegar and water into a bowl; mix them into a solution; soak cloth and/or socks in this solution and administer as follows:

Place soaked cloth on irritated area. When cloth dries or warms up replace it with a newly soaked one.

Repeat until irritation or rush is calmed down.

Should irritation increase, immediately wash area with fresh water then place a lukewarm or at room temperature fresh water compress.

Creation: the act of creating; act of producing or causing to exist. The fact of being created.

Celebration; **R**eality; **E**ase; **A**bility;
Trust; **I**nspiration; **O**neself; **N**ewness
Courage; **R**ealization; **E**xistence;
Application; **T**reasure; **I**nsight; **O**neness; **N**ascence

Creativity creation exercise

Ingredients:
A note-book, or a writing paper block
A pen
Procedure:
1. Find a place and a time when and where you feel comfortable, free and safe.
2. Take the note-book and pen. Arrange them so you can begin the process.
3. Sit down, take a deep breath (inhale through your nostrils, exhale through your mouth), with your passive (non-dominant) hand start writing whatever comes out.
Remember, "I am here to create creativity, nothing else is important nor matters." Do not slow or stop for any reason, add, change, erase or read your writing.
When a blank comes up, you may want to choose between:
a. Setting your look on a fixed point on a blank wall, and focusing on deep and peaceful breathing, till a change occurs or 5 minutes passes by. Repeat this daily till a change occurs. Or,
b. Writing a single character (digit, letter), word, or phrase repeatedly till a new one comes out.
4. Repeat daily for six months and more.
Remember you are precious and so is your time. Creating a change and its assimilation is essential and important to happiness and health. Begin to honour and respect, literally, naturally, primitively, simply, sincerely and truthfully take, treat and walk your words, wishes, wills, thoughts, dreams, decisions, agreements, authenticity and actions.

Criticism: the act of passing severe judgment, censure, faultfinding. Critical comment.

Core; **R**emedy; **I** am; **T**enderness;
Inner-self; **C**riterion; **I**sland; **S**implicity; **M**irth

E.S.T. Exercise - see: pp. 5

Cry: to utter inarticulate sounds, esp. of lamentation, grief, or suffering, usually with tears. To weep, shed tears, with or without sound. To shout, yell. To beg or plead for, implore.

Creation; **R**ay; **Y**oung
Chapter; **R**emembrance; **Y**ield
Credence; **R**evival; **Y**es

Culture
: the act or practice of cultivating the soil, soul. A particular form or stage of civilization. *Sociol.* The sum total of ways of living built up by a group of human beings and transmitted from one generation to another. The quality in a person or society that arises from an interest in and acquaintance with what is generally regarded as excellence in arts, letters, manners, scholarly pursuits, etc. Development or improvement of the mind by education or training.

Cord; **U**nity; **L**ove; **T**reasure; **U**tterance; **R**emedy; **E**ndowment

Cure
: a method or course of remedial treatment, as for dis-ease. Successful remedial treatment, restoration to health.

Credibility; **U**biquity; **R**esult; **E**steem
Core; **U**p-growth; **R**elief; **E**nvironment
Cuddle; **U**sher; **R**eadiness; **E**den

Curse
: the expression of a wish that misfortune, evil, etc., befall another. A formula or charm intended to cause such misfortune to another. A profane oath. An evil that has been invoked upon a person. Something accursed. The cause of evil, misfortune, or trouble.

Court; **U**gliness; **R**udeness;
Self-incriminating evidence/perception; **E**xpression

CURSE is one letter short of **COURSE**

Goodbye curse coarse course
Welcome blessings course
Blessed is the blesser

Along the way of transforming my relationship with my mother into a blessed one, I began to transform my relationship with other family members. It dawned on me that as I do with her and with them, I can do with every body in my life. I started thinking that I am blessed with a family whose members are the most adorable, amazing, charming, generous, kind and loving people in the world and to express that truth my way. When I heard cynical and skeptical remarks, I shut them up then and there with "They are yours, not mine, I have the best and the most…" I began ending telephone conversations with, "I love you." I began and ended my letters to them with blessings and loving words. When the cry of one of them burnt hell in me, I called and asked, "What is the matter? Why are you raising hell?" Between the lines I heard: agony. From that time onwards, all that mattered to me in my relationship with him was to befriend and love him. After the words of the other cut my heart with a knife, time and time again, for two long years, we met on Sukkoth holiday; I went ballistic and left feeling raging mad to later send him an "Anger Clearing Letter"(See: pp. 18). In the last paragraph of my letter, I suggested we let by gone be by gone and open a new leaf in our relationship. In his answer I read that… YES, a peace treaty, same as did Begin and Saadat, Rabin and Hussein. I have since lived to enjoy the bliss of our success in achieving it.

On my birthday, my sister-in-law sent me a blessing from my brother's cellular telephone. Then and there, I returned my thanks to her. Before I put the cellular telephone down on the shelf, I heard the SMS ring-tone. I opened it, and saw this time my brother phrased and sent his personal blessing. My heart filled with bliss and mirth and a happy smile spread on my face, from ear to ear.

On our next meeting, on the last Saturday of the month, I arrived with a song in my heart, ready and willing to live sheer happiness. This Saturday filled my heart, soul and spirit with gratitude to my family members, life's miracles and wonders.

E.S.T. exercise for blessing creation

Materials:
Cannabis, cotton, or linen thread.
Procedure:
1.   Cut the thread to a 15-20 cm (0.5-0.6 ft) long piece.
2.   Tie a knot while you say/sing, out loud, the following sentence: "I feel gratitude Source (Almighty, Creator, Devine presence, Father, Heaven, Holy inspiration, Mother, Omnipresence,

Providence, Sacred spirit...) that the same way I tie this knot evil is shut out forever towards (person's name, idea, reason, plan, situation, will, wish) until I myself open this knot with my own hands."

Repeat three times.
3. Throw the thread with the three knots into the waste bin.
4. When you leave home/office take out the waste bag with the thread and dispose of it into the garbage can outside the building.

Custom: a habitual practice; the usual way of acting in given circumstances. A practice so long established that it has the force of Law; 2nd nature.

Creation; Up; Simplicity; Tangibility; Ocean; Merriness

Cynic: a person who believes that only selfishness motivates human actions and who disbelieves in or minimizes selfless acts or disinterested points of view. One of a set of Greek philosophers of the 4th century B.C. that the essence of virtue is self - who advocated the doctrines that virtue is the only good control, and that surrender to any external influence is beneath the dignity of man.

Calamity; Yield; Next; Irritation; Cancer
Contrariety; Yard; Negativity; Incriminating; Clamor
Comfort; Youth; Nurture; Intuition; Creativity

Cynicism: cynical disposition, character, or belief. A cynical remark. Any of the doctrines or practices of the Cynics.

I found my way out from cynicism in   **The Four Agreements**[6]
1. Never assume, opine, postulate, suppose or take for granted.

When in doubt, clear, inquire, investigate, verify. When unsure, ask, clarify, make clear and make sure. Assumptions, inferences and suppositions create fictitious films or scenarios.
2. Be true to your word, honour it, respect it, stand up to it and walk it.

One's words are state of being and state of mind reflection and perception.

Be truthful, sincere, honest, genuine, and authentic.

Honouring, respecting, standing up to and walking my/your word is honouring and respecting, standing up to my/yourself. Be coherent; mean and speak your idea, intention, opinion then act on it and walk it.

A word is a belief energy that create e-motions and reality.
Declaration is an arrow to destination; A destiny creator.

3.	Acknowledge and walk the truth: that at each and every moment you are doing the best; that in the doing new ideas can come up and that acting on these new ideas and following a new idea is a way to do better, excel and succeed.

4.	Maintain a non-participant observatory approach and attitude remembering to never take things personally. Words express and reflect their speaker's perception.

D

Dare: an act of daring, challenge, confront with courage.

Dream; **A**ction; **R**ealization; **E**cstasy
Dart; **A**udacity; **R**evelation; **E**fficiency
Desire; **A**bility; **R**elief; **E**ffectiveness
Devotion; **A**ffection; **R**eward; **E**lasticity
Dedication; **A**dmiration; **R**evival; **E**ndowment

In English class, during a school year at Mevu'ot Iron boarding school, we were divided into three grades, 'Below Average - behinders', 'Average - normals' and 'Advanced - fore-runners'. I was allocated to the 'normals' class. One day I approached my English teacher and asked her to let me join with the 'fore-runners' class. She told me that since my average test mark was 8, it prevented her from complying with my wish. I then set the conditions and terms for a contract with her. She would let me join the 'fore-runners' class, should my average test mark be lower than 8 during the 1st semester, I would come back to her class. She agreed. I finished high school in the 'fore-runners' class.

When I studied English Expression in writing, Literature and Poetry at Menashe College, Hadera one of the papers I presented made the teacher call me aside to tell me he cannot accept such a paper because in class my abilities manifested differently. I asked for a second chance, he gave it to me, and this time the grade he gave me filled me with sheer happiness.

Dare more dread less

Darkness: the state or quality of being dark. Absence or deficiency of light. Wickedness or evil. Obscurity, concealment. Lack of knowledge. Lack of sight, blindness.

Dare; **A**cknowledgment; **a**wareness;
Ray; **K**indness; **N**ewness; **E**ase; **S**pirit; **S**pectacle

Death: the end of life; the total and permanent cessation of all the vital functions of an animal or plant. The state of being dead. Extinction, destruction.
Spiritual death: loss or absence of Divine Grace.

Deliverance; **E**nthusiasm; **A**uthenticity; **T**ruth; **H**appiness

> The extent to which one fears death is the extent to which one is a walking dead among the living

> Dare living life to it's fullest
> Dread not death

Decision: the act of making up one's mind. A judgment, as one formally pronounced by court. Something that is decided, resolution. The quality of being decided, firmness.

Delight; **E**ncouragement; **C**larity;
I am; **S**ureness; **I**nnovation; **O**neness, **N**ewborn

> Decision making and responsibility taking is the name of the game of problem solving

> See: Addiction, pp. 14
> Cancer, pp. 31
> "Zvia come", pp. 44
> Curse, pp. 60
> Ego, pp. 75
> Power Of The Word, pp. 171
> Self, pp. 200
> Wisdom, pp. 250
> Zero, pp. 260

Deed: something that is done, performance, or accomplishment; an act. Action or performance, esp. an illustrative of intentions, promises, or the like.

Dedication; **E**cstasy; **E**steem; **D**elight

Delight: a high degree of pleasure or enjoyment; joy; rapture. Something that gives great pleasure.

Dream; **E**njoyment; **L**ove; **I**ntegrity; **G**ratitude; **H**ealth; **T**reasure

Depression: dejection, sadness, gloom, dullness or inactivity.

Depth; **E**nlightenment; **P**urity;
Reflection; **E**ssence; **S**elf; **S**anity; **I**nner; **O**asis; **N**ascence

E.S.T. Exercise - see: pp. 5

Key-phrases/words: *Preliminary rounds*: depressed, ach, sorrow, pain, frustration, loss... *Positive affirmation rounds*: all is in divine and in perfect orchestration, order and timing, I choose to feel calm, confident, happy and joyful, I freely flow, I am motivated, I am protected and relaxed, I act on inspiration...

Desire: a longing or craving. An expressed wish, request. Sexual appetite or a sexual urge. A state of lack, not having, want.

Deluxe; **E**volution; **S**oul; **I**nspiration; **R**elief; **E**nthusiasm

Despair: loss of hope; hopelessness.

Dream; **E**nthusiasm; **S**incerity;
Peace; **A**ffection; **I**nner-self; **R**emedy

E.S.T. Exercise - see: pp. 5

Key-phrases/words: *Preliminary rounds*: depressed, despair, desperate, hopeless, lost, powerless... *Positive affirmation rounds*: I choose to feel calm, I am protected, I am safe, I am motivated, I am supported, I am ability, I am creativity, I am resourceful...

Destiny: something that is to happen or has happened to a particular person or thing; lot or fortune. The predetermined course

of events. The power or agency that determines the course of events.

Declaration; **E**ase; **S**erenity; **T**ruth; **I**ntuition; **N**ewness; **Y**ield

Destiny is an end result of a destination's declaration
(be the declaration conscious or subconscious)

The 2nd Agreement[(6)]

Be true to your word, honour it, respect it, stand up to it and walk it.

One's words are state of being and state of mind reflection and perception.

Be truthful, sincere, honest, genuine, and authentic.

Honouring, respecting, standing up to and walking my/your words is honouring and respecting, standing up to my/yourself. Be coherent; mean and speak your idea, intention, opinion then act on it and walk it.

A word is a belief energy that create e-motions and reality.
Declaration is an arrow to destination; A destiny creator.

Diarrhea: *Pathol.* An intestinal disorder characterized by abnormal frequency and fluidity of fecal evacuations. Also: Diarrhoea (LL and Gk: a flowing through).

Disgust; **I**nflammation; **A**bnormality;
Rivalry; **R**eflection; **H**ot-temper; **E**xit; **A**dversary

E.S.T. Exercise - see: pp. 5

Key-phrases/words: *Preliminary rounds*: anger, anxiety, enflamed; enraged; fear stricken, hysterical, nervous, panic, poisoned, sick of… *Positive affirmation rounds*: I now choose to be calm, chill out, cold-minded; relaxed, peaceful…

Difference: the state or relation of being different; dissimilarity. An instance or point of unlikeness or dissimilarity. A significant change in a situation. A distinguishing characteristic; distinctive quality, feature, etc.

Daylight; **I**nnovation; **F**reedom; **F**riskiness; **E**ssence; **R**elief;
Enthusiasm; **N**ascence; **C**reation; **E**ternity

Dignity: formal, grave, or noble bearing, conduct, or speech. Nobility or elevation etc.

Dare; **I**ntegrity; **G**ratitude; **N**ewness; **I**nvention; **T**ruth; **Y**es

Diligence: constant and earnest effort to accomplish what is undertaken; persistent exertion of body and mind. Care, caution.

Desire; **I**nspiration; **L**ove; **I**ntimacy;
Gift; **E**nlightenment; **N**ow; **C**uddle; **E**nthusiasm

Dis-appointment - **Disappointment**: the act or fact of dis-appointing. The state or feeling of being dis-appointed. A person or thing that dis-appoints.

Dearness; **I**nspiration; **S**atisfaction;
Awareness; **P**lay; **P**ower; **O**ption; **I**nside;
Nobility; **T**urn; **M**ake; **E**xistence; **N**earness; **T**urn-point

 Which appointment did I dis-... or miss?

E.S.T. Exercise - see: pp. 5

Key-phrases/words: *Preliminary rounds*: disappointed, frustrated, lost... *Positive affirmation rounds*: it is a learning experience only, I can today achieve, do, make it, succeed...

Dis-cover-y - **Discovery**: the act or an instance of discovering. Something discovered. Law, compulsory disclosure, as of facts or documents.

Dare; **I**nner; **S**elf; **C**ome; **O**utside; **V**itality; **E**ra; **R**ealization;
Yard

**Each day
and every moment
is suitable to dis-cover
authenticity, brilliance,
decency, excellence, genius,
honesty, integrity, love, serenity,
sincerity, success, living truth and truthfulness well-being.**

Dis-ease - **Disease**: a condition of the body in which there is incorrect function resulting from the effect of heredity, infection, diet, or environment; illness, sickness, ailment. Any deranged or depraved condition, as of the mind, society, etc. Decomposition of a material under special circumstances.

Drive; **I**ntegrity; **S**avour; **E**ase; **A**wareness; **S**hift; **E**steem

> E.S.T. Exercise - see: pp. 5
> Pre-sent Present Presents - see: pp. 6
> H.P.T. - see: pp. 7

Diversity: the state or fact of being diverse; difference, unlikeness. Variety, multiformity. A point of difference.

Devotion; **I**ntegrity; **V**alue; **E**steem;
Relief; **S**erenity; **I**ntuition; **T**rust; **Y**es

Do: a festive social gathering; party. Dos and don'ts, customs, rules, or regulations.

Dedication; **O**pportunity
Delight; **O**rchestration
Desire; **O**rder
Devotion; **O**re
Dignity; **O**ption
Diligence; **O**riginality

Dread: terror or apprehension, as of something in the future;

great fear. A person or thing dreaded. Held in awe or reverential fear.

Dare; **R**each out; **E**levation; **A**ward; **D**elight

Dread: are, bad, be, bead, bed, dad, dare, dead, dear, ear, read, red (traffic light)…

DARE is one letter short of **DREAD**

Freeze: on a summer holiday, in my primary school era, I escorted a companion to visit her ex-teacher. The host opened the door, instructed my companion to go see her ex-teacher in their bedroom and me to stay with him. He started nearing me as my companion walked through the living room's doorway, on her way to the bedroom. Looking at him I walked backwards till my back was against the closet door. Once my back was backed with the closet I stood still, reading his body language, obeying its "be quiet" order. He then held out his other hand, inserted it under my clothes, caressed, felt, sensed, touched my intimate parts.

Flight: on a 12th grade summer holiday I traveled with a friend to Eilat. On our first night there we went to a pub on the seashore. I dared, 1st time in my life, to drink beer. I drank a bottle of Goldstar and then a bottle of Guinness. By early dawn I felt sick. I went to the sea, walked in, bent down to vomit. A man came behind me. I felt his hands caress, feel and sense their way from my back to my breasts. I ran out of the sea to my friend, woke her up, urged her to rush, to arrive at the central bus station to board the 1st bus to Tel Aviv.

Fight: in my early 20s I arrived at a meeting point in Haifa, to meet a man. While waiting, a man, about my age, walked up to me and started talking with me. After sometime, I accepted this man's invitation to go over to his place. He invited me to sit on the bed and he sat on a chair. He later moved to sit beside me. When his lust overcame his brains and he would not accept or respect my no, in body language to begin with and out-loud to end it with, I kicked him in his privates.

E.S.T. exercise

1. Find a place and a time in which you feel comfortable, free and safe to practice emotional and spiritual transformation. You may practice while walking, sitting or lying down. Sit with your back straight, head up, both your feet firmly on the floor/ground. Lie down with your legs, back and head straight on a mattress, floor or ground (i.e. all body parts are within mattress frame, no bent knees, nape or neck). Use a pillow to ease stress and tension in knees, or

rolled towel under the nape (head resting on mattress). You are here to experience change, be open to awareness, listen to your e-motions.

2. Set the jug and glass within easy reach, the paper, pen or pencil on a desk or a firm surface on which you are comfortable to write. On the paper: draw a 10 - 0 e-motion scale, 10 = strongest e-motion, 0 = zero e-motion.

3. Write down the words and/or phrases that came up while you were listening to your inner self. These words and phrases are your key-words and key-phrases to insert in the following sentences:

Although I…(*) I completely and deeply love myself.
Although I…(*) I whole heartedly honour myself.
I deeply and fully for-e-give and accept myself although…(*).

4. Start gentle tapping with one hand's fingers tips on the outer-side of your other hand (The Karate chop point), or gently massaging - in a clockwise-direction - your sore-chest points marked S in the chart). While gently tapping with your finger tips on the Karate chop point or massaging the sore-chest points start saying, out loud, the key-phrases and key-words you wrote down in stage 3 above.

Let words flow freely and refrain from corrections.

Repeat this step until you feel ready to move to the next stage.

5. Move to repeat, saying out loud, the key-phrases and/or key-words you wrote in stage 3 above while gently tapping with your fingers tips on the following points:

1 Top of the head (Chakra 7)
2 Depression above eyebrows/nose ridge (Chakra 6)
3 Eye brow inner side rim
4 Eye side rim
5 Eye lower rim
6 Under the nose (depression)
7 Chin (depression)
8 Clavicle bone (v shape - Chakra 5)
9 Under the armpit (man: nipple line, woman: bra strip line)
10 Ribs 7-8 (L: over spleen, R: over liver)

6. Take a deep breath, close your eyes and listen to your emotional body. What pain/emotional level are you in now?
Write it down.

(*) fill with key-words, key-phrases

Repeat stages 4, 5 & 6 until you feel relieved or ZERO e-motion.

Should a new emotional wave well up, flow through stages 3, 4, 5 & 6 with new key-phrases and key-words it brought up.

Dream
: a succession of images, thoughts, or e-motions passing through the mind during sleep. An involuntary vision occurring to a person awake. A vision voluntarily indulged in while awake; day-dream, reverie. An aspiration, goal, aim.

Day; **R**eality; **E**xistence; **A**spiration; **M**ake
Divinity; **R**ecreation; **E**nthusiasm; **A**ward; **M**iracle

> Dreams come true,
> manifest, materialize
> and are realized from
> our inner-self
> to whom the imaginary
> and real are one, the same

> Dream BIG
> Dream FAR
> Dream HIGH

Dream world is where one can safely create, change, and receive information, know-how and knowledge for self-growth, transformation and success. It's an amazingly excellent, great, marvelous, splendid and wonder-full media to create in and with.

In a dream in January 2009, I came to my father to tell him that my mother died. I walked along a wide corridor with bright white walls and shining stainless steel metal bars. Along the way, one wide handle-free door after another opened for me to freely walk straight through. Where am I? A hospital? A Nursing Ward? I entered a room, on the left, with bright white walls and a single bed. I approached the bed and saw my father lying on it. He was covered with a spotless white sheet (in deep sleep? dead?). On his legs I saw a pile of clothes. I picked up each garment, and saw a white cashmere sweater of my mother's, that I loved dearly. I woke up feeling confused. What was my dead father doing lying in that bed? He died in 1992. Surely he knows mom died, so what is he doing here now? What is the message this dream is bringing me as I am going through the 2nd proof reading of the Hebrew version of The Challenge? (See: Cancer, pp. 31)

Happy dream creation exercise

Ingredients:
Colour chalks, paints, pens, pencils
Sketch paper, or canvas
Procedure:
Before lying in bed to sleep:
1.   Think of happiness, what does it feel and look like?
2.   Draw / sketch / paint a happy picture.
3.   Put the picture where you can watch it, lying in bed, or under your pillow.
4.   Gently shake loose your arms and legs, from hip to toes, shoulders to finger tips. Lie in bed, close your eyes, take three deep breaths (inhale through your nostrils, exhale through your mouth) and in your mind ask the good, happy and pleasant events, occasions, occurrences of the day to come forth, re-feel them, allow and let them re-fill and refresh you.

On a day when there is no memory of a good, happy, or pleasant event of yours, ask your family members or your friends if they had one. Ask he/she to share it and tell it to you. Connect with hers/his good, happy, pleasant event as if it were yours, thus making it yours.

Follow and practice this procedure with children waking up from a nightmare.

Drink: beverage. Any liquid that is swallowed for nourishment or to quench thirst. A draft of liquid. Alcoholic liquor. Excessive indulgence in alcoholic liquor. To take in through the senses; esp. with eagerness and pleasure.

Divinity; **R**ay; **I**nnovation; **N**eatness; **K**indness

Duty: something that one is expected or required to do by moral or legal obligation. A moral or legal obligation.

Deluxe; **U**ttermost; **T**reat; **Y**ippee-do-da

On a Sunday, I arrived with the kids from the kindergartens, walked into the kitchen and saw the sink and its neighbouring surface loaded with dishes. I felt exploited, angered and boiled. A juicy curse began to emerge through my clenched teeth. I stopped to consult with myself. "One moment, it's true that I agreed to help with the children's dishes, not the dishes that accumulated from the day I left until today. Yet truth is, I love washing dishes, so what is the true cause for the anger? What do I care…" Washing the dishes turned into a sheer delight.

> Love transforms duty into delight, hell into heaven on earth

Dwarf: a person who is considerably smaller than the average in stature or size, esp. one who is not normally proportioned.

Dance; **W**isdom; **A**ll-ways; **R**elish; **F**abulousness

Dye: a colouring material or matter. Colour or hue, esp. as produced by dyeing. Of the deepest or blackest dye, of the most extreme or the worst sort. To become coloured or absorb colour when treated with a dye.

Dedication; **Y**outh; **E**cstasy
Delight; **Y**ield; **E**steem

In my blond dye epoch, I happily turned on the TV after cleaning the flat. The screen filled with 'snow'. I called the cable's technical support. The technician came right away, walked straight over to the TV, bent down, picked up the plug, inserted it into the socket, turned the TV on and wonder of wonders, all is well. After I saw the technician out, I rolled with hearty-laughter at my 'blond' moment.

E

Ease: freedom from labour, pain or discomfort. Freedom from concern or anxiety; a quiet state of mind. Freedom from difficulty or great effort; facility. Freedom from financial need; plenty: a life of ease. Freedom from stiffness, constraint, or formality.

Eden; Action; Satisfaction; Ecstasy
Elevation; Affection; Serenity; Efficiency
Embrace; Affluence; Simplicity; Elation
Enthusiasm; Appreciation; Sincerity; Endurance
Exertion; Ascension; Solemnity; Euphoria
Expansion; Awareness; Stimulation; Existence

Be easy about it and with yourself. Learn to accept, respect and take yourself with ease.

See: laughter, pp. 136

Effort: deliberate exertion of physical or mental power. A strenuous attempt.

Ease; Fairness; Freedom; Omnipresence; Reality; Treasure
Essence; Festivity; Free spirit; Other; Recreation; Truth
Esteem; Faith; Fare; Origin; Relaxation; Trust

E.S.T. Exercise - see: pp. 70

Ego: the 'I' or self of any person; a person as willing, thinking, feeling, and distinguishing itself from the selves of others and from objects of its thought.

Elaboration; Gentleness; Ocean
Elevation; Gratitude; Opportunity
Evolvement; Gift; Option

Easy does it; **G**race; **O**utcome

> An Ego-free me has no abyss to fall into and multitude ways to follow and walk along to a heaven on earth reality

> See: Self, pp. 200
> Zero, pp. 260

> E.S.T. Exercise - see: pp. 70

Embrace: to clasp or take in the arms; press to the bosom; hug.

Equilibrium; **M**iracle; **B**lessing;
Relief; **A**ffection; **C**onfidence; **E**xpansion

'Welcome' and 'farewell' with my mother were from a safe distance until the end of our telephone call on my way from Tel Aviv to Hod Hasharon. **Me**, "I love you." **She**, "So why doesn't it sound like it?" **Me**, "I don't know how it sounds to you, I know that I love you." In reality these sentences opened a door to action: a natural, primitive gesture of affection and love. I began to embrace my mother every time we met or separated. At the beginning she turned stone-like. With time, she began to return my embrace with a hug until, in her last years, her embrace expressed her powerful love and we laughed asking, "Who loves whom more."

> Embrace instead of embarrass

> An embrace from love dismantles barriers, dissolves a hard as a rock heart, melts ice, and softens rigidity, roughness, stiffness, toughness

E-motion - Emotion: an affective state of consciousness in which bliss, happiness, joy, mirth, anger, fear, hate, sorrow, or the like, is experienced, as distinguished from cognitive and volitional states of consciousness: usually accompanied by certain physiological changes, as increased heartbeat, respiration, or the like,

and often overt manifestation, as crying, shaking, or laughing. An instance of this, as joy, love, mirth, sorrow, fear, or hate.

Energy-motion, Management;
Option; Talent; Inspiration; Origin; Nascence

> E-motion is energy in motion asking for a new direction, seeking relief, a way out
>
> E.S.T. Exercise - see: pp. 70

Endeavour: to exert oneself to do or effect something; make an effort; strive. To attempt; try. A strenuous effort; attempt.

Enthusiasm; Neatness; Delight;
Ecstasy; Ability; Value; Outlet; Relief

Energy: the capacity for vigourous activity; available power. The habit of vigourous activity; vigour as characteristic. The ability to act, lead others, effect, etc., forcefully.

Elation; New; Enthusiasm; Remedy; Gratitude; Yes
Expansion; Nascence; Equality; Rest; Greatness; Youth
Effect; Nobility; Efficiency; Road; Gladness; Yield

Enthusiasm: lively, absorbing interest; excited involvement. An activity in which such interest is shown.

Energy	Exuberance	Evolution
Naturalism	Navigation	Niceness
Treasure	Trust	Truth
Honesty	Honour	Humanism
Unity	Up	Utility
Sanity	Self	Softness
Innocence	Integrity	Initiative
Affection	Ability	Attitude

Serenity   **S**tamina   **S**uccess
Mind   **M**otivation   **M**ake

Epilepsy: *Pathol.*

A dis-order of the nervous system, usually characterized by loss of conscious with/without fits of convulsions, caused by traumatic experience, a shocking experience. Gratitude bend, dis-regard, dis-tortion, negation, twist.

Equilibrium; **P**ractice; **I**ntegrity; **L**ove; **E**ase; **P**eace; **S**ong; **Y**ield

The move from Ma'anit primary boarding school to Me'vuot Iron secondary and high boarding school replaced asthma with epilepsy Petit Mal fits. Sometime after I moved from Ma'anit to Hod Hasharon the Petit Mal turned into Grand-Mal to later disappear for good.

After my 2nd Grand-Mal fit I began forgetting the lunch time pill. In the following check up, after the blood test, the Neurologist accepted my request to skip this pill. I then started forgetting the night time pill and once more the neurologist accepted my request, after reading the blood test results. Then I progressed to forget the once daily pill, and this time the neurologist declined my request. I left our meeting feeling furious. Years later I realized this 'forgetfulness' was my inner-self way to reveal to me I healed. I began to pay attention, research and study 'forgetfulness', asking myself, "Did I really forget, or…?"

Twenty years later, fits and medicines free, I once again met the same neurologist and closed a circle.

From the clinic: When I began my way as a reflexology practitioner a young woman came for treatment. She told me that her epilepsy fits began after she witnessed a violent explosion by her father. Her fits duration, frequency and manifestation prevented her from integrating in a healthy life cycle and style. Shortly after she felt good at having found a job, our ways separated. Years later we coincidently met and I heard she since married, and feels very content with her job.

E.S.T. Exercise - see: pp. 70

Key-phrases/words: *Preliminary rounds*: abused, ashamed, blame, deprived, embarrassed, fear stricken, helpless, paralyzed, regret, scared shitless, shame, shocked, wounded, unaccepted, undeserving, unworthy… *Positive affirmations rounds*: accepted, appreciated, competent, deserving, grateful, loved, protected, powerful, safe, successful, valuable, worthy.

Err-or - **Error**: a deviation from accuracy or correctness; a mistake, as in action or speech. Belief in something untrue; the holding of mis-taken opinions, perceptions, principles, stand-points or viewpoints. The condition of believing what is not true. A moral offense;
wrongdoing, sin.

Exit; **R**emedy; **R**ight; **O**pportunity; **R**evival
Excitement; **R**evelation; **R**oad; **O**rder; **R**oyalty
Ecstasy; **R**edemption; **R**espect; **O**ptimism; **R**out

E.S.T. exercise to dis-cover a hidden truth
1. Get a notebook and a pen.
2. Find a place and a time where you feel at ease, protected and safe.
3. Write the first word that comes to mind and continue with each word or phrase that follows. Write freely, disregard, ignore, over-come and over-look grammar, phrasing, style 'conventions', 'laws', 'rules'. Give yourself a break. Do not read what you wrote, seek logic, search for phrasing or spelling errors or mis-takes.
4. Finish writing after you've written a few lines, or sentences and more, and you feel it's enough, it's right and put the notebook in a safe place.
5. Proceed to follow new ideas or with your pre-planned schedule.
6. Approximately half an hour before you go to sleep, or on another day, take the notebook, go and sit where you feel at ease, protected and safe. Adopt the approach, attention, attitude and awareness of a non-participant observer sitting on top of a high fence or way up in the bleachers watching the young playing on the ground.
   Open the notebook and read what you wrote.
   When finding an 'error', close your eyes, focus on your breath, and dedicate attention, awareness and time to ask and wonder, "What is revealed to me now?" "What is my inner-self showing or telling me?"
   The first word, or sentence, that comes up is the correct and true answer, whether you understand it, are puzzled by it, or you find no connection, logic explanation to it or can make sense of it. When you cannot make sense of the answer, concerned or puzzled by it - ask for inspiration to enlighten you with a message/words that you

can make sense of, understand, use.

Escape: to slip or get away, as from confinement or restraint; gain or regain liberty. To slip away from pursuit or peril; avoid capture, punishment, or any threatened evil.

Ease a cap/cape?; **S**incerity; **C**hance; **A**bility; **P**ower; **E**volvement

Examination: inspection, inquiry, investigation. The act or process of testing pupils, candidates, etc., as by questions. The test itself; the list of questions asked.

Expansion; **X**ebec; **A**musement; **M**ind;
Insight; **N**ew; **A**nchor; **T**rust; **I**n; **O**ption; **N**ext

An examination, inspection, inquiry, investigation, test allows and lets me satisfy primitive instincts to delve, explore, reconsider, review a belief, date, know-how, pattern, piece of information, way to grow and thrive. When I remember that this is the one and only root of the matter there goes away and out failings and failure to freely and naturally bring along and in science and success; a room is made for success successions.

For the parent that you are: please dare reconsider your approach, attitude, perception and response to your passing of examinations; be them in your life's university, past or present private or public kindergartens and schools. When you perceive yourself as a failure or you take exam results for what they really and truly are: a way for you to find out what you know, what works or does not work for you, what you perhaps need still learn to grow and thrive? your child will do the same for you are your child's raw-model to become, follow and grow into and up to, teacher in life and schools schooling and university studies.

E.S.T. Exercise - see: pp. 70

Shame and shyness - see: pp. 207

In my last years in Ma'anit I studied English expression, literature and poetry for a B.A. degree. One lesson the teacher asked us to present a paper with 2,500 words. For three weeks I sat down, wrote and threw what I wrote to the waste bin, until out of anger and frustration, I presented my 1,000 words paper. The teacher returned my paper and said he cannot accept such paper having in class heard and seen… I answered him that what I can express with 500 words I cannot express with 2,500 and asked him to let me present him with a new paper, words limitation free. He agreed. I then presented him with a new paper and was the happiest student when I saw the grade.

In the early 1980's I registered for Economics, Labour and Employment Relations studies in Tel Aviv University. In the first trimester we studied Economics and with all my hate of this field, I passed the tests and reached the second trimester in which we studied Labour and Employment Law. I slept through the first three lessons, so I informed the university of my decision to quit. My request for the relevant tuition fee refund was granted.

At this time, one of my acquaintances said, "I have the connections in a famous industry and I shall get you in there." He asked me to come up with a certificate evidencing I finished 12 years of school. When I received the certificate I saw it included my high school marks: average in most fields, very good in English.

One of my colleague students in Huna joined me for my first year in Reflexology studies. In one of the times we studied for a test, she told me that she finished her university studies thanks to her alliance (b.h.m.). He wrote all her papers. During our meetings, before each examination, we declared joyfully laughing out loud, "We are now learning the best we can, we have all the knowledge, we easily pass this test and every test." Miracles and wonders began to fill our school year.

In the last semester in the first year of Reflexology studies I heard the teacher's talk with one of the students. The teacher reminded the student that if she doesn't hand in reports she will not receive her diploma. The student answered her, "I don't know what to do, I have no one to ask, I don't know how…" The teacher suggested she go and ask me. Why did she suggest she come to me? When I heard that one of the criterions to receive the diploma was to hand in 100-120 reports before the school year ends I calculated the weekly quantity, and so by that time I had handed in nearly 130 reports. The week after school year ended I was asked to come and collect the diploma.

In 2008 my eldest brother, David, brought me documents he collected from our mom's home, among them was a gymnastics and sports 10th grade certificate with a 'good' certificate and medal.

> Early planning and preparation opens a door to who is wise - the one foreseeing the outcome and a way to successfully pass exams

Ex-pensive-ness - **Expensiveness**: entailing great expense; very high-priced; costly.

Exploration; **X**ylophone; **P**assion; **E**nlightenment; **N**et; **S**ense; **I**nvention; **V**alue; **E**thics; **N**icety; **E**nrichment; **S**ight; **S**atisfaction

Experience: a particular instance of personally encountering or undergoing something. The process or fact of personally observing, encountering, or undergoing something. Knowledge gained from what one has observed, encountered, or undergone. To meet with, feel, undergo.

Evolution; **X**erox; **P**leasure; **E**ra; **R**eality;
Innovation; **E**xistence; **N**ewness; **C**reativity; **E**cstasy

Eye: the organ of sight, in vertebrates, typically one of a pair of spherical bodies contained in an orbit of the skull. Sight, vision. Appreciative or discriminating visual perception. Look, glance, or gaze. An attentive look, close observation, or watch. Regard, view, or intention. Manner or way of looking at a thing, estimation, opinion. A centre of light, intelligence, influence, etc.

Elation; **Y**outh; **E**vergreen
Every-body; **Y**es; **E**steem

F

Failure: the act or an instance of failing or proving unsuccessful; lack of success. Non-performance of something due, required, or expected. An insufficiency; a subnormal quantity or quality. Deterioration or decay, esp. of vigour, strength, etc. a condition of being bankrupt by reason of insolvency.

Fare, **f**air, **f**rankness; **A**bility; **I**ntuition;
Love; **U**nity; **R**esourcefulness; **E**nthusiasm
Fun; **A**rdour; **I**nnovation; **L**aughter; **U**niqueness; **R**espect; **E**lation

Pre-sent present presents

1. Find a place and a time where you feel protected and safe.
2. Lie down, sit or stand with your back and head in a straight line.
3. Gently shake your arms and legs loose to clear stress.
4. Take a deep breath, calmly exhale, let all negativity and tension leave.
5. Take another deep breath and say out loud, "I am one with all there is"[3], calmly exhale.
6. Take 2-3 deep breaths, calmly exhaling, while listening to your body language, to what it reveals to you.
7. Take a deep breath and say, out loud, "I now connect with my soul and spirit energy and feel it."
8. Take another deep breath. Calmly exhale and begin to return to sense your surroundings and say out loud, "I feel calm, love, peace and success."
9. Open your eyes, welcome back, nurture that feeling of divine ease, love, peace and success.

Faith: belief in anything, as a code of ethics, or the occurrence of a future event. A system of religious belief. Confidence or trust in a person or thing. Belief that is not based on proof. Belief in Holy-spirit or in doctrines or teaching of religion. The obligation of loyalty or fidelity to a person, promise, engagement, etc.

Fate; **A**ll; **I**nnocence; **T**oken; **H**armony
Festivity; **A**ward; **I**nnermost; **T**ool to enjoy; **H**eaven on earth

Faith creates fate, self-esteem self-evidence

Fake: anything made to appear other than is actually is. A spurious report or story. A person who fakes; a faker.

Faking it is making it; **A**wareness; **K**ey to kingdom; **E**xistence

To the inner-self imaginary and real are one, thus by and via faking it is the way the law of attraction yields. To fake is a way to programme, set and use the imagination to create a reality; make the inner-self manifest a. the negative, traditionally and widely used interpretation of fake (fear or lie come true, to counterfeit, misrepresent); b. the positive, new way in which a dream come true, wish happen, materialize and is realized.

Believing, dancing, drawing, feeling, playing, saying, sensing, sketching, speaking, talking, thinking, visualizing, walking it is making it.

Fare: the price charged for transporting a passenger. A paying passenger. Food, diet. State of things. Experience of good or bad fortune. Travel.

Fertility; **A**dvancement; **R**e-ward; **E**ndowment
Freedom; **A**nswer; **R**e-phrase; **E**ase

Fate: something that befalls a person; fortune; lot.

Faith; **A**ssembly; **T**reasure; **E**mpowerment
Freedom; **A**bundance; **T**rust; **E**volution
Fun; **A**ll the way; **T**hankfulness; **E**cstasy
Fare(in)well; **A**dmiration; **T**elepathy; **E**xistence

Fate is faith is self-esteem perception's self-evidence

Fault: a defect or imperfection; flaw; failing. An error or mistake. A misdeed or transgression. Responsibility for failure or

wrongful act.

Fun; Award; Usher; Love; Treasure
Frankness; Aspect; Utility; Lesson; Truth
Faith; Awareness; Unity; Life; Trust

E.S.T. Exercise - see: pp. 70

Fear: a distressing e-motion aroused by an impending pain or by the illusion of danger, evil, etc. Anxiety; solicitude.

Forthcoming; Evolution; Assessment; Respect
Fairness; Ease; Awareness; Rejuvenation
Fare; Encouragement; Alert; Red-light
Freedom; Establishment; Attention; Reward
Free-spirit; Equilibrium; Affection; Relief

Dread - see pp. 69

Fear creates a reality that justifies it is one message, power of the word creating a reality is another.
How is that?

I came to this world being and feeling fearless. Talks of dangers, risks, terror, time and time again, gave fear authority and power. Feeling, hearing and sensing the other's fear nourishes one's fear, makes it expand and grow, sets a fear impulse pattern that turns to be the controller and the ruler of one's life. Now what do you want? For fear to go on being your controller and dominant ruler in creating scenes such as the following ones? Or...

> In a family that hired me to nurture her children, the father came home, ordered the children to go out to the backyard garden or upstairs to their rooms. He then invited me to sit on the couch and started to share memories from his early adolescent holidays at the Black sea's beach. "My family went on summer holiday to the same beach; where German families were having their holidays. The Germans were sitting on the beach drinking and playing cards, not paying attention to what their children were doing... I came alone to Israel...." A few days later it dawned on me that my family name and my way of interacting with his children awakened these memories of his and I wondered if they are behind his

'the best defence is attack' mannerism with me.

One late afternoon he came home and found the front gate was unlocked. I then heard "I told you to never leave the gate unlocked… don't let my 4 year old be out of your sight. You have no idea what he does. You cannot trust him, he runs out into the street without telling us. We were at an event and he ran out into the parking lot, he could have been hit by a car."

"When we were on our holiday in Eilat, after we put the children to sleep, we went down to mingle. Suddenly I saw my man come rushing up to me after he saw that our 7 year old had come into the hall and heard that she was looking for us because when she woke up she saw that our 4 year old was not in his bed. We went looking for him all over the hotel and out in the parking lots and street and found him walking along the curb-stone of the swimming-pool. Just imagine what could have happened if he had fallen into the water" I heard his wife say after they safely returned from this holiday.

See: Child, pp. 42
Terror, pp. 229
Young, pp. 258

E.S.T. Exercise - see: pp. 70

Key-phrases/words: *Preliminary rounds*: afraid to death, frozen like an iceberg, paralyzed, helpless… *Positive affirmation rounds*: I choose to let fear go, all is in divine and perfect order and timing, calm, peaceful, I give myself permission to hold the reins with my own two hands, protected, safe…

Female
: a human being of the sex that conceives and bears young; a woman or girl. of, pertaining to, or characteristic of this sex; feminine: female charm, female suffrage.

Festivity; **E**lation; **M**agic; **A**ffection; **L**ove; **E**cstasy
Fun; **E**legance; **M**astery; **A**scent; **L**aughter; **E**nthusiasm
Flow; **E**steem; **M**erriness; **A**rt; **L**eadership; **E**xcellence
Frankness; **E**ase; **M**ake; **A**ttitude; **L**ight; **E**volution
Free-spirit; **E**xpansion; **M**otivation;
Affluence; **L**ivelihood; **E**soteric knowledge
Fellowship; **E**lasticity; **M**ake; **A**rdour; **L**ife; **E**quilibrium

Festival: a day or time of celebration, marked by feasting, ceremonies, or other observances. A periodic commemoration or celebration. A period or programme of festive activities, cultural events, or entertaining. Gaiety, merrymaking.

Freedom; **E**poch; **S**ensuality;
Treasure; **I**ntuition; **V**ivacity; **A**wareness; **L**ove

Fight: a battle or combat. Any contest or struggle. An angry argument or disagreement. Boxing: a bout or contest. Ability or inclination to fight. To contend in any manner; strive.

Fear; **I**nterest; **G**uard; **H**abit; **T**rance;
Fellowship; **I**ntelligence; **G**ratitude;
Hear no evil, see no evil, speak no evil; **T**rip

> Which Is my call and choice: Fight OR thrive?

> E.S.T. Exercise - see: pp. 70

Key-phrases/words: *Preliminary rounds*: angry, frustrated, helpless, hopeless, hurt, offended, powerless, vict-I'm... *Positive affirmations rounds*: calm, confidence, love, peace, protected, relief, safe...

Fixation: *Psychoanal.* a partial arrest of emotional and instinctual development at an early point in life. A preoccupation or obsession; compulsive absorption or involvement.

Free **f**low; **I**ndependence; **X**ebec;
Accord; **T**enderness; **I**ntegrity; **O**asis; **N**ew

> E.S.T. Exercise - see: pp. 70

Key-phrases/words: *Preliminary rounds*: imprisoned, stuck, helpless, worthless, weak... *Positive affirmations rounds*: calm, capable, deserving, flowing, free, gifted, skilled, talented, trained, valuable, worthy...

Flight: swift movement, transition; or progression. The act, manner, or power of flying. A journey into or through outer space.

Friendship; **L**ove; **I**ntelligence; **G**ratuity; **H**armony; **T**ime

For(e)-give-ness - Forgiveness: to pardon a perceived as offense or an offender. To grant free pardon for or remission of (an offense, debt, etc.); absolve. To give up all claim or account of; remit (a debt, obligation, etc.).

Frequency; **O**riginality; **R**esistance, **r**elief; **G**enuine; **I**ntegrity; **V**acation; **E**nthusiasm; **N**ew; **E**xpression; **S**ong of **s**ongs; **S**hift

Foul: a violation of a rule of a sport or game. A collision or entanglement. Something that is foul.

Freedom; **O**rder; **U**tterance; **L**ove

Foul play: self-deception, destruction, murder, assassination, homicide, treachery, unfairness.

Which rule am I violating?
Who am I deceiving or destructing?
Which/whose self is murdered?

Fraction: a part as distinct from the whole of anything; a portion or section. A very small part of anything; minute portion. A very small amount; a little bit.

Fruit; **R**ail; **A**uthenticity;
Charisma; **T**reasure; **I**ndividuality; **O**rigin; **N**eatness

Fracture: a break, breach, or split. The characteristic manner of breaking: The breaking of a bone, cartilage, or the like, or the resulting condition.

Fragility; **R**evelation; **A**bility;
Course; **T**ruth; **U**nity; **R**emedy; **E**ase

E.S.T. Exercise - see: pp. 70

Key-phrases/words: *Preliminary rounds*: broken, shattered; weak... *Positive affirmations rounds*: connect; elasticity; health, perfect harmony; unity; tie together; ...

Fragment: a part broken of or detached. A portion that is incomplete or unfinished: fragments of a poem. An odd piece, bit or scrap.

Freedom; Redemption; Affection; Gift;
Miracle; Endowment; Nurture; Treasure, trust, truth

In secondary school we were divided to three levels, in mathematics, and I studied with the 'Below Average' group. When we reached fractions studies I sincerely and truly wanted with all my heart and might to figure out and learn how, in the name of Holy-spirit, I can assemble, deduct, divide, multiply fragments. I recall that in one of the classes my questions made the teacher say, "You know it very well and you are doing it on purpose to disrupt my class, now get out." Then and there I set my self free from mathematics. The Principal threatened, "If you don't go back to mathematic lessons you shall be assigned to labour work." I joyfully read books outside of class until the happy end of my high school days.

In the high inflation cycle that swept through Israel in the 1980ies, a partner (a lawyer, in his 30ies) and I (an export/import clerk, in her 20ies) were challenged to find Bank Leumi's Interest formula for the company's account. The partner keyed his formula into VisiCalc (the electronic calculating sheet), to yield a result that was different from the one showing in the Bank's report page. He then took his Texas Instruments calculator, efficiently and effortlessly keyed the values and... the result matched with the one in the Bank's report page. How is that? What's happening here? I sat beside him, exploding with excitement. When he invited me to key my formula, the result on the screen matched with the one in the Bank's report page. The partner, that showed and taught me ways out of mathematic questions, leaped from the chair, as though a snake bit him, hit the table so the computer flew up in the air, and said, "Never again dare tell me that you don't know mathematics, that in secondary and high school they did not teach you mathematics." Years later I realized that mathematics doing and knowing and mathematical mind are different things.

Fraud: deceit; trickery, or breach of confidence, used to gain some unfair or dishonest advantage. Any deception or trickery.

Fun; **R**ectitude; **A**uthenticity; **U**sher; **D**are

> E.S.T. Exercise - see: pp. 70

Key-phrases/words: *Preliminary rounds*: betrayed, deceived, lied to, tricked… *Positive affirmations rounds*: authentic, honest, sincere, transparent, truthful, valuable, worthy…

Freedom: the state of being at liberty rather than in confinement or under physical restraint. Exemption from external control, interference, regulation, etc. Power of determining one's or its action. *Philos.* the power to make one's own choices or decisions without constraint from within or without; autonomy; self-determination.

Fertility; **R**apture; **E**ssence; **E**quality; **D**are; **O**asis; **M**iracle
Fascination; **R**eality; **E**volution;
Elation; **D**elicacy; **O**bservance; **M**irth
Frequency; **R**efreshment;
Enthusiasm; **E**quilibrium; **D**ay; **O**ffering; **M**astery

Freshness: quality or state of being fresh.

Festivity; **R**eliability; **E**cstasy;
Self; **H**onesty; **N**ew; **E**ssence; **S**weet; **S**port

Fright: sudden and extreme fear; a sudden terror. A person or thing of shocking, grotesque, or ridiculous appearance.

Friendship; **R**emedy; **I**sland; **G**rowth; **H**and; **T**ruth

> E.S.T. Exercise - see: pp. 70

Key-phrases/words: *Preliminary rounds*: afraid, boneless, fear-stricken, insecure, like a leaf in a storm, terrorized, unsure… *Positive* *affirmations rounds*: calm, deserving, free, immuned, protected, safe, strong, valuable, worthy…

Fruition: attainment of anything desired; realization of good results: the fruition of one's labour. Enjoyment, as of something attained or realized. The state of bearing fruits.

Fun; Relaxation; Unity; Intuition;
Truth; Innovation; Order; Navigation

Frustration: the making of (action, intention, plan, etc.) worthless or of no avail; defeat; baffle; nullify. Side-effect of dis-appointment.

Fruit; Recreation; Usher; Selection; Trust;
Right; Award; Treasure; Inspiration; Ongoing; Next

E.S.T. Exercise - see: pp. 70

Fun: something that provides mirth or amusement; enjoyment; playfulness.

Feast; Usher; Nourishment
Finesse; Uniformity; Nutrition

Fury: unrestrained or violent anger, rage, passion or the like. Violence; vehemence; fierceness.

Freedom; Utmost; Relief; Youthfulness

G

Gaiety: quality or state of being gay, bright appearance, festivity.

Gratitude; **A**ttitude; **I**dentity; **E**ssence; **T**ruth; **Y**outhfulness

Gall: something bitter or severe. Bitterness of spirit; rancor. Bile. Impudence.

Garden of Eden; **A**djustment; **L**ife; **L**ove

E.S.T. Exercise - see: pp. 70

Key-phrases/words: *Preliminary rounds*: angry, annoyed, bitter, sour,... *Positive affirmations rounds*: easy going, flowing, free, good...

Gall bladder stone

Generosity; **A**ttunement; **L**everage; **L**and
Being grace; **L**esson; **A**ffection;
Dedication; **D**elight; **E**nergy; **R**espect
Success; **T**aste; **O**ption; **N**ewness; **E**nergy-motion;

Gall bladder and liver cleansing
Frequent anger, bitterness, sourness remedy

Ingredients:
Citrus juice squeezer
Crystal glass
Fresh, mellow, ripe yellow lemon
Olive Oil (cold pressed, acidity value up to 1.8)

21 days procedure:
Women in fertility cycle are to begin procedure on cycle's 7th day.

Every day, half an hour before your first drink or meal, squeeze fresh lemon juice and mix it with olive oil into a homogenous mixture, drink to health.

Begin with 1 table spoon each, proceed to 2 table spoons each.

Gall bladder stones, severe constipation

Ingredients:
Citrus juice squeezer
Crystal glass
Fresh, mellow, ripe and yellow lemons.
Large size strainer
Olive Oil (cold pressed, acidity value up to 1.8)

3 days procedure:
Women in fertility cycle are to follow this procedure between cycle's 7th-28th day.

Place strainer near the toilet seat.

Every night, two and a half hours after your last drink or meal, squeeze fresh lemon juice, fill half of the crystal glass with the freshly squeezed lemon juice and half with the olive oil. Mix the lemon juice and olive oil to a homogenous mixture, drink to your health and lie down. Mentally prepare yourself to liquidity feces. When time comes, place the strainer under your rump, and when done, look for the stones in it.

Game
: an amusement or pastime. Fun, sport of any kind. A competitive activity involving skill, endurance, or chance on the part of two or more persons who play according to a set of rules; usually for their own amusement or for that of spectators.

Gratitude; **A**ffection; **M**otivation; **E**volution
Gladness; **A**ffluence; **M**astery; **E**xpansion

Gastritis
: *Pathol.* Inflammation of the stomach, esp. of its mucous membrane.

Gaiety; **A**ttunement; **S**ource; **T**aste; **R**emedy; **I**ncarnation; **T**enderness; **I**sland; **S**erenity, **s**implicity, **s**incerity, **s**uccess

E.S.T. Exercise - see: pp. 70

Key-phrases/words: *Preliminary rounds:* burning acidity, burning hell, crazed, enraged, raving mad, sour... *Positive affirmations rounds:* calm, chill, cool, easy digestion, easy going, flow freely, good, happy, peaceful, taking it easy...

Gate
: an opening permitting passage through an enclosure. Any means of access or entrance. A mountain pass.

Gift; Awareness; Treasure; Eloquence

Generosity
: readiness or liberality in giving. Freedom from meanness or smallness of mind or character. Largeness or fullness; amplitude.

Grace; Existence; Nearness; Elegance;
Reality; Oasis; Simplicity; Innovation; Treat; Yield

Good
: profit; worth; benefit. Excellence or merit; kindness. Moral righteousness; virtue.

Gentleness; Originality; Ocean; Desire
Growth; Oxygen; Order; Delight
Gem; Openness; Opportunity; Development
Genesis; Own; Outcome; Dream

Grace
: elegance or beauty of form, manner, motion, or action. A pleasing or attractive quality or endowment. Favour or good will.

Gesture; Relief; Amplitude; Charisma; Ease
Glow, Revelation; Award; Creativity; Elation

Gratification
: the state of being gratified; great satisfaction. Something that gratifies; source of pleasure or satisfaction. The act of gratifying.

Greatness; Rapture; Aspect; Treasure; Image; Fun; Identity;
Comfort; Ardour; Truth; Implementation; Origin; Nobility

Gratitude: the quality or feeling of being grateful or thankful.

Gift; **R**evival; **A**wareness; **T**ime;
Influence; **T**ide; **U**sher; **D**eluxe; **E**xpansion

Growth: the act or process, or manner of growing; development; gradual increase. Size or stage of development. Completed development. Development from a simpler to a more complex stage.

Gaiety; **R**ipple; **O**pportunity; **W**isdom;
Tenderness; **H**ear no evil, see no evil, speak no evil

Grow into: **a**. to become large enough for. **b**. to become mature or experienced enough for.
Grow out of: to become too large or mature for; outgrow.
Grow up: **a**. to be or become fully grown. **b**. to come into existence; arise.

You may want to consider the following remedy and experience it before rushing to artificial or laboratory made growth hormones.

Growth and immunity system acceleration
Fun, rest, whole-hearted happiness, joy and laughter are essential and vital components.
Sleep - light and sound free:
Adult: night-time sleep: 9 hrs and more; day-time: 2 hrs.
Child: night-time: 8 hrs and more; day-time: 2 hrs and as much as he/she feels like and needs.
Baby: as much as he/she feels like and needs.

Exercise
Height: measure height the day you begin, keep the note with the measurement in a safe place, measure again a year later, and calculate the difference between the two measurements.
Immunity system: keep present laboratory test results in a safe place, take same laboratory test three months later, compare difference between the two.
Babies: Once daily, father/mother, tap gently and lovingly for half a minute to a minute on your baby's chest centre (rib

cage, over thymus gland^(*))
Children and grownups: One-three times per day, 3-5 minutes boxing (with both fists alternately) or tapping on chest center (rib cage, over thymus gland^(*)).

Grudge: a feeling of ill will or resentment.

Grace; **R**elief; **U**nity; **D**evelopment; **G**ain; **E**ntity;

E.S.T. Exercise - see: pp. 70

Guilt: the fact or state of having committed an offense, crime, etc. esp. against moral or penal law; culpability. Conduct involving the commission of such crimes, wrongs, etc.; criminality. A feeling of responsibility or remorse for some real or imagined offense, crime, etc.

Gratitude; **U**plift; **I**nnocence, **i**ntegrity; **L**ove; **T**ruth;
Genuine; **U**niformity; **I**nstallation; **L**oyalty; **T**hank you

E.S.T. Exercise - see: pp. 70

Key-phrases/words: *Preliminary rounds*: ashamed, blamed, embarrassed, guilty, guilt complex, shame, unworthy... *Positive affirmations rounds*: authenticity, honesty, integrity, serenity, sincerity, valuable, worthy...

Gum: the firm, fleshy tissue covering the alveolar parts of either jaw and enveloping the necks of the teeth.

Greatness; **U**ltimate; **M**iracle
Gladness; **U**nity; **M**otivation

Remedies

♦ Quit alcohol, beverages, sodas drinking; baking, cooking or storing drinks and foods in aluminium dishes or aluminum foil, sugars rich

---

^(*) The thymus is a specialized organ in the immune system. The functions of the thymus are the production of T-lymphocytes (T cells), which are critical cells of the adaptive immune system, and the production and secretion of thymosins, hormones which control T-lymphocyte activities and various other aspects of the immune system. One of its most important roles is the induction of central tolerance.

drinks and foods - other than fruits; excessive sweets easting; smoking..

♦ Have your amalgam fillings, root canals, teeth and wisdom teeth extractions checked redone or replaced by a biological dentist. They all can create aches, bleedings, infections and other manifestations in the gums, jaw bones, nape, neck, pharynx, throat, and in some cases cancer.

Gum bleeding:

E.S.T. Exercise - see: pp. 70

Key-phrases/words: I spit blood, I am bleeding, hurting...

Salty sea water rinsing; Lemon leaf: chewing and massage, Zinc nutritional supplement.

Gum infection:

E.S.T. Exercise - see: pp. 70

Key-phrases/words: *Preliminary rounds*: Blazing mad, boiled, chasing my tail like a dog; Inflamed with ambition/desire/passion, raving mad... *Positive affirmations rounds*: apprentice, student, trainee, I choose to educate myself, I choose to learn, I choose to reprogramme myself, I open to re-wire my nuero pathways...

CO-Q-10, Zinc, Vitamin C; Clove buds infusion(*) and/or Sage and/or salty sea water rinsing; Clove bud and Juniper berry pure essential oils, silica with sea salt crystals; Aloe vera - break/cut the leaf and apply the gel to the infected area.

Application:
Prepare a synergy from the Clove bud and Juniper berry pure essential oils.
    Add sea salt crystals to the silica and mix together. Dip the tooth-brush bristles in the silica with the sea salt crystals. Drip 1-2 drops of Clove bud and Juniper berry pure essential oils synergy, attentively, intentionally and gently massage the gums by holding the tooth brush bristles at 45°, from the gum along the tooth (6-10 times each tooth or group of teeth). Attentively and gently brush the tongue and inner mouth walls. Rinse with sea-water.

Gingival: gums massage, once daily, 2-3 minutes.

(*) Clove bud infusion: place 2 grams (0.07054 ounces) of clove buds in a crystal bowl, pour 500 ml (2 1/2 glasses) boiling hot water into the bowl, cover with glass top, let it infuse for 30 minutes. Store in the refrigerator or in a cool dark and dry place.

H

Habit: customary practice or use. A particular practice, custom, or usage. Compulsive need, inclination, or use; addiction. A dominant or regular disposition or tendency; prevailing character or quality.

Heart; **A**ffection; **B**eauty; **I**nnocence; **T**reasure;
Hear no evil, see no evil, speak no evil;
Awareness; **B**alance; **I**nnovation; **T**ruth
Harmony; **A**wareness; **B**reath; **I**ntuition; **T**rust

Habitat: the native environment of an animal or plant; the kind of place that is natural for the life and growth of an animal or plant.

Happiness; **A**ssurance; **B**each; **I**ncentive; **T**reat; **A**rt; **T**aste

Habitation: a place or residence; dwelling; abode. The act of inhabiting; occupancy by inhabitants. A settlement or community.

Heaven on earth, **h**umor; **A**lways; **B**est; **I**dentity;
Thanksgiving; **A**sset; **T**act; **I**magination; **O**cean; **N**eatness

E.S.T. Exercise - see: pp. 70

Key-phrases/words: *Preliminary rounds*: afraid, blocked, restrain, stuck, fixed with nails, frozen to death, paralyzed... *Positive affirmations rounds*: calm, confident, free to create my own new..., choose to freely create..., I allow my system to let it out, I give my self permission to let it go from each and every cell and cell receptor site, from every fiber in my being, body, mind, soul and spirit, inspired motivation, inspired action, love, peace...

Happiness: good fortune, pleasure; contentment; joy, aptness or felicity, as of expression.

Home; **A**ffection; **P**resence; **P**eace;
Integrity; **N**ascence; **E**lation; **S**afe-place, **S**ong
Horizon; **A**wareness; **P**rosperity; **P**otential;

Innermost; **N**eatness; **E**nrichment; **S**ecurity; **S**ureness
Hardihood; **A**pproach; **P**arty; **P**assion;
Intelligence; **N**ew; **E**ssence; **S**acredness; **S**weet

> E.S.T. Exercise - see: pp. 70

Key-phrases/words: I choose to have an amazingly happy day. Happiness is my true nature. I deserve happiness, I am entitled to happiness, I claim my happiness and intend to enjoy a happy day. I give myself permission for inspired motivation, inspired action, love, peace. I am open to clearing whatever blocks or resist happiness, inspired motivation and action at a cellular level and from every fiber of my being, body, mind, soul and spirit…

Hardness: a relative degree or extent of the quality or state of being hard.

Heart; **A**ffluence; **R**ipple; **D**elight;
Nurture; **E**nthusiasm; **S**olemn; **S**erenity

> Starting now eggs, only, boil and harden

Hard drug: any drug that is physiologically addictive and physically and psychologically harmful, such as heroin.

Harmony; **A**wareness; **R**ide; **D**etermination;
Destination; **R**oad; **U**nity; **G**ladness, **g**race

Hard-fisted: stingy, miserly; close fisted. Tough-minded; ruthless: hard-fisted gangsters.

Home; **A**ffection; **R**elief; **D**ay
Festivity; **I**nspiration; **S**helter; **T**ruth; **E**volvement; **D**ivinity

Hard-handed: having hands hardened by toil. Oppressive; cruel.

Happiness; **A**ssistance; **R**esilience; **D**evotion
Higher-self; **A**ttunement; **N**ext; **D**ream; **E**lasticity; **D**esire

Hard-head: a shrewd, practical person. A blockhead.
Hard-headed: practical, shrewd, not easily moved or deceived. Obstinate; stubborn; willful.
Hard-head manifestations: cervical deformation and disks eruptions, face, neck and upper back muscles cramps and paralysis,

frozen shoulder, shoulder pain, stiff neck. Cervical vertebrates , shoulder joint sclerosis.

Health; **A**rdour; **R**evelation; **D**edication
Harvest; **E**cstasy; **A**udacity; **D**eliverance;

E.S.T. Exercise - see: pp. 70

Key-phrases/words: *Preliminary rounds*: hard-headed, stubborn, thick head... *positive affirmations rounds*: elasticity, flexibility, I love when things easily, freely and naturally fall into my lap, one at a time, being open minded, open to new ideas, open to new ways, freely flow, inspired motivation, inspired action...

Additional exercises

Stand or sit with your back, chin and head straight.

Exercise 1:
♦ Bend one of your elbows, place fingers tips on shoulder joint cavity of this arm.
♦ Turn your face towards this arm, fix your look at the elbow's edge.
♦ Begin to turn your arm and shoulder joint **forward** while:
1. Your gaze is fixed at elbow's edge to your best ability.
2. Your concentration and focus are on creating as flowing a movement as you can while drawing as large a circle with your elbow as you possibly can.

Feel and listen to your shoulder and neck muscles e-motion and story.

Repeat three times before you proceed to do it with your other arm.

Proceed to do the above **backwards**, with each arm.

Exercise 2:
♦ With your back straight, chin and head up, gaze fixed straight forward, attentively and intentionally turn your head to one side as far as you possibly can pain, stress, strain or tension free. Feel and sense every muscle in your chest, shoulder belt and neck.

Remain in this position for a peaceful count of 1-2-3.

Begin turning of your head back, with same attention, focus and intention, until you look straight ahead.

Repeat three times.

Proceed to do the above to the other side.

♦ With your back, chin and head straight, gaze fixed straight forward, attentively and intentionally lower your head **backwards** in as round an arch-like angle and as far as you possibly can, pain,
stress, strain or tension free.

Feel and sense every muscle in your chest, shoulder belt and neck.

Remain in this position for a peaceful count of 1-2-3.

Begin raising your head back, with same attention, focus and intention, until you look straight ahead.

Repeat three times.

Proceed to do the above **forward**, in as round an arch-like angle as you possibly can, all the way for the chin to touch the neck.

Exercise 3:
♦ Exercise 1 above, with straight arm.

Exercise 4:
♦ Lie on your stomach, exhale while you uplift your shoulders until shoulder blades touch each other. Inhale while you let them come down and rest. Repeat 10 times x 3, once daily.

Exercise 5:
♦ Lie on your stomach, breath out while you stretch your arms forward and raise your upper back with your spine in a straight line with your back and head. Breath in while you let them come down and rest. Repeat 10 times x 3, once daily.

Exercise 6:
♦ Roll a towel, place it on the bed, length-way or width way, place your back or upper chest on the rolled towel and let it rest until you feel relief. Move the towel side-ways, down/up until you feel rested and peaceful. Falling asleep during this procedure is welcomed.

Hard-hearted: unfeeling, unmerciful, pitiless.

Heaven on earth; **A**musement; **R**elief; **D**elight

Hurray; **E**ase; **A**ffection; **R**evival; **T**reasure; **E**nthusiasm; **D**rink

E.S.T. Exercise - see: pp. 70

Key-phrases/words: *Preliminary rounds*: ache, agony, broken heart, harm, hurt, repression, offence, oppression, pain, sorrow, suffering... *Positive affirmations rounds*: blissful, calm, confident, ease, happy, open heart, protected, safe, whole hearted joy, laughter, love, and peace...

Hard-ship - hardship: a condition that is pain or stress full to endure; suffering; deprivation; oppression. An instance or cause of this; something hard to bear.

Happiness; **A**ttunement; **R**eflection; **D**ream;

Serenity, **s**implicity, **s**ail; **H**arbor; **I**nstance; **P**leasure

E.S.T. Exercise - see: pp. 70

Key-phrases/words: *Preliminary rounds*: abused, burdened, deprived, oppressed, pain, suffer... *Positive affirmations rounds*:

calm, ease, peace, relief...

Hardihood: hardy spirit or character; determination to survive; fortitude. Strength; power; vigour. Boldness or daring; courage.

Harmony; **A**bundance; **R**elaxation; **D**elight;
Integrity; **H**eart; **O**pportunity; **O**ngoing; **D**are

Harmony: agreement; accord. A consistent, orderly, or pleasing arrangement of parts; congruity.

Heaven on earth; **A**ffection;
Relief; **M**otivation; **O**ption; **N**eatness; **Y**outh

Hate: intense dislike; extreme aversion or hostility.

Head; **A**lternative; **T**reat; **E**valuation
Hear no evil, see no evil,
speak no evil; **A**lliance; **T**reasure; **E**levation-time
Horizon; **A**llure; **T**hanksgiving; **E**thics

E.S.T. Exercise - see: pp. 70

Key-phrases/words: *Preliminary rounds*: hate, dislike, hostility, detest... *positive affirmations rounds*: calm, confident, forgiving, generous, kind, love anyway/anyhow, peaceful...

Head: the upper part of the body in man, joined to the trunk by the neck, containing the brain, sinuses, eyes, ears, nose, and mouth. The head is considered as the centre of the intellect; mind; brain. The position or place of leadership, greatest authority, or honour. A person to whom others are subordinate; director of an institution; leader or chief. A person considered with reference to his mind, disposition, attributes, status, etc. The part of anything that forms or is regarded as forming the top, summit, or upper end. The foremost part or front end of anything or a forward projecting part.

Hello; Energy-motion; Authenticity; Delight

Health: the general condition of the body or mind with reference to soundness and vigour. Soundness of body or mind; freedom from dis-ease or ailment. Vigour, vitality.

Happiness: Endurance; Attraction; Love; Togetherness; Harmony

Heart: a hollow, muscular organ that by rhythmic contractions and relaxations keeps the blood in circulation throughout the body. The centre of the total personality, esp. with reference to intuition, feeling, or e-motion. The vital or essential part; core.

Humour; Exuberance; Aptness; Relaxation; Tune
Humbleness; Enthusiasm; Attitude; Respiration; Trophy
Hardihood; Elegance; Art; Resourcefulness; Touch
Honesty; Essence; Awareness; Retreat; Time

Heartache: emotional distress; sorrow; grief; anguish.

Herald; Entity; Approach; Revelation;
Tenderness; Alleviation; Charisma; Harvest; Enthusiasm

Heartbreak: great sorrow, grief, or anguish.

Hug; Equity; Affection, Revival; Treasure
Breathe; Respect; Alleviation; Kindness; Endowment

In January 2005 one of my brothers called me up and asked me what I know about our mom receiving 70,000 NIS bonus. A few days later my other brother called me up and I heard that I am invited, with our mother, to a Friday dinner. When he opened the door for us I heard his wife called from the kitchen "ask them,... 70,000 NIS bonus." The following Friday our mother called me up and left a message on the answering machine "where are the papers you stole from me this time," I called her up. I heard my brother answered the telephone and that the papers were found. On Sunday I arrived for my weekly 'mother's day'. I saw a pile of papers on the dining table and heard mother said "throw them out."

I started sorting them out and in one of them I recall that I read "… 70,000 NIS addition to the … NIS annual bonus…" i.e. 70,000 NIS divided by the number of our mother's community members = mother's part. I put that paper in my bag and we continued with our day in which I started hearing her express and talk of her heartache and anger, "how could they." When I came home I wrote on a sticker "Here is the answer to your question." I glued the sticker on the page and tele-faxed it to my brothers.

In our following 'mother's days' she talked about being better off without her sons' visits, not wanting to hear from her sons, not knowing how she could come to her 90 birthday party that my brothers organized and produced, that her brother did not want to hear, see nor talk with her sons. Three months of good talking to, implorations and reassurances: "I am here for you and with you;" "I shall be there with you;" "if this is my brothers' way to honour you you shall come to this birthday party," walking my words, yielded her coming to her 90 birthday party in which she sat with her back turned to her sons, their families and the stage; her brother sat at the very far corner of the hall; one of my cousins saw and sensed the distance and came up to me to ask what happened. I confirmed her impression, and said I shall tell her another time.

Shortly after this birthday party my mother was hospitalized. Her complaints and the symptoms she described were ones coming from an aching and broken heart. She never again spoke or talked with me of her sons' not coming over, of missing her sons' and her grandchildren's visits.

In autumn one of my nieces married, when I came to kiss her mother she (the mother) turned her face away. During dinner time the cousin (that came up to me in my mother's 90 birthday party) came over, we walked over to the Bougainvillea, and through an opening to the other side, where I freely and peacefully answered her questions, opened my heart and poured some of it's ache out.

In one of my talks with one of my brothers I heard that he called our mom's brother to invite him to our mom's 90 birthday party and her brother refused to talk with him. I recall from another call that we had that he told me that our other brother also concluded "it is impossible to talk with you = me." This sentence added oil to a burning fire in my relationship with our other brother who in our mother's burial service turned his back to me; then in front of the hundreds of people that surrounded our mother's grave his wife joined him in breaking into my words; a few months later he answered my question with: "You are stirring up bigotry and hate," **me**: "Can you forgive me?" **him**: "No;". In 2011 this brother's son-in-law letter and later this brother's wife's words burnt hell in my heart. In 2012 I opened up to casually tell him that I still dream of... he expressed his upset and I did too, in one sentence.

> "When there is no one to tap you on your shoulder tap on your shoulder yourself"
> - Pesia Frankfurt

E.S.T. Exercise - see: pp. 70

Key-phrases/words: *Preliminary rounds*: abuse, anger; pain, sorrow, grief, sadness, anguish, anxiety, frustration, procrastination; burdened; endangered; offended; insulted; at a loss; lost; fear; desperation, depression... *Positive affirmation rounds*: comfort, happiness; delight, gratitude; forgiveness; acceptance; dare; joy; love; peace, plea-sure; pleasure...

H.P.T. - see: pp. 7
Pre-sent present presents - see: pp. 83

Letting Go fun exercise

Materidals:
Paper to write on
Pen or pencil
A jug with water
Crystal glass

♦ Find a time and a place where you feel protected and safe.
♦ Write down every sentence and word that angers, humiliates, hurts, pains, shames or up-sets you.
♦ Recite out loud or in your heart each sentence or word then say, out loud or in your heart "not so bad".
♦ Recite out loud or in your heart each sentence or word then say, out loud or in your heart "I love you".
　　Drink water to cleanse and purify;
　　Repeat until you feel ease or at peace.

Heaven: the abode of Holy-spirit, the angels, and the spirits of the righteous after death. A place or state of supreme happiness.

Heart; **E**cstasy; **A**llure; **V**itality; **E**ssence; **N**est

Here; **E**quity; **A**ll; **V**igour; **E**xtraordinariness; **N**ature

Heaviness: the state or quality of being heavy; weight; burden.

Hi-story;
Ease; **A**scension;
Valour; **I**ncarnation;
Nobility; **E**ra; **S**pirit; **S**unshine

Hell: the place or state of punishment of the wicked after death; the abode of evil and condemned spirits. Any place or state of torment or misery. Anything that causes torment or misery, esp. severe verbal censure; a tongue-lashing. A perception and a state of mind.

Happiness; **E**ase; **L**ight; **L**ove
Heaven on earth; **E**vergreen; **L**iberty; **L**oyalty

Hematoma: -mas, -ma-ta. *Pathol.* A swelling filled with extravasated blood. Also haematoma.

Health; **E**ye; **M**atter; **A**ttention; **T**ime **O**f **M**y **A**llowance

A Word Keeps The Doctor Away
On January 21, 2011 I woke up on the tar road after I rode bicycles and a van that overtook me collided with the left side of my head. **In month 5 (July 2011) U.S. findings** of the haematoma in the left thigh **were 4.6 x 1.2 cm**. I heard the a male surgeon say an operation can result in infection and was then referred to an orthopaedist. In the 24rd month (December 2012), a sharp pain in the haematoma area woke me in the middle of the night. I touched it and was overwhelmed to feel and sense that it turned into a grapefruit shape and size. A female surgeon then told me that in addition to it being an aesthetic issue it can also turn to an infection. She referred me to an US, suggested a simple procedure with simple and speedy recovery. **In month 25**

(January 2013) U.S. findings were 7 x 4 cm. I overcame my fear, set a date for the procedure and **in month 26 (March 2013)** a male surgeon with angelic approach and touch cut the thigh open and inserted a sterile rubber glove, he cut to serve as drain. **He recommended to take the rubber glove out in 2-3 days**. The rubber glove was taken out **after Eight days**. The female surgeon estimated that **it will take a week to two weeks time** to what I believed would be the happy end. **The cut healed in less than seven hours. The hole shape in the thigh turned into a hill shape within two more weeks**. In **month 28 (May 2013) US findings were 7 x 7 x 2.6 cm, a bigger size than ever before**. In month 29 (June 2013) I arrived for a more complex procedure, the nurses refused to let me in and told me the decision is up to a doctor. Two surgeons came over, said "Haematoma? I am not operating," and walked away. The Professor came, said "Haematoma? I am not operating, it can become a terrible infection.", and walked away. The March 2013 surgeon came, repeated his decision "Revision of cavity and drainage" and walked away. The nurses then repeated their verdict and vanished in all four directions, leaving OR staff members in the arena. Between the hammer and the anvil anger simmered and raging mad me drove home and on the spot wrote an angry letter to the Minister of Health and the Hospital Manager. A week later a colleague suggested all happened for a good cause and that there is another way to heal. **In Month 29 (June 2013) I made decision that a surgeon's knife shall never again cut me open; if my body could create it it can let it go. I added guided imagery to my daily E.S.T. tapping, ease replaced the pressure, the haematoma shape and size changed some**. A week later another colleague suggested I enrich, my already low animal products and carbohydrates diet, with a green mash for breakfast. **With E.S.T. tapping, and the green mash as the 1st course for breakfast within two more weeks the haematoma size significantly contracted**. **In month 31 (August 2013)** the grapefruit like shape and size turned to a flat, small and thin potato like. **In month 32 the aesthetic issue of the haematoma resolved**; leaving the scar from the surgery as an aesthetic issue and me to believe that had I found the way to heal before the surgery the happy end would have left me scar free.

October 20, 2013 U.S. findings are intended and premeditated results of choice making, responsibility taking, following, living and walking up to new ideas and ways;

letting go of hanging or holding on to the four corners of chronic chronology comfort altar; a safe basis and a solid ground to believe in and hold on to continuous infection free recovery.

See: Western Galiliee Hospital - Nahariya US findings and surgery report, pp .108-109

An open eye and mind, Choice making, Decision and responsibility taking, combined together with life loving makes the difference in a problem solving

See: Miracle, pp. 150
Power Of The Word, pp. 171

Remedies

E.S.T. Exercise - see: pp. 70

Key-phrases/words: *Preliminary rounds*: trauma, terror, poor me, miserable me, loss of control, injured me, hurting and hurt full me, helplessness... *Positive affirmations rounds*: I choose to let the hurt out of each and every cell in my body and capillary in my body, blood, e-motions, soul and spirit, my body created this trauma and thus can heal itself. I give, let and permit myself to heal, relax, take it easy and transform...

♦ **Guided imagery**
♦ **Green mash**

Green leaves: chard (part/whole leaf), lettuce (1 and more spine free leaves), leaves from 5 and more branches of coriander, dill, parsley, peppermint or spearmint;

Green fruits / vegetables: half and apple, 1-2 celery stalk with leaves, a small cucumber or equal, green onion;

Fill a blender cup with the fruits, leaves and vegetables, add one glass of filtered fresh water and let it blend to a creamy, delicious and refreshing mash. Eat immediately after preparation, before any drink (other than water) or food.

For variation I added one and more of: a mellow and ripe avocado (third-half of a fruit), a mellow ripe banana (yellow from bottom to top, dark spots, easy peeling), thick slice of beet, cabbage leaves, garlic (1-3 cloves), a thick slice of kohlrabi, half a lemon, pips free (my colleague adds the lemon juice only), onion (small one or equal) radish (small whole one or equal), spinach leaves, alfalfa sprouts, broccoli sprouts, cress sprouts, fenugreek sprouts and

other sprouts, cold pressed organic coconut oil (2 table-spoons).
♦ **Holistic massage with emphasis on Haematoma**
♦ **Homeopathy**

Notes: In the mid seventies I started a low coffee diet, in the late nineties I took out preservatives including salt and sugar, industrialized and/or processed drinks, and foods. Since 2011 I gradually reduced animal products and carbohydrates.
The green mash moved the following budwig[(*)] delicacy to serve as breakfast 2nd course:
4 table spoons Flaxseed oil,
8 spoons Goat Yoghurt (3.5%, or so, fat)
Blended with Hand (Stick) blender to homogeneous liquid.
To the homogeneous liquid I add: 1 table-spoon Cranberries, 1 table-spoon blueberries OR 7 and more strawberries (in their season), 1 table-spoon almonds, 7 Apricot kernels, 1 mellow and ripe banana (when having the green shake with avocado and vice versa).
   This delicacy should also be eaten immediately after preparation to enrich cells and cells membrane with oxygen.

January 28, 2013 US findings

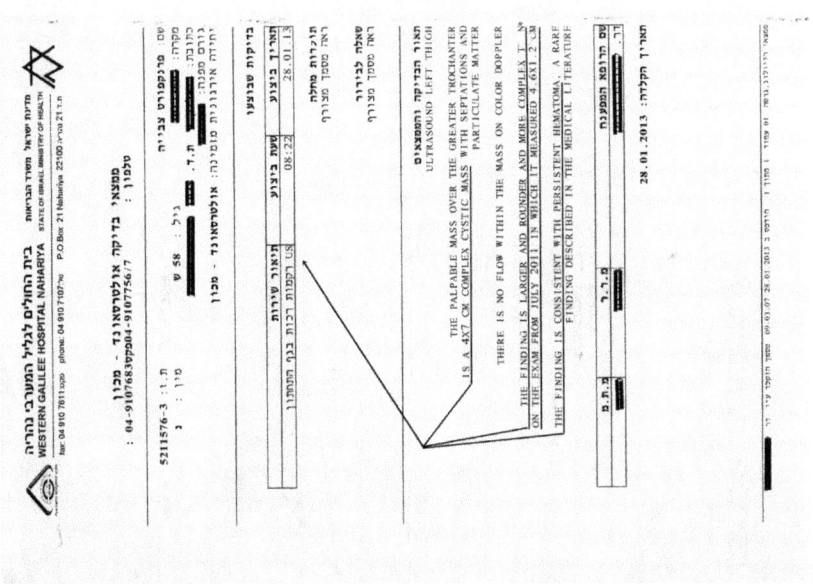

[(*)] Johanna Budwig (http://www.budwigcenter.com/) used organic quark or Kefir. Bill Henderson, in How to CURE Almost Any CANCER at Home for $5.15 a Day discussed Organic Cottage Cheese (2% fat); recommends a Hand (Stick) blender; explains how the blending process transform the cow milk to a non-allergen, non animal product, which empowers the flax seed oil qualities. My colleague reported excellent results with goat yoghurt. More information on the budwig protocol and dairy products use .is at http://curezone.com/forums/am.asp?i=1205557

March 11, 2013 Post surgery report

May 20, 2013 Post surgery US findings

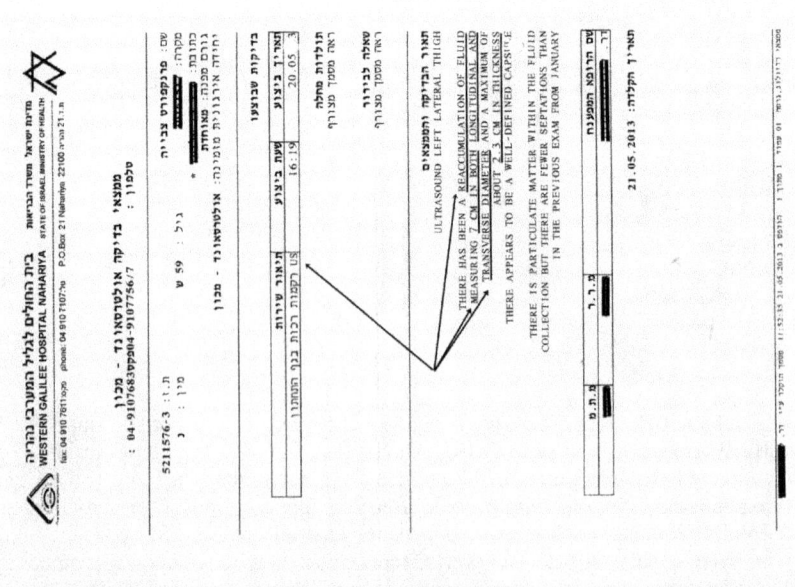

October 20, 2013 US findings - 4 months after decision making

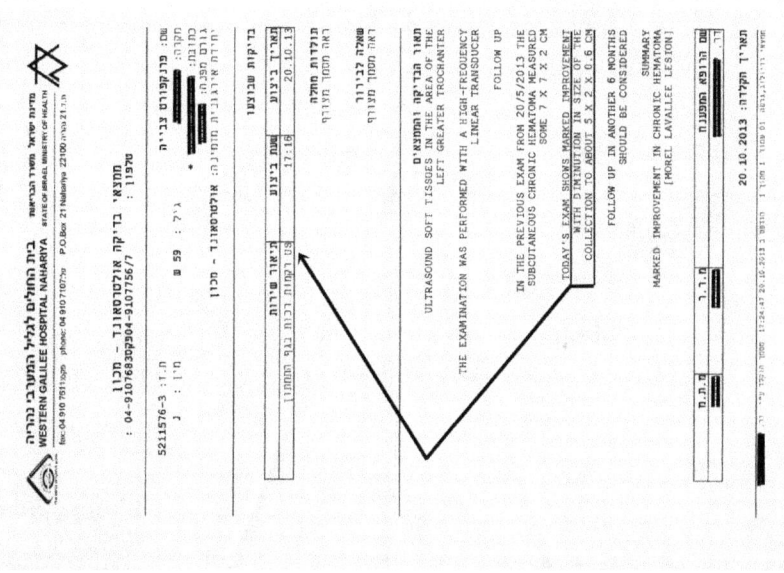

Here: this place. This world; this life; the present. Now; all right.

Hallelujah; **E**arth; **R**emedy; **E**xultation

Hi-story - **History**: the branch of knowledge dealing with past events. The record of past events, esp. in connection with the human race.

Hush; **I**ncarnation; **S**elf; **T**uition; **O**ption; **R**evelation; **Y**ield
Honesty; **I**s; **S**atisfaction; **T**rophy; **O**rigin; **R**eality; **Y**es

E.S.T. Exercise - see: pp. 70
Key-phrases/words: *Preliminary rounds*: angry, fear driven, hysterical, suffering, traumatized... *Positive affirmation rounds*: free choice, conscious choice, change; realization; let go; freedom; free from; free of; new story, my story, hi story...

Holiday: a day fixed by law or custom on which ordinary business is suspended in commemoration of some event or person.

Any day of exemption from labour.

Here; **O**pportunity; **L**ove; **I**'m; **D**elight; **A**ffection; **Y**acht

Home
: a house, apartment, or other place of residence. The place in which one's domestic affections are centred. Any place of residence or refuge.

Heart; **O**asis; **M**odesty; **E**nthusiasm
Happiness; **O**rchard; **M**odel; **E**levation
Honesty; **O**rchestration; **M**astery; **E**xtraordinariness

See: Power, pp. 171

Home is where love and peace coexist and reside in divine harmony

Honesty
: the quality or fact of being honest; uprightness, probity, or integrity; Truthfulness, sincerity, or frankness; Freedom from deceit or fraud.

Harvest; **O**mnipresence; **N**ew; **E**ra; **S**implicity; **T**ruth; **Y**es

A client came in after regular office hours carrying a gas heater for repair. I put the receptionist hat on, diagnosed the impaired part, handed him a repair receipt, and told him he'd be contacted and informed when to come and pickup the heater. I thought to myself, "His name is familiar to me," and asked myself, "From when or from where do I know his name from?"

Herein is the story:

The customer is right… sometimes[11]
By Gabriel Strasman, Ma'ariv

Who said the customer is not right? In recent days we were proved in … factory that not only is the customer right, but that it is said with a smile and is attended to in an exemplary fashion.

A client came to the factory carrying a gas heater for

ignition repair, the secretary that welcomed the client told him, the repair price is "20 Shekels, come back in two days... "

First act:
Two days later the client came back and met with another secretary that after keying on the keyboard keys of the computer on her desk, informed him the repair will cost him "166 shekels."

The conversation developed as follows:

Client: "I was told the price for the repair will be 20 shekels. I can understand an estimate mistake can occur, but a price demand eight times higher than what was said at the beginning seems way exaggerated."

Secretary: "Sorry, this is the price."

Work manager present on scene: "It cannot be that you were told 20 shekels. Here is the leaflet (shows the client a printed page) and in it it says the price of the part replaced before work cost is five and a half dollars."

Client (seeing the printed page): "But it cannot be that you shall treat a client so. I drove a distance of 15 km from my home to repair the thermocouple, because I bought the heater from you a few years ago. Had you told me in advance, that the repair price would be 166 shekels, I might not have left the heater here for repair at all."

Work manager: "I am sorry, but this is the price."

In the meantime the secretary that did the account came in with the factory manager.

Manager (smiling): "What is the matter?"

The client explains.

Manager: "Who told you the price of the repair will be 20 shekels?"

Client: "The beautiful and tall secretary that I see now."

(Miracle of miracles - the beautiful and tall secretary walks into the office).

Second act:
Client: "Shalom to you, maybe you remember me, I was here the day before yesterday (yes, sure). Perhaps you remember also how much you said the repair of the thermo-couple will cost?"

Secretary: "Yes, 20 shekels."

(General astonishment).

The manager asks the secretary to walk with him to an adjacent office.

A minute passes by and the manager returns and addresses the client: "It is all right, you shall pay 20 shekels, as you were told."

Client (a little embarrassed): I hope you do not intend to punish the secretary for her mistake, if she was mistaken. If a sum should be added, I will add it, but 166 shekels ..."

Manager: "No, Sir,

you are right, pay 20 shekels."

Screen.
Five minutes continuous
audience applause

Authenticity, honesty, integrity simplicity, sincerity, truth yield

The answer that came brought a smile:
I remembered the reporter's name from my afternoons and weekends with my parents, in which I loved reading his articles in Ma'ariv. I was the Export/import clerk that quoted the part's purchase cost. I was not punished. Years later I realized that honest truth brought the factory reputation money doesn't bring.

Hope: the feeling that what is desired is also possible, or that events may turn out for the best. A particular instance of this feeling: *the hope of winning*. Grounds for this feeling in a particular instance: *There is little or no hope of recovery.*

Heart; **O**pening; **P**ace; **E**xpansion
Heaven; **O**mnipresence; **P**assion; **E**xuberance

Host-ility - Hostility: a host-ile state, condition, or attitude; enmity; antagonism. A host-ile act. Opposition or resistance to an idea, plan, project, etc.

Hostel, **O**pportunity; **S**ense, **T**enderness,
Innovation, **L**oyalty, **I**ntegrity; **T**reat; **Y**ield

E.S.T. Exercise - see: pp. 70

Key-phrases/words: *Preliminary rounds*: aggression; anger, fear, trauma… *Positive affirmations rounds*: out of danger, protected, safe, secured…

See: Foul play, pp. 88

Humility: the quality or condition of being humble; modest sense of one's own importance, rank, etc.

Heart; **U**sher; **M**easurement; **I**ntegrity; **L**ove; **I**dentity; **T**act; **Y**es

E.S.T. Exercise - see: pp. 70

Key-phrases/words: *Preliminary rounds*: arrogant, smart-alecky...
Positive affirmations rounds: I choose to be humble, I am modesty, I radiate and vibrate modesty...

Hunger
: a compelling need or desire for food. The painful sensation or state of weakness caused by need of food. A strong or compelling desire or craving. To have a strong desire.

Herald; **U**tmost; **N**avigation;
Gratitude; **E**xpression; **R**esourcefulness

Husband
: a manager. A prudent or frugal manner. To manage, esp. with prudent economy. To use frugally; conserve: to husband one's resources. Careful or thrifty management. The management of domestic affairs or of resources generally. A married man, esp. considered in relation to his wife. Archaic: to be or become a husband to; marry. To find a husband for. To till; cultivate. Husbandry: the cultivation and production of crops and animal: agriculture; farming. The science of raising crops or food animals.

Hurray, **U**ltimateness, **S**erenity;
Brotherhood; **A**ttitude; **N**avigation; **D**elight
Heaven on earth; **U**sher; **S**implicity;
Balance; **A**scension; **N**ew; **D**ominion
Hear no evil, see no evil, speak no evil;
Unity; **S**avouriness; **B**ridge; **A**llure; **N**ascence; **D**esignation

Hub, Hun, us, un, sad, san, sand, bad, ban, band, bud, bus, bush, an, and, ad, ah, nub, dash, dab, dub, dun...

> Hus(h)band
> now in and out come my
> alliance, associate, friend,
> love, lover, partner,
> significant other,
> soul-mate

Practice 1:
Materials:

A note book or paper block.
Pen or Pencil.
Procedure:
♦ Find a place and a time where you feel at ease and safe.
♦ Lie down, sit or stand with your back and your head straight up.
♦ Close your eyes, focus on your breath.
1. Run the word 'husband' in your mind, feel, observe, sense, test and watch it.
2. Start playing with the word, create new words from its letters.
3. Ask for a new definition, phrase or word to replace 'husband'. Open your eyes and write it or them down.
4. Close your eyes, feel and sense the new definition, phrase or word.
> Let the one that feels and vibrates best, comfort, ease, good, peace set and sink in.

Practice 2:
Every time you hear the word "husband" say quietly and peacefully in your heart or out loud "delete, disperse... (new definition, phrase, or word, example: my partner, my significant other)."
> Repeat six months and more and watch your relationship gradually change and turn.

Hypocrisy: a semblance of having desirable or publicly approved attitudes, beliefs, principles, etc. that one does not actually possess.

Hello; **Y**oung; **P**otency; **O**nword,
Curiosity **R**ise; **I**ntegrity; **S**incerity **Y**ield

> See: Fraud, pp. 90
> Lie, pp. 138

Hypo: from Greek: meaning "under," the opposite of hyper.

Hyster-i-a(m) - Hysteria: an uncontrollable outburst of e-motion, often characterized by irrationality, laughter, weeping, etc. A psychoneurotic order characterized by violent emotional outburst, disturbances or sensory and motor functions, and various effects due to autosuggestions.

Health; **Y**ield; **S**ensibility; **T**reasure;
Earth; **R**elief; **I**ntegrity; **A**wareness
Heart; **Y**outh; **S**ense, sensuality, serenity, simplicity,
sincerity; **T**enderness; **E**ase; **R**enaissance; **I**nnocence; **A**rdour

Hyster: from Greek meaning "uterus," used in the formation of compound words. Also, esp. before a vowel (Gk, comb. form of hystéra).

Hyster-Ia(m)

E.S.T. Exercise - see: pp. 70

Key-phrases/words: *Preliminary rounds*: hysterical, out of my mind, crazy, raving mad, scared to death, scared shitless… *Positive affirmations rounds*: calm, courage, I love being in control, in my senses, peaceful, rational…

I

Ice: the solid form of water, produced by freezing; frozen water.

Island; **C**ore; **E**ducation
Innovation; **C**rown; **E**xcellence

Ice cream: a frozen cream.

Imagination; **C**reation; **E**ndowment
Caress; **R**esilience; **E**xpression; **A**rt; **M**anifestation

> Ice cream
> I scream

Ill-temper - Ill-temper: bad, or irritable disposition.

I am; **L**ife; **L**ove;
Transformation; **E**xcitement,
Make; **P**ersistence, **p**rivilege; **E**ase; **R**emedy

> E.S.T. Exercise - see: pp. 70

Key-phrases/words: *Preliminary rounds*: craze, ill-tempered, raving mad, short circuit, short fuse, … *Positive affirmations rounds*: calm, clear and cold-minded, good, happy, love, peace…

Ill-us-i-on - Illusion: something that is perceived by producing an impression. A perspective.

I'm; **L**ad; **L**ady; **U**niformity; **S**incerity; **I**nfinity; **O**ffering; **N**ature

> A vision blocked by prejudice?
> A message or a sign mal-interpreted?

Illustration: L. (s, of illustrâtiô) spiritual enlightenment.

Intuition; **L**ight; **L**ibido; **U**tensil; **S**tar; **T**ruth;
Reservoir; **A**ttunement; **T**reat; **I**ssuance; **O**bjectivity; **N**ewness

Imagination: the act of imagining. The faculty of imagination. The faculty of producing ideal creations consistent with reality, as distinct from the power of creating illustrative or decorative imagery. Ability to meet and resolve difficulties; resourcefulness. *Psychol.* The power of reproducing images stored in the memory under the suggestion of associated images or of recombining former experiences to create new images.

Inspiration; **M**ake; **A**ffection; **G**ift; **I**nitiative; **N**urture;
Awareness; **T**hanksgiving; **I**nnermost; **O**mnipotence; **N**exus

See: Fake, pp. 84

Immunity: the state of being immuned from or insusceptible to a particular dis-ease or the like.
Exemption from any natural or unusual liability.

Integrity; **M**irth; **M**astery; **U**nity;
Niche; **I**nfluence; **T**ranquillity; **Y**ield

See: Growth, pp. 95

I'm-possibility - Impossibility: condition or quality of being impossible. Something impossible.

I'M; **P**otency; **O**rigin; **S**incerity; **S**erenity; **I**nnovation; **B**rilliance;
In-capacity; **L**ove; **I**mmunity; **T**angibility; **Y**outhfulness

I'm possibility
I'm possible

I'm-potency - Impotency: the condition or quality of being impotent; weakness. Complete failure or serious impairment of sexual power, esp. in the male. Obs. Lack of self-restraint.

Indulgence; Miracle; Persistence;
Orchestration; Tune; Energy; Nurture; Creativity; Yard

> I'm potency
> I'm potent

I'm-pulse - **Impulse**: the influence of a particular feeling, mental state, etc.; *to act under a generous impulse*. Sudden, involuntary inclination prompting to action. An impelling action or force, driving onwards or inducing motion. The effect of an impelling force; motion induced; impetus given.

Inside; Motivation; Peace; Usefulness; Life; Savour; Existence

Infection: the act or fact of infecting. The state of being infected.

Intuition; Nascence; Free spirit; Excitement;
Custom; Treat; Innovation; Ongoing; Newness

> In-(ef)fect-I-on?
> What is in effect?
> Who is in effect?

> E.S.T. Exercise - see: pp. 70

Key-phrases/words: *Preliminary rounds*: a blazed, blazing, boiling, burning with…, cool, raving… *Positive affirmations rounds*: calm, chill, ease, heal, relief…

♦ Synergy Master Blend pure essential oil. Parents that used it with their children reported that their children did not consume antibiotics.

Inferiority complex: *Psychiatry*, intense feeling of inferiority producing a personality characterized either by extreme reticence or, as a result of over compensation, by extreme aggressiveness. Lack of self-esteem, feeling of inadequacy, lack of self-confidence.

Influence; Notch; Freedom; Esteem; Radiance; Inspiration;

Orchestration; **R**evelation; **I**ndulgence; **T**rait; **Y**ield
Confidence; **O**ption; **M**asterpiece;
Projection; **L**ove; **E**volvement; **X**ylophone

> E.S.T. Exercise - see: pp. 70

In-flam(e)-mat(e)-i-on - Inflammation: the act or fact of inflaming. The state of being inflamed. *Pathol.* Redness, swelling, pain, tenderness, heat, and disturbed function of an area of the body, esp. as a reaction of tissues to injurious agents.

Intuition; **N**urture; **F**low; **L**ove; **A**lliance; **M**etabolism;
Mastery; **A**ttunement; **T**reat; **I**nnovation; **O**ption; **N**ext

> What is in-flam(e)?
> Who is in-flam(e), inflame(ed)?

Early one spring, my gums started bleeding profusely along with a strong toothache. Hereinafter is part of the letter I sent to the dentist:

… In our last Wednesday meeting I was glad to hear you defined my state 'normal'.
I heard you were interested in the way and the mile-stones to heal my ear, gums and sinus inflammation.
At the beginning of the millennium I replaced tooth paste with pure essential oils, silica and Dead Sea salt crystals.
In 2004, a few months after I began spiritual correction with Nira's classic homeopathy counseling, Avinoam expressed his opinion, "Your wisdom tooth should be pulled out" and revealed to me that there is another treatment with laser that costs approximately 2,000 NIS, "And why pay 2,000 NIS for a treatment for a tooth" whose existence in the body is above, beyond or unknown to human knowledge and wisdom?
I arrived at your clinic for 2nd opinion - which Zahi gave.
Zahi recommended a root canal and Shulamit moved us a step forward when together with Zahi we concluded, that actually and why not, we shall settle for a conservative ordinary tooth filling.
I was the happiest person on earth to discover that the mountain turned into a mole hill. The tooth was corrected with an ordinary filling.
In 2005 I arrived at your clinic once again, this time I heard Zahi say the pain is from the neighbouring tooth and the only way is a root

canal. We did it from beginning to end. Along the root canal process our ways met and Zipi continued to clean plaque twice yearly.

07.03.2007, Zipi said, "There is an inflammation, in our next meeting we shall see if we need antibiotics."

21.03.2007 On my way to my meeting with you I bought nutritional supplements and consumed the 1st dose.

You suggested opening the tooth for drainage, explaining to me that the root canal had failed to yield fruit, and showed me 3 locations, the old two and a new one, at the bottom, between the root's top.

22.03.2007 I called Lihi in your clinic, told her of the amazing change I felt and suggested we meet in three months time, thinking the X-ray will prove which change occurred and that to open the tooth is a way we can always follow later.

A week later I called you, we talked briefly and we agreed that a week or two after Pessach I will call you. I did so.

06.06.2007 we met again, this time I heard, "Normal, see you in six months."

The mile-stones - Ingredients:
♦ Attention, courage, creative thinking, faith, listening, set of beliefs, willingness and will-power.

Synergies:
♦ For cleaning the gums, mouth walls, teeth and tongue:
♦ Silica powder
♦ Dead Sea Salt crystals

Pure Essential Oils:
♦ Clove bud
♦ Juniper berry

Water from the Mediterranean sea

Nutritional supplements:
Zinc drops
Co Q-10 soft-gels

Tooth picks, dental floss, manually operated instrument for gum massage.

The way - application:
From the beginning of the millennium, every day began with:
♦ Dipping the toothbrush bristles in a mixture of silica and Dead Sea salt crystals.
♦ Dripping 1-2 drops of pure essential oils synergy: clove bud and juniper berry.
♦ Massaging, to the best of my ability and understanding, every tooth I could reach within my mouth.
♦ Teeth that evoked rejection were given additional attention and were approached from another angle.
♦ Tooth pick cleaning.
♦ Tap water rinse.

♦ At this stage, on days I felt a certain pressure, I add a finger massage to the walls, gums, tongue, and soft tissue under the lower jaw and the chin.

♦ 1-4 times per week I massaged the gums with the mechanical massage instrument.

♦ Once every two weeks I changed the tooth pick cleaning to a dental floss one.

After my last meeting with Zipi and on my way to our March meeting I added:

♦ Co. Q-10,

♦ Zinc (liquid).

About a week after our March meeting, secretions started flowing out of the nostrils, and a week later out of the right ear. I heard that water from the Mediterranean sea is a tested medicine for gum inflammation. I then replaced the tap water rinse with Mediterranean sea water and also rinsed my nostrils.

♦ I began to replace the tooth pick with dental floss x 1 per week.

Why only once a week?

♦ Because my teeth are crowded, it required a forceful approach that cut the gums, causing them to bleed.

♦ With the dental floss I could not reach the rear molars.

♦ With a tooth pick I am able to reach all teeth.

In the first days, progress was felt every few hours.

First the ear healed, then followed the sinuses and the gums.

The treatment with nutritional supplements began with a daily dosage of:

♦ 120 mg Co Q-10 (one when my day started, another in the evening).

♦ 45 drops of liquid Zinc (10 under the tongue, 5 on pain point x 3 times per day)

♦ I reduced the Zinc, according to feeling.

At the end of April, after I noticed I occasionally skipped a Co Q-10 dose, I changed to:

♦ 90 mg Co Q-10 (30 mg soft-gels, 1 when my day started, 1 in the evening, 1 at night)

♦ 23 mg Zinc (1 lozenge per day).

Both products of Puritan's Pride Inc., Oakland, New York, U.S.A.

Thanks to your findings, yesterday I reduced the Co Q-10 dosage to 60 mg per day, and I continue with all other.

Sum up:

♦ Blood flows continue to erupt, sometimes from deep in the throat, sometimes from the pharynx, sometimes from the gums, occasionally from all these together.

♦ The seismographic activity lessens and disappears. Cry bursts are replaced with more and more whole hearted laugh outbursts.

♦ The red colour is analogue to the red light in a traffic light: stop, look around, investigate, study, weigh, reach a decision; act on it, and follow the way chosen.

How true, why else did I start spitting blood when I left the previous life's routine and pattern, thus choosing and deciding to follow the heart?

What is Inflammation? In flame fear cornered in a cell's corner, instead of courage driven flow and move.

> E.S.T. Exercise - see: pp. 70

Key-phrases/words: *Preliminary rounds*: angry, blazing hell, burning with desire, had enough of..., inflamed, fed up, sick of..., *Positive affirmations rounds*: calm, chill down, chill out, cool, cool down, heal, fine, let go of..., taking it easy, well...

♦ Synergy Master Blend pure essential oil. Parents that used it with their children reported that their children did not consume antibiotics.

In-flue-nce - In-fluence - Influence: the capacity or power to produce effects on others. The action or process of producing effects on others. A person or thing that exerts influence.

Irresistible; **N**eed; **F**ervour; **L**ove;
Uniformity; **E**ase; **N**est; **C**hoice; **E**poch

Influenza: *Pathol*. An acute, dis-ease, characterized by general prostration, occurring in several forms, usually with nasal catarrh and bronchial inflammation.

> In-flue?
> Influenced?

> E.S.T. Exercise - see: pp. 70

Key-phrases/words: *Preliminary rounds*: influenced, helpless, powerless, sick of... tired of..., *Positive affirmations rounds*: I am influence, I love to influence, I claim my power, I take the power, I now choose to hold the horses reins, be the driver, rider and surfer...

Initiative: an introductory act or step; leading action. Readiness and ability in initiating action; enterprise. One's personal, responsible decision.

I'm-potency; Nascence; Integrity; Tenderness; Innovation;
Authority; Truth; Inside; Veni, vidi, vici, Exuberance

Inspiration: an inspiring or animating action or influence. Something inspired, as a thought. A result of inspired activity. A person or thing that inspires. *Theol.* A divine influence directly and immediately exerted upon the mind or soul of man. The drawing of air into the lungs; inhalation.

Insight; Navigation; Source; Performance; Intuition; Readiness;
Aspiration; Trust; Incarnation; Opportunity, option; Newness

> So God created mankind
> in his own image, in the image of God he
> created them; male and female he created them.
> Genesis 1:27

In-spirit I am
I am spirit

Integrity: adherence to ethical and moral principles; soundness of ethical and moral character; honesty.

Innermost; Nest; Truth; Experience,
Gladness; grace; Reality; I am; Thank; You

Intimacy: the state of being intimate. A close, familiar and usually affectionate or loving, personal relationship. A detailed knowledge or deep understanding of a place, subject, period of history, etc. an act or expression serving as a token of familiarity, affection, or the like. A sexually familiar act; a sexual liberty. Privacy, esp. an atmosphere of privacy suitable to the telling of a secret.

Integrity; Nudity; Treat; Island;
Mirth; Assembly; Credibility; Yield
Indulgence; Nest; Trust; Inspiration;
Motivation; Awareness; Comfort, Yard

Intimidation: fear inspiration. Overawe or cow, esp. with a forceful personality or superior display of fluency, fame, wealth, etc. A force to or deter from some action by induced fear.

Immunity; **N**ewborn; **T**ake; **I**n one's hands; **M**ystery; **I**nterest; **D**elight; **A**ssertiveness; **T**ime; **I**ntelligence; **O**ccasion; **N**erve[*]

Intuition: direct perception of truth, fact, etc., independent of any reasoning process; immediate apprehension. A fact, a truth, knowledge, etc. perceived in this way. A keen and quick insight. The quality or ability of having such direct perception or quick insight.

Integrity; **N**est; **T**reasure; **U**nion; **I**nsight; **T**ruth; **I**nnermost; **O**ne; **N**exus

> See: Creation, pp. 58

---

[*] Strength, vigour, or energy

J

Jail: a prison, esp. one for the detention of persons awaiting trial or convicted of minor offense.

Just-ice; **A**ttunement; **I**nsight; **L**esson
Jubilation; **A**dventure; **I**ntuition, **L**oveliness

Jam: A mass of objects, vehicles, etc... jammed together or otherwise unable to move except slowly: a traffic jam.
A preserve of whole fruit, slightly crushed, boiled with sugar.

Joy; **A**dventure, **M**astery

Which jam do I choose now?
Joyful, playful and sweet jam session

Jealousy: jealous resentment against a rival, a person enjoying success or advantage, etc. or against another's success or advantage itself. Mental uneasiness from suspicion or fear of rivalry, unfaithfulness, etc. as in love or aims. Vigilance in maintaining or guarding something. A jealous feeling, disposition, state, or mood.

Joy; **E**arnestness; **A**ll ways; **L**ove;
Opportunity; **U**pgrade; **S**atisfaction; **Y**es

E.S.T. Exercise - see: pp. 70

Key-phrases/words: *Preliminary rounds*: jealous, envious, jaundiced; green eyed, yellow eyed, heartburn, suspicious, dis-trust, mis-trust, doubt, mis-doubt, grudge ... *Positive affirmations rounds*: calm, confident, peaceful, trust, trustworthy, valuable, worthy...

Joy: the e-motion of great delight or happiness caused by something good or satisfying; keen pleasure. A source or cause of keen pleasure or delight. The expression or display of glad feeling;

festive gaiety. State of happiness or felicity.

Journey; **O**ngoing; **Y**outh
Jolly; **O**utlet; **Y**es

Jubilation: a feeling of joy or exultation. The act of rejoicing or jubilating; exultation. A joyful or festive celebration.

Juice; **U**ltimate; **B**liss, **I**nside; **L**avishness;
Ardour; **T**ruth; **I**ncarnation; **O**xygen; **N**ecessity

Just-ice - Justice: The quality of conforming to principles of reason, to generally accepted standards of right and wrong, and to man made stated terms of law, rules, agreements, etc. in matters affecting persons who could be wronged or unduly favoured. Rightfulness or lawfulness, as of a claim: to complain with justice. The administering of deserved punishment or reward. The maintenance or administration of what is just according to man made law. A judge or magistrate.

Joy; **U**nity; **S**ense; **T**reat; **I**ntuition; **C**reativity; **E**levation

> Between a vict-i'm and a vict-or
> is just-ice or wisdom
>
> What is my call? Choice?
> Just-ice?
> A just wisdom in and on every stage, step and way?

Just-if-i-ca(tio)n - Justification: a reason, fact, circumstance, or explanation that justifies or defends.

Jubilation; **U**tility; **S**atisfaction, **s**ensuality; **T**reasure;
Innovation; **F**aith to **f**ate; **I**nstinct; **C**reation; **A**ward,
a-word; (**T**ruth; **I**'m; **O**h thank you); **N**ature's law

> Act more
> Justify, doubt, suspect, worry less
>
> E.S.T. Exercise - see: pp. 70

K

Keep: sustenance; support.

Kindness; **E**ra; **E**ducation; **P**rosperity

Keeping: Due or logical conformity with or of associated things, qualities, etc. Care or charge. Observance. Maintenance; custody. Reservation for future use.

Kindle; **E**xuberance; **E**quilibrium;
Pleasure; **I**ntegrity; **N**ew-born, **G**ladness

Kick: the act or an instance of kicking. Potency. Vigour, energy, or vim.

Key; **In**-stance; **C**uriosity; **K**now-how

Kidney: either of a pair of bean-shaped glandular organs in the back part of the abdominal cavity that excrete urine. Constitution or temperament. Kind, sort, or class.

Kiss; **I**ntegrity; **D**elight; **N**est; **E**xultation; **Y**ield

Contrition, fear, pangs of conscience, remorse, some foods and M.D. prescribed medicines cause kindney dis-comforts, dis-eases, mal-function.

Kidney stones: *Pathol.* A stone, or concretion, composed principally of oxalates and phosphates, abnormally grown in the kidney resulting from excessive admonition, fear, harsh self-criticism, judgment or righteousness, hesitancy, insecurity, regret, remorse, reproach.

E.S.T. Exercise - see: pp. 70

Key-phrases/words: *Preliminary rounds*: admonition, agony, fear stricken, morbid, mortified, regret, remorse, reproach, self-correction, self-criticism, self-guilt, self-pity, self-punishment, self-torment, suffering... *Positive affirmations rounds*: calm, confident, honest, peaceful, relaxed, safe, serene, sincere, wise…

Remedies

Clove bud infusion (See: Gum infection, pp. 97), drink one glass per day.

Small and tiny kidney stones

Replace artificial drinks, coffee, soda, tea with fresh filtered water, take 2-3 small sips at a time, chew and mix water attentively and intentionally with saliva, then swallow. Drink one glass during an hour from wake up time to sleep time and bring yourself as quickly as you can to an experienced and skilled reflexology practitioner or a body-masseur. When urinating pay attention to urine colour and smell, listen to the sound of the stone hitting the toilet's wall.

Repeat procedure the following day together with a reflexology or a body-massage session should you feel unsure or if pain's frequency and strength seem similar to the ones on the previous day.

For vibrant health please make tap freshly filtered water your favourite drink for good.

Medium and large kidney stones

Replace artificial drinks, coffee, soda, tea with fresh filtered water, take 2-3 small sips at a time, chew and mix water attentively and intentionally with saliva, then swallow.

Prepare and drink, every day until you feel pain-free for 7 days and nights, fresh **Indian corn hair** infusion[*]. Take 2-3 small sips at a time, chew and mix infusion attentively and intentionally with saliva, then swallow. Drink one glass during an hour. 2-3 glasses a day.

For vibrant health please make tap freshly filtered water your favourite drink for good.

Kin: a person's relatives collectively; kinfolk. Family relationship or kinship. A group of persons descended from a common ancestor. A relative or kinsman. Someone or something of the same or similar kind.

Kindness; **I**nsight; **N**ectar
Kiss; **I**nnovation; **N**ewness

---

[*] Indian corn hair infusion: put a heaping teaspoon of Indian corn hair in a crystal glass, fill with boiling water, cover with glass saucer and allow to soak (infuse) for 10 minutes and more. Do not sweeten. Drink to health.

Kindness: the state or quality of being kind. A kind act. Kind behaviour. Friendly feeling; liking.

Kingdom; **I**nitiative; **N**ature; **D**evotion;
Navigation; **E**nergy; **S**uccess; **S**atisfaction

Kiss: a touch with the lips; the act or an instance of kissing.

Keep; **I**t; **S**imple and straight, **S**weetheart
Kindling; **I**mmediate, **S**afety; **S**mile
Kindness; **I**s; **S**ecurity; **S**urety

A kiss from affection to a hurt part, scratch or wound together with an authentic, loving and sincere expressiuon of interest in what one can do to ease the hurt, is all a baby or a child need to heal and happily move on.
A kiss from true love cure's hurt, and costs nothing.

See: Love, pp. 143
Sex, pp. 202

Know: in the know *informal*, having inside information. Syn., know, comprehend, understand, imply being aware of meaning.

Kindle; **N**ow; **O**mnipresence; **W**onderful, **w**onder

Know-how: knowledge of how to do something; faculty or skill for a particular activity.
Knowledge: acquaintance with 'facts', self-evidence 'truth', or principles, as from study or investigation; general erudition. Acquaintance or familiarity gained by experience.
You know, you know what I mean: are expressions describing and manifesting a barrier, a block, perhaps a brake, spiritual, mental, e-motional constipation, handicap, hide-away, inhibition, lack of, lack in, scarcity; or a fear of freely and naturally expressing my/yourself, peacefully, safely and whole-heartedly speaking my/your mind out loud. Bare and simple knowledge and naked truth is that the other party is not me/you, thus cannot nor does not know what's inside my/your mind, what does I/you think, nor mean or intend, nor needs

to figure it out, guess, strain or stress to find out. You are welcome to daily practice: Authenticity, pp. 20, Ego, pp. 75, Foul play, pp. 88, Honesty, pp. 112, Integrity, pp. 125, No, pp. 158, Presence, pp. 176, Respect, pp. 193, Self, pp. 200, Simplicity, pp. 212, Sincerity, pp. 212, Wisdom, pp. 250 Yes, pp. 258, Zero, pp. 260 and the following E.S.T. exercise to come out and grow out and up from this custom.

E.S.T. Exercise - see: pp. 70

Key-phrases/words: *Preliminary rounds*: I am blocked, I am afraid, I lack the confidence... *Positive affirmations rounds*: I am safe, I am protected, I am able, I can speak freely and naturally, I am free to be, express and speak my true-self, I am attractive, appreciated, authentic, honoured, loved, loving, protected, safe, truthful...

L

Labour/**Labor**: productive activity, esp. for the sake of economic gain; work; toil. A job or task done or to be done. The pains and efforts of childbirth; travail. The period of these.

Liberty; **A**spiration; **B**ridge; **O**pportunity; **U**sher; **R**evelation

E.S.T. exercise
1. Find a place and a time in which you feel comfortable, free and safe to practice emotional and spiritual transformation. You may practice while walking, sitting with your back straight, head up, both your feet firm on the floor/ground, or lying down with your legs, back and head straight on a mattress, floor or ground (i.e. all body parts are within mattress frame, no bent knees, nape or neck). Use a pillow to ease stress and tension in knees, or rolled towel under the nape (head resting on mattress). You are here to experience change, be open to awareness, listen to your e-motions.
2. Set the jug and glass within an easy to reach distance, the paper, pen or pencil on a desk or a firm surface and on which you are comfortable to write. On the paper: draw a 10 - 0 e-motion scale, 10 = strongest e-motion, 0 = zero e-motion.
3. Write down words and/or phrases that came up while you were listening to your inner self. These words and phrases are your key-words and key-phrases to insert in the following sentences:
Although I…(*) I completely and deeply love myself.
Although I…(*) I whole heartedly honour myself.
I deeply and fully for-e-give and accept myself although…(*).
4. Start gentle tapping with one hand's fingers tips on the outer-side of your other hand (The Karate chop point), or gently massaging - in a clockwise-direction - your sore-chest points (marked **S** in the chart on pp. 134). While gently tapping with your finger tips on the Karate chop point or massaging the sore-chest points start saying, out loud, the key-phrases and key-words you wrote down in stage 3 above.
   Let words flow freely and refrain from corrections.
   Repeat this step until you feel ready to move to the next stage.
5. Move to repeat, saying out loud, the key-phrases and/or key-words you wrote in stage 3 above while gently tapping with your

---
(*) fill with key-words, key-phrases

finger tips, on the following points:
1. Top of the head (Chakra 7)
2. Depression above eyebrows/nose ridge (Chakra 6)
3. Eye brow inner side rim
4. Eye side rim
5. Eye lower rim
6. Under the nose (depression)
7. Chin (depression)
8. Clavicle bone (v shape - Chakra 5)
9. Under the armpit (man: nipple line, woman: bra strip line)
10. Ribs 7-8 (L: over spleen, R: over liver)

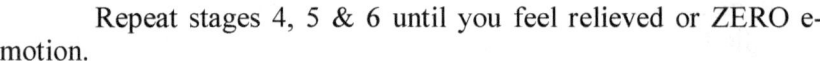

6. Take a deep breath, close your eyes and listen to your emotional body, what level are you in now?

Write it down.

Repeat stages 4, 5 & 6 until you feel relieved or ZERO e-motion.

Should a new emotional wave well up, flow through stages 3, 4, 5 & 6 with new key-phrases and key-words it brought up.

Pre-sent present presents

1. Find a place and a time where you feel protected and safe.
2. Lie down, sit or stand with your back and head in a straight line.
3. Gently shake your arms and legs loose to clear stress or tension.
4. Take a deep breath, calmly exhale, let all negativity and stress leave.
5. Take another deep breath and say out loud "I am one with all there is"[3], calmly exhale.
6. Take 2-3 deep breaths, calmly exhaling, while listening to your body language, to what it reveals to you.
7. Take a deep breath and say out loud "I now connect with my soul and spirit energy and feel it."
8. Take another deep breath. Calmly exhale and begin to return to sense your surroundings and say out loud "I feel calm, love, peace and success."
9. Open your eyes, welcome back, nurture that feeling of divine love, peace and success.

H.P.T.[4]
Heart Point Technique

Find a place and a time where you feel at peace and protected.
Lie down, sit or stand with your back, chin and head straight up.
1. Raise an arm up to the sky, straight up and to its full length. Close your eyes, focus on your breath, unite with the universe till you feel it's enough or sense energy streams; heat waves, gentle bites at your fingers tips; spontaneous, involuntary, or unconscious move of the raised hand.
2. Lower your hand, gently and tenderly cap your head top with it. Ask for divine light to shed it's rays on the cause, reason or story behind the scene. Let it flow, run the film, watch each frame.
3. Lower your hand to gently touch the depression point above your eyebrows/nose ridge (Chakra 6). Ask for divine assistance and guidance in transforming the cause/ reason/story to a one that brings you joy, fills your heart with peace.
4. Lower your hand to gently, lovingly, softly and tenderly cap your heart. Express appreciation, forgiveness, gratitude and thankfulness to both old and new. Let them rise to climax and your heart fill with joy, peace, tranquillity.
5. Raise your hand to gently, lovingly and tenderly cap the consolidation point (upper neck) run both films, starting with cause/reason/story one then continue to run the one that brings you joy, fills your heart with peace.

Lamentation(s): the act of lamenting or expressing grief. A lament.

Livelihood; **A**ppreciation; **M**astery; **E**nthusiasm; **N**avigation; **T**reat; **A**ll; **T**reasure; **I**ntuition; **O**utput; **N**est; **S**uccess

E.S.T. Exercise - see: pp. 133

Lash: the flexible striking part of a whip. A swift stroke or blow, as with a whip. Something that goads or pains in a manner compared to that of a whip. A violent beating or impact, as of waves or rain, against something.

Love; **A**ttunement; **S**erenity;
Hear no evil, see no evil, speak no evil, **h**umbleness

Laugh: the act or sound of laughing. Have the last laugh, to prove ultimately successful after a seeming defeat.

Life; Amusement; Uniqueness; Gratitude; Heart

Laughter: the action or sound of laughing. An experiencing of the e-motion expressed by laughter. An expression or appearance of merriment or amusement, esp. mirth or derision.

Lavishness; Affection; Usher; Gift;
Honesty; Treasure; Exultation; Riches

E.S.T. exercise to create and develop a whole hearted laughter

1. Find a place and a time where you shall feel at ease, protected and safe.
2. Lie down or sit with your back straight. Gently shake loose your arms and legs, from hip to toes, shoulders to finger tips to clear aches and stress from nape, neck, shoulders, upper, middle and lower back.
3. Begin to force out, imitate or mimic artificial laugh gestures, sounds and voices. Repeat until you hear, feel or sense your voice changed.
4. Repeat for 21, and more, consecutive days and whenever you feel sad, stressed, tired, or worried.

Internet surfers: a warm recommendation to join Willie Skratter[9] laughing baby.

A laughter coming out from the heart with all it's might and power is a cure to aches, dis-comforts and dis-eases pains.
Learn to laugh at your mis-takes and yourself, take it easy.

Law: a rule or principle of proper conduct sanctioned by man's conscience, concepts of natural justice, or the will of a deity: a moral law. Any rule or injunction that must be obeyed: having a good and nourishing breakfast was an absolute law in the household. A rule or manner of behaviour that is instinctive or spontaneous: the law of self-preservation. A commandment or a revelation from Holy-Spirit. The controlling influence of such rules: the condition of society brought about by their observance: maintaining law and order.

Leniency; **A**spect; **W**ard, **w**ord
Life; **A**dventure; **W**ill-power
Love; **A**uthenticity; **W**isdom
Law of attraction, **A**ffection, **W**ay

The Law Of Attraction
is a metaphysical idea in which like attracts like; i.e., negativity yields a prejudice perceived as 'here is the proof, self-evidence - see it with your own eyes'. Positivity does the exact same thing. According to the law of attraction phrases like "I need more… = I am not… = I don't…" allow me/you to remain captivated and secure in the 'need = lack = scarcity = want'. When I/you want to change I/you should centre, fix and focus my/your attention, awareness, intention and mind on the goal which is my/your new out of the box belief and perception in which I/you create a new state of mind and thinking pattern, i.e. I am, be-in - being, having, believing it is aligning, creating, making it, and making me see it come true instead of repeating and recycling the conclusion, 'fact', 'outcome', 'result' "I shall believe it when I see it." When I/you acknowledge and own the hurt/hush/negative/no no, adopt, get accustomed to my/your new programme and set with phrases such as "I am ability," "I am happiness," "I can…" "dreams come true" the universe aligns it in line, brings it along and manifests it for me/you to see it.

See: Fake, pp. 84
Loyalty, pp. 145

Leave: permission to do something. Permission to be absent, as from duty. The time this permission lasts. A parting; departure; farewell.

Legality; **E**arnestness; **A**ppreciation; **V**ivaciousness; **E**legance

Length: the linear extent of anything as measured from end to end. The measure of the greatest dimension of a plane or solid figure. Extent in time; duration. A large extent or expanse of something.

Leisure; **E**xultation; **N**ew; **G**reatness; **T**ruth; **H**ome

Letter: **a**. an energy form, wave; **b**. one of the marks or signs conventionally used in writing to represent speech sounds, alone or in combination; an alphabetic character; **c**. a collection of words, phrases or sentences. **d**. a communication in writing addressed to a person or a number of persons.
A person who lets, esp. one who rents out property.

Life, **l**ove; **E**ssence; **T**rust; **T**reat; **E**nthusiasm; **R**emedy

In 1998 a medium suggested I add the letter ׳ to my first name. She asked that I do not ask her for the reason. I added that letter to my name, had it changed in my Id card, to later find out it changed my spirit.

A few years later another medium asked me for my name. I asked her if she asks for my second name too. When she heard it her face twisted. When she repeated it I heard "Ric-la? What kind of name is it? " In Hebrew ric means empty; la means for/to her. When I came to the Ministry of Interior affairs, before 7 years passed by from the 1st change (the 7 years period slipped out of my mind), I heard the clerk said: "the change you made a couple of years ago is minor, so I can do this change too." She did so for me to find out that this delete changed my world.

To right a spirit - change a letter
To change the world - change a word

Lie: a false statement made with deliberate intent to deceive; a falsehood. Something intended or serving to convey a false impression; imposture.

Loyalty; **I**nnermost truth; **E**xit

For our inner-self the imaginary and the real are one. People expressing their inner world truth - in which imaginary and real are one - are not liars. We are not born false, hypocrites or liars. There are people that learnt from a model figure to be false, hypocrites, liars. When I/you think I/you hear a lie, it's time to stop, ask my/your self did I hear a lie? Is it a lie, or…? What is blocking my/your way to truth hearing and telling?

The 2nd Agreement[6]

Be true to your word, honour, respect, stand up to it and walk it.

One's words are state of being and state of mind reflection and perception.

Be truthful, sincere, honest, genuine, and authentic.

Honouring, respecting, standing up to and walking my/your words is honouring and respecting, standing up to my/yourself. Be coherent; mean and speak your idea, intention, opinion then act on it and walk it.

**A word is a belief energy that create e-motions and reality.
Declaration is an arrow to destination; A destiny creator.**

See: Authenticity, pp. 20
Fake, pp. 84
Honesty, pp. 112
Hypocrisy, pp. 116
Sincerity, pp. 212
Truth, pp. 237

Life: an action or stimuli and the reaction to it. The condition that distinguishes animals and plants from inorganic objects and dead organisms, being manifested by growth through metabolism, reproduction, and the power of adaptation to environment through changes originating internally. A corresponding state, existence or principle of existence conceived of as belonging to the soul. The general or universal condition of human existence. Any specified period of animate existence. A living being. Animation; liveliness. Resilience; elasticity.

Latitude; **I**nfinity; **F**airy-tale; **E**go-free
Love; **I**nn; **F**reedom; **E**xistence
Luxury; **I**nnovation; **F**un;
Extreme sport of my call and my choice

♦ **Life perceived as dangerous, or hard brings along and calls for dangers and hardships.**
♦ **Life being easy, fun full, protected, safe and secure are perceptions and perspectives.**

Both abide by The Law of Attractionin in which negative attracts negative and positive attracts positive (see: Law, pp. 136**).**

Light: something that makes things visible or affords illumination: all colours depend on light. The radiance or illumination from a particular source, as a candle, light-bulb, or the sun. Daybreak or dawn. Daytime. A measure or supply of light; illumination. A particular light or illumination in which an object seen takes on a certain appearance. The aspect in which a thing appears or is regarded. A gleam or sparkle, as in the eyes. Mental or spiritual illumination or enlightenment. A person who is an illuminating or shining example; luminary. A light-house. A traffic light.

Life; Intuition; Gratitude; Heart; Treasure
Love; Intelligence; Glory; Heaven on earth; Time
Lesson; Instinct; Greatness; Harmony; Treat

Limit: the final or furthest bound or point as to extent or continuance. A boundary or bound, as of a country or district.

Load; Ignorance; Mark; Impertinence; Turn
Livelihood; Integrity; Motivation; Interest; Truth

E.S.T. Exercise - see: pp. 133

Line: a long mark of very slight breadth, made to divide an area, determine a direction, distribution, or limit, depict an object, etc. something occurring naturally or coincidentally that resembles such a mark. Such a mark imagined as lying on a surface or extending in space in order to understand the direction, distribution, limit, etc., of something.

Link; Innovation; Nature; Enthusiasm

Live-r - **Liver**: 1. *Anat*. A large, reddish-brown, glandular organ located in the upper right side of the abdominal cavity, divided by tissues into five lobes, and functioning in the secretion of bile and various metabolic processes. A dis-eased condition of the liver. 2. A person who lives in a manner specified: He was always a high liver. A dweller or resident; inhabitant (live + er).

Lust; **I**nhibition; **V**anity; **v**ulture; **E**go; **e**-motion;
Ramification; **r**atification ˜
Laughter; **I**ntegrity; **V**ivacity; **E**ase; **R**elief
Livelihood; **I**nteraction; **V**alidity; **E**ssence; **R**est

Live - rrrrrr?
Live-ly? Li li li

The liver symbolizes ability, to be active, in charge, in command, a general and a leader. Holding on to excessive or extreme in any of these, may manifest in aggression, anger, foul language, hostility, hyper-action, hypocrisy, hysteria, irritation (commonly referred to as allergy), and violence eruptions.

Liver cleansing
E.S.T. Exercise - see: pp. 133

Key-phrases/words: *Preliminary rounds*: angry, mad, hostile, hysterical, irritated, jealous, envious, jaundiced, green eyed, narrow eyed and minded, yellow eyed... *Positive affirmations rounds*: calm, cheerful, confident, easy going, happy, I choose to be in command, I enjoy and love being in command and in control, peaceful, protected, safe, secured...

Aggression clearing letter
1. Find a time and a place where you feel comfortable, free and safe,.
2. It is important to keep a free and intuitive flow, do not stop to correct or read what you write, else you stop to think, "What more do I want to let go and out of my system."
3. Take a pen and paper, sit down and start writing in the following format:
To (reason, person, situation)
free intuitive flow...
Signature
Date
4. Tear your letter to pieces.
 Burn the pieces (optional).
 Throw pieces and/or ash to waste bin.
5. Discard, when going out, into the trash can.
 Repeat this procedure three days in a row.
 On days 2 and/or 3, should nothing come out, write
To (reason, person, situation)

your signature and the date
and follow steps 4, 5.

More remedies

Ingredients:
Citrus juice squeezer
Crystal glass
Fresh, mellow, ripe, yellow lemon
Olive Oil (cold pressed, acidity value up to 1.8)
21 days procedure:
Women in fertility cycle are to begin procedure on cycle's 7th day.
Every day, half an hour before your first drink or meal, squeeze fresh lemon juice, mix with olive oil into a homogenous mixture, drink to health.

Begin with 1 table spoon each, proceed to 2 table spoons each.

Herbs:
Dandelion, Devil's Claws nutritional supplements, **Milk Thistle** (Silybum) seeds: Infusion: put 1 teaspoon of seeds in a crystal glass, pour boiling hot water over it, cover with glass saucer, let it rest for 10 minutes and more, drink to health.

Rosemary, Summer savoury, leaves (dry or fresh), lavishly mix with your already broiled or cooked vegetables or fresh vegetable salad. Infusion: put 1 teaspoon of Summer savoury, with or without 4-6 Rosemary leaves, in a crystal glass, pour boiling hot water over it, cover with crystal glass saucer, let it stand for 10 minutes and more, drink to health.

Drink two and more glasses per day in cycles of three weeks drinking, one week holiday (free from drinking).

Freshly prepare each glass.

Apple vinegar 5% (natural, non-pasteurized), 1 table spoon mixed in a crystal glass filled with lukewarm water, as 1st drink of the day. Please note that apple vinegar drains out minerals, amongst is salt. Lack of salt may manifest in attacks of crazed and violent behaviour. When consuming apple vinegar on a daily basis It is essential to maintain a diet with minerals rich foods, such as almonds, cabbage, nuts, seaweed, spinach.

Longing: prolonged, unceasing, or earnest desire. An instance of this.

Love; **O**bedience; **N**est; **G**race; **I**nnocence; **N**ascence; **G**rowth

Laughter; **O**verture, **N**ext, **G**arden; **I**ndulgence; **N**avigation, **G**rid

Loss: detriment or disadvantage from failure to keep, have, or get: to bear the loss of a robbery. The state of being deprived of or of being without something that one has had: to suffer the loss of one's friends. The coincidental or inadvertent losing of something dropped, misplaced, stolen, etc.: to discover the loss of a document. A losing by defeat; failure to win: the loss of a bet. Failure to make good use of something, as time; waste. Failure to preserve or maintain: loss of engine speed at high altitudes. Destruction or ruin: the loss of a ship by fire.

Let go; **O**rder; **S**erenity; **S**hift
Love, **l**uster; **O**pportunity; **S**heer; **S**uccess

See: Mourning, pp. 154

E.S.T. Exercise - see: pp. 133

Key-phrases/words: sadness, deep sorrow, lost, at a loss, helpless, powerless, useless…

Love: a strong prediction or liking for anything. The object of this liking. A profoundly tender, passionate affection for a person of the opposite sex, an animal; an object or an occupation. A feeling of warm personal attachment or deep affection, as for a parent, child, or friend. A person toward whom love is felt; beloved person; sweetheart.

Misconceptions of love
* Affectionate concern for the well-being of others. Truth: Do you feel good or happy when you are affectionately concerned for the well-being of the other? No, you do not. What you do feel is concern. Concern is worrying and both come from being in fear or feeling insecurity. When you are fearing or insecure your good judgment and perceptions are impaired. What good can you do when your jugdement and perception are impaired? You can do no good. You cannot be concerned and loving at the same time same as you cannot be awake and asleep at the same time. So you may as well let go of concern, to be in love and loving.
* I love you when you do as I say. You may as well say I will hate or kill you if you don't do as I say.

* I hit you because I love you. You may as well say this is all too much for me. I don't know what to do about it.
* I punish you because I love you. You may as well say I cannot deal with what you just did or say.
* Hit her/him to show her/him that you love her/him. You may as well say I hate your guts, you are the worst nightmare I could ever come up with.
* Sexual passion or desire, or its gratification; see: Sex. pp. 202.

True meaning of love

An unadulterated and unconditional love is being in love and loving, all the time.
* I love you.
* I love you anyhow, anytime and anywhere.
* I love you when you are bad and when you are good.
* I love you when in happiness and health and when in sickness and sorrow.

Life; **O**rder; **V**ivaciousness; **E**nthusiasm

Lesson; **O**pportunity; **V**alour; **E**ssence

Lenience; **O**bedience; **V**ict-OR-y; **E**xistence

Livelihood; **O**bservance; **V**ehicle; **E**ndurance

Longevity; **O**cean; **V**irtue; **E**volution

Lordship; **O**ffer; **V**igour; **E**verlastingness

Loyalty; **O**neness; **V**alidation; **E**xuberance

Lift; **O**asis; **V**alue; **E**steem

Luxuriance; **O**ngoing; **V**ision; **E**uphoria

Light; **O**ncoming; **V**itality; **E**xclusivity

Lyricism; **O**ption; **V**ulnerary; **E**xcellence

Leadership; **O**penness; **V**oyage; **E**arth

Luminosity; **O**ptimism; **V**astness; **E**ase

Line; **O**riginality; **V**ocation; **E**den

When in my twenties, I fell in love with a supplier, to nearly 30 years later, realize that his image was engraved on my heart's table. Here is how and what happened.

Towards the end of the millennium, I started to drive to the beach on a pretty regular basis. I walked along the sea shore, fooled and played with the sea waves. One Shabbat evening in autumn 2003 I went out of my way (I wore a T-shirt) and out of course (I climbed up a staircase). I saw one of the regular runners, whose image along the years attracted my attention time and time again, come downhill and down the staircase I was climbing up. I heard, "When you change give us a notice so that we know its you." I stopped at the top of the staircase, turned around, smiled and my body language asked, "Were you talking to me?" "Yes, you are the one with the red bathing suit. Are you staying here some more? Will you wait for me on the bench? I am running and will return within 20 minutes'" he added. I answered, "Yes, I am staying, I will wait for you." He returned before 20 minutes were up. I smiled once more. When we got up for each to go her/his way he told me his name. The bells started ringing. The following Sunday I met a friend whose line of business was the same as the supplier's one. I told him that on Friday I met a man I remember from my distant past and he helped me to remember. I heard him say, "But I am not sure, I don't want to be wrong." I asked, "Is it true that he Is approximately 1.85 metres high, with beautifully carved facial lines, always dressed in a three piece suit style?" "Yes," he answered and I concluded, "Then, this is the same one I met on Shabbat evening." I decided this time I shall open my heart, reveal to him and make with him what I did not dare do then - and so I did.

Being in love IN
Falling in love OUT

Every moment is a perfect momentum to follow my heart and act on it's word

See: Tongue, pp. 233

Loyalty: the state or quality of being loyal; faithfulness to commitments or obligation. Faithful adherence to a sovereign, a government, cause, or the like. An example or instance of faithfulness, adherence, or the like: a man with fierce loyalties.

Love; **O**ffering; **Y**ield;
All ways; **L**et; **T**ruth; **Y**es

See: Fake, pp. 84
Law, pp. 136

M

Mad: Informal, a period or spell of anger or ill-temper. Mad-ness: the state of being mad, insanity. Senseless folly. Frenzy, rage. Intense excitement or enthusiasm.

Mastery; **A**dventure; **D**are
Motivation; **A**wareness; **D**elight

E.S.T. Exercise - see: pp. 133

Key-phrases/words: *Preliminary rounds*: angry, raving mad,… *Positive affirmations rounds*: at ease, calm, cool, in control, peaceful, relaxed, responsible, taking it easy…

Marvel: a person or thing that arouses wonder, admiration, or astonishment.

Mystery; **A**uthenticity;
Revelation; **V**ict-OR-y; **E**ssence; **L**ivelihood.
Magic; **A**isle; **R**eflection, **V**ivaciousness; **E**cstasy; **L**eisure

Marvel and wonder more to effortlessly transform anxiety into enthusiasm burning hell into heaven on earth

Maturity: the state of being mature; ripeness. Full development; perfected condition.

Manifestation; **A**uthority; **T**rust; **U**niformity;
Reliability; **r**esponsibility; **I**ntuition; **T**reasure; **Y**outh

Meditation: an engagement in thought; reflection; contemplation; cogitation.

Miracle; **E**nergy; **D**rive; **I**ntuition; **T**rait;
Agency; **T**reat; **I**magination; **O**pportunity; **N**ascence

Memory: the mental capacity or faculty of retaining and reviving impressions, or of recalling or recognizing previous experiences. This faculty as possessed by a particular individual: To have a good memory. The act or fact of retaining mental impressions; remembrance; recollection. A mental impression retained; recollection.

Mastery; **E**ase; **M**ake; **O**ptimum; **R**elief; **Y**ield

In my forties, with Ofira and Perla's encouragement, I decided to come to my mother and open my heart. I asked, "Please help me bring up happy childhood memories." "There are none," I recall I heard. "Maybe there is one from when you were in 3rd grade. We went together with father to Tel Aviv, to the zoo, perhaps to a film too." I shared sorrowful memories (See: Dread, pp. 69). We agreed that the memories of one are not the memories of the other. Along the way, I decided I want to create happy memories with my mother. Thereafter, this was the will power that motivated every management and move in my relationship with my mother and others.

A few years later, I came over to celebrate Pesach (Passover) evening with my mother. While I was in the shower, I felt tired. I asked my mother if she would come help me comb my hair. She stopped what she was doing, came (practically running) over and combed my hair with love and tenderness that moves me to this day. A happy and profound heart moving memory was created inside me.

Ideas and thoughts manifest in matter, physical entities and things

Memory development exercise

Instruments:
A crystal glass, with fresh filtered water at room temperature or lukewarm
A note-book or a writing paper-block
Pen

Procedure:
1. Before going to sleep, take a crystal glass, fill it with fresh filtered water at room temperature or lukewarm.

2. Place the crystal glass with the water, note book or writing paper-block and pen by your bed-lamp, on a table, or a dresser near your bed.

3. Sit on your bed-side, take the crystal glass in your hand, say out loud, or in your heart, "I have a good memory, I remember my dream when I wake up." Drink some water.

Repeat three times.

Lie in your bed and let sleep peacefully engulf you.

4. When you wake up, be it 'in the middle of the night' or any other time, immediately write down what you remember, be it a single digit, a letter, a symbol, a word, a phrase, or a story.

Repeat daily, for six months and more.

Happy memory creation

Exercise 1:

Instruments:

Writing paper and tools, or any electronic device with a programme for writing.

Procedure:

Find a place and a time where you feel at ease. Lie down or sit with your spine straight, inhale deeply (through your nostrils) and exhale peacefully (through your mouth) a couple of times.

Sit down and start writing what you want your happiness, health, love, relationships, and career to become with yourself, and every person, matter or thing in your life.

Read it out loud once daily.

This is your dream.

Bless it, feed it, give it light, give it water, hold on to it, honour it, keep it safe, keep it warm, let it grow, nurture it with love from your heart. Let it reflect in your actions, deeds, eyes, hands and heart. Share it when ready.

Exercise 2:

Instruments:

Happy occasion notebook

Pen or pencil

Procedure:

At the end of each day, for 21 days straight, open your happy occasions notebook and write in it: full day/date/hour (example: Tuesday, June 18, 2018, 18:18) and all the happy occasions you can recall and remember in each day.

On the 22nd day read all that you wrote, examine and observe the difference between day 1 and day 21.

Repeat whenever you feel it's time to attract, create and establish happiness, a sense of gratitude and success.

Exercise 3:

Find a place and a time where you feel at ease and safe. Close your eyes, focus on your breath, inhale through your nostrils and gently exhale through your mouth three times. Listen to your breath and sense it. Is it freely, naturally and peacefully flowing all the way to the belly, or blocked, emotionally loaded, flat?

When your breathing is flowing freely, naturally and peacefully, move your focus to your thoughts. Allow them to freely fly, run, pass across the screen of your mind. Look at them, observe and study them. What are they revealing to you? What information do they bring to your mind? What are they telling you about yourself? Your thinking patterns? Your perceptions? If the knowledge is on a scale of young-old, continue your self exploration.

The goal is to create a change in perception, to connect with the young free flowing and happily youthful you.

If your breath is flat or heavy (emotion loaded, constricted, blocked) continue to focus on your breathing, directing and navigating it to the block until you feel that your breath freely flows. Move your focus to your thoughts and visions when breath flows freely.

Memory absence or loss

Absent mind, memory loss, poor memory result from stress and/or food and metals poisoning, heavy and long term medication use.

For aches, pains, stress, tension, worries relief practice Letting Go fun exercise, pp. 105 and E.S.T exercise, pp. 133.

♦ Find with your local GP and/or Herbalist foods and herbs from nature's garden that replace pharmaceutical laboratories medications.
♦ Chew, eat, smell and sniff Basil leaves; eat coconut oil.
♦ Metal cleaning procedures.
♦ Replace negating and negativity with acceptance and positivity.

Mentality: mental capacity or endowment; intellectual character.

Mankind; **E**steem; **N**urture; **T**alent;
Art; **L**ove; **I**ntention; **T**angibility; **Y**es

Mercy: compassionate or kindly forbearance shown toward an offender, an enemy, or other person in one's power; compassion, pity, or benevolence. An act of kindness, compassion, or favour.

Miracle; **E**lation; **R**evival; **C**reation; **Y**ield

Milestone: a stone functioning as a mile post. A significant event, as in hi-story or in a person's life.

Magic; **I**dentity; **L**ife; **E**nthusiasm;
Sanity; **T**reasure; **O**ption; **N**ewness; **E**xistence

Mind: the agency or part in a human or other conscious being that creaate e-motions, perceives, reasons, understands, wills etc. *Psychol.* The totality of conscious and inner-self mental process and activities of the organism. The faculty of reasoning or understanding; intelligence. Reason or sanity: To loose one's mind. Opinion or intention: To change one's mind. Psychic or spiritual being, as opposed to matter. A conscious or intelligent agency or being: An awareness of a mind ordering the universe. Remembrance or recollection: Former days were called to mind. Attention; thoughts: He can't keep his mind on his studies.

Maintenance; **I**nteraction; **N**urture; **D**elight

The human mind works like a comnputer. It contains data and old programming. When you ask a computer for an answer - do you beat it down, break it for coming up with a wrong answer or not coming up with the answer?
Did you notice that when your mind does the exact same thing you tend to beat, hit or run yourself down?
To let go of beating, hitting or running yourself down and to programme your mind to an abuse, accuse, blame, guilt, punishment, reproach free conduct pracrtice Letting Go fun exercise pp. 105 and E.S.T. exercise, pp. 133.

Miracle: an event in the physical world that surpasses all known human or natural powers and is ascribed to a divine or supernatural cause. A wonder; marvel.

Mind **m**omentum; **I**ntuition; **R**eflection;
Attunement; **C**onsciousness; **L**ove; **E**cstasy

I boarded a bus, feeling glad I had time to take a shower, change and take it easy beforehand and over an hour to enjoy the scenery along the way. After a couple of bus stops, I felt a cramping pain in my stomach. Calm down, relax. The memory of recent months raised the question: "What am I going to do now?" I felt my stomach turn inside out as another wave of cramps welled up. Various ideas crossed my mind. One of them questioned my ability to clean up, with a bottle of water and A-4 paper sheets. Another questioned: "Will the driver (of the bus I will board to go on) agree to let me on without charging me?" The bus stopped to drop off a soldier. I decided I had better get off too and did so. The bus stop was dark and empty, no one around - perfect! I went behind the bus stop to ease the tension out. I felt thankful that earlier that day, I followed the notion to walk back into my apartment to get the bottle of water. Sitting there in the dark I asked myself, "Where does it say I must clean up with tissue or toilet paper?" Primitively I washed my self clean and considered the possibilities, only to realize the bus-driver had stopped at an out of the way bus stop. Once more I filled with uplifting energy. I'll take a bus to one of the central bus stations and there I'll board the bus to reach my destination. "What if the driver (of the bus I shall board to reach my destination) is the miserable and nervous one?" I remembered to call Nira to set a new time for our meeting. In divine and perfect order and timing, the miserable and nervous driver drove up to the bus-station, stopped the bus, opened its door. There were two men among the women waiting to board the bus. The first one accepted and respected my wish to board the bus before me, the second, dressed in black from top to bottom, did not. I boarded the bus, with a smile from ear to ear and Good evening coming out of my mouth. I saw the miserable and nervous bus driver's face light up with a smile. I handed the ticket to him and said, "I earlier got off because I felt bad. May I continue the rest of the way with this same ticket?" He looked down at the ticket he held in his hand, "Sure, you can," I heard him say as he handed the ticket back to me.

This course of events was one result of marveling abilities, beautiful and good people and things coming my way. Thank you, Holy Spirit, for this miracle, for making me realize I am able, and can be filled with inspiring appreciation and uplifting joy. For showing me goodness reflects through others.

Miser
: a person who lives in wretched circumstances in order to save and hoard money. A niggardly, avaricious person. Obs. A wretched or unhappy person

My; **I**mpression; **S**ort; **E**xistence; **R**eflection
Make, **I**nnovation, **S**elf; **E**xchange; **R**eassurance

Mis?
Er(r)?
MISER is one letter short of MISERY
M(y) RISE to a new rung

E.S.T. Exercise - see: pp. 133

Key-phrases/words: *Preliminary rounds*: hard headed, fear stricken, miserable, poor me, stuck, wretched me... *Positive affirmations rounds*: abundant, broad minded, happy, mirthful, open minded, open to receive, resourceful, rich...

Mis-take
- **Mistake**: an err-or caused by a missing attention, conception; focus, integrity, perception; sincerity; understanding.

Mastery; **I**nn; **S**implicity; **T**ruth; **A**ffection; **K**indle; **E**ase

E.S.T. exercise to dis-cover mis-take is in the eye of the beholder

1. Get a notebook and a pen.
2. Find a place and a time where you feel at ease, protected and safe.
3. Write the first word that comes to mind and continue with each word or phrase that follows. Write freely, disregard, ignore, over-come and over-look grammar, phrasing, style, conventions, laws, rules.
    Do not read what you wrote, do not seek logic, do not search for phrasing or spelling err-ors or mis-takes.
4. Finish writing after you have written a few lines, or sentences and more.
    Put the notebook in a safe place.
5. Proceed to follow new ideas or with your pre-planned schedule.
6. Approximately half an hour before you go to sleep, or on another day, take the notebook, go and sit where you feel at ease,

protected and safe, adopt the attention and attitude of a non-participant observer sitting on top of a high fence or way up in the bleachers watching the young playing on the ground.

Open the notebook and read what you wrote.

When finding an 'err-or', close your eyes, focus on your breath, and dedicate attention and time to ask yourself and wonder, "What is being revealed to me now?" "What is my inner-self showing or telling me?"

The first word, or sentence, that comes up is the true answer, whether you understand it, are puzzled, or you cannot find any connection, logic, or make sense of it.

Mood: a person's emotional state or outlook at a particular moment. A person's disposition in dealing with others at a particular moment. An emotional response or attitude toward something seen, heard, or otherwise experienced. Moods, fits of e-motion, esp. of sullenness or gloom.

Motion; **O**ption; **O**dyssey; **D**elight

MOOD spelt backwards is doom

Frequently changing mood reflects ego mannerism, a habit of excessive judgment, hyster-ia, insecurity, or harsh self-criticism.

E.S.T. Exercise - see: pp. 133

Key-phrases/words: *Preliminary rounds*: run myself down, underestimate myself... *Positive affirmations rounds*: accept, acknowledge, appreciate, honour, own, respect, value...

Morality: conformity to the rules of right or virtuous conduct. Moral quality or character. Virtue in sexual matters; chastity. Lesson: teaching, instruction, lecture, discourse, talk, sermon, recitation, assignment, exercise. Drama: play, melodrama, pageant, vaudeville, re-view.
Ethics: virtue, moral climate.
Virtue: goodness, righteousness, saintliness, godliness.

Make; **O**ne; **R**e-vision;
Align in line; **L**ove; **I**ntegrity; **T**ranquillity; **Y**outh

Mourning: sorrowing, lamentation. The conventional manifestation of sorrow for the death, or loss of a person, an animal, or an object.

Magnificence; **O**verture; **U**biquity;
Ripeness; **N**ext; **I**nspiration; **N**est; **G**rowth

Allow and let yourself a wholehearted grief and mourning, for repressed grief and mourning rush to bring out a rash and come out and up in dis-ease.

MORNING is one letter short of MOURNING
GOOD DAY is my call, choice and greeting

N

Naïveté: also called naiveness, the quality or state of being naïve; artless simplicity. A naive action, remark, etc.

Nature; **A**ll; **I**nstinct; **V**ivacity; **E**nthusiasm, **T**reasure; **E**xistence

Narrow: A narrow part, place or thing. A narrow part of a valley, passage, or road. Narrows: a narrow part of a strait, river, ocean, current, etc.

New; **A**wareness; **R**evival; **R**elaxation;
Option; **W**ings to freely flow and fly

Narrow-hearted: petty.
Narrow-mind - small minded: intolerant, mean-spirited, one-sided, having or showing a prejudiced or an extremely conservative and morally self-righteous mind, short-sighted, nearsighted.

E.S.T. Exercise - see: pp. 133

Nature: the particular combination of qualities belonging to a person, animal, thing, or class by birth, origin, or constitution. The instincts or inherent tendencies directing conduct. The material world, esp. that part unaffected by man. Plants, animals, geographical features, etc... The original, natural, uncivilized condition of man. A primitive, wild condition; an uncultivated state.

Neatness; **A**ffection; **T**reasure; **U**niformity; **R**eality; **E**xpansion

Second nature: an acquired habit, mindset, perception or tendency that is so deeply ingrained as to appear automatically.

State of mind; **E**nthusiasm; **C**are-free; **O**ngoing; **N**ature; **D**elight
Navigation; **A**ttentiveness; **T**ruth; **U**nity; **R**eset your programme;
Evolution

Nausea: sickness at the stomach. Esp. when accompanied by a loathing for food and an involuntary impulse to vomit. Extreme disgust; loathing; repugnance.
A sensation reflecting an emotional or spiritual evolvement turmoil, a time to let go of emotional or spiritual conditions, customs, habits, manners, patterns, sets or ways that no longer benefit or serve one's wellbeing, and wellness.

Naïveté; **A**lign in line; **U**niverse; **S**implicity; **E**lation; **A**lliance

E.S.T. Exercise - see: pp. 133

Key-phrases/words: *Preliminary rounds*: afraid, bitter, detest, disgusted, fear stricken, had enough of, loath, sick of, sour, swept in a turmoil ... *Positive affirmations rounds*: all is in divine and perfect orchestration, all is well, I allow myself to calm down, chill out, uplift, in harmony, at peace, relax...

Navigation: the act or process of navigating. The art or science of plotting, ascertaining, or directing the course of a ship, aircraft, or one his own life and way.

Newborn; **A**ssessment; **V**ision; **I**ntuition; **G**aiety;
Assertiveness; **T**rack, **I**nsight; **O**pportunity; **N**ascence

Necessity: something necessary or indispensable; the necessities of life. An imperative requirement or need for something: the necessity for a quick decision. An unavoidable need or compulsion to do something: by necessity or need rather than by free choice. A state of being in difficulty or need; poverty choice and strait: a family in dire necessity. *Philos.* The quality of following inevitably from logical, physical or moral laws.

Nerve(*); **E**scapade, **C**reativity; **E**volution;
Serenity; **S**ystem; **I**nsight; **T**wist and shout; **Y**outh

---

(*) Strength, vigour, or energy

Neck
: the part of the body of an animal or human being that connects the head and the trunk. The slender part near the top of a bottle, vase, or similar object.

Neatness; **E**quilibrium; **C**hoice; **K**indness

Nerve
: strength, vigour, or energy. Firmness or courage under trying circumstances.

One or more bundles of fibers forming part of a system that conveys impulses or sensation, motion, etc., between the brain, solar plexus, or spinal cord and other parts of the body.

Nicety, **n**est; **E**ase; **R**evelation; **V**itality; **E**ssence

Dare nerve

See: Examination, pp. 80

Night-mare
- **Nightmare**: a terrifying dream in which the dreamer experiences feelings of helplessness, extreme anxiety, sorrow, etc. a condition, thought, or experience suggestive of a nightmare in sleep.

Nature; **I**nnocence; **G**ratitude; **H**eart;
Transformation; **M**agic; **A**wareness; **R**elief; **E**nlightenment

The Dream world is where one can safely create, change, and receive information, know-how and knowledge for self-transformation, growth, expansion, development, prosperity and success. It's a marvellous and splendid media to act in and with (See: Dream, pp. 72; Fake, pp. 84).

For a child waking up from a night-mare

Every evening before you bless your child and give your good night affectionate, graceful and kind caress and kiss, ask the child to share the day's events, happy, sad, stressful, and all. Attentively listen to every word, and ask matter-of-fact questions rather than correct, right, or reproach your child.

On an evening that your child shares sad or sorrowful events encourage the child with happy, joyful and loving memories from your life and ask the child to draw or sketch a happy and merry picture, perhaps find a picture projecting happiness and joy. Suggest the child put it under the pillow and wish happy dreams in a pleasant and sweet sleep.

For the child that is within mature me
Instruments:
Colour chalks, paints, pens, pencils
Sketch paper.
Procedure:
Before lying in bed to sleep:
1. Think of happiness. What does it feel and look like?
2. Draw / sketch / paint what to you is a happy picture.
3. Put the picture where you can look at it while lying in your bed, or under your pillow.
4. Lie in bed, close your eyes, take three peaceful breaths (inhale through your nostrils, exhale through your mouth) and in your mind call the good, happy and pleasant events, occasions, occurrences of the day to come forth. Re-feel them, allowing and letting them refill and refresh you.

On a day with an annoying, sad or sorrowful event allow yourself to express your e-motions, and ask your family members or your friends if they have one. Ask he/she to share it and tell it to you. Connect with hers/his good, happy, pleasant event as if it were yours, thus making it yours.

Follow and practice this procedure with children remembering a nightmare.

> See: Memory development exercise, pp. 147
> Happy memory creation, pp. 148

No: a denial or refusal.

Negativity; **O**ut
Nest; **O**penness
Newness; **O**xygen
Next, **O**ption

Each and every human-being is born with human intelligence and deserves to be considered, perceived, seen and treated as having it and worthy. A no followed by reason can be reasoned by the other party. It can also be an opening for a dialogue, learning and a new -

learned - decision. A no with no reason is a denial, insult, offense and refusal to human intelligence.

> NO
> is an opportunity to
> ON-ward a new direction
> A possibility to
> ON-word a new way
>
> See: Child, pp. 42
> You know, pp. 131

Noise: sound, esp. of a loud, harsh, or confused kind. A sound of any kind. Loud shouting or clamour. An electric disturbance in a communication system that interferes with or prevents reception of a signal or of information. Obs. Rumour or common talk, esp. slander.

Next; **O**pening; **I**ncarnation; **S**tream; **E**volution

> E.S.T. Exercise - see: pp. 133

Key-phrases/words: *Preliminary rounds*: noise, confused, harassed, disturbed, nervous, restless, stressed, worried... *Positive affirmations rounds*: calm down, chill out, in harmony, at ease, at peace, in peace, peaceful...

Nose: the part of the face or facial region in man and certain animals that contains the nostrils and the organs of smell, and functions as the usual passageway for air in respiration and, in man, in the modification or modulation of the voice.

Nirvana, **n**urture, **n**utrition;
Opportunity, **o**ption, **o**pening;
Spirit, **s**oul, **s**ense, **s**pace, **s**afety;
Entrance and **e**xit, **e**volution, **e**nthusiasm

O

Occupation: a person's usual or principal job or business. Any activity in which a person is engaged. Possession, settlement, or use of land or property.

Openness; **C**reation; **C**omfort; **U**niqueness; **P**lea-sure;
Affection, **a**lleviation; **T**rait; **I**nnovation; **O**mnipresence; **N**ewness

Operation: the act or an instance, process, or manner of functioning or operating. A process of a practical or mechanical manner. *Surg.* A process or act of operating on the body of a patient.

Occasion; **P**resence; **E**lation; **R**eflection;
Awareness; **T**op; **I**ntuition; **O**rchestration; **N**eatness

> What is my call and choice?
> To be operated by a surgeon?
> To operate to the best of my ability?
> To have an operation completed?

Opportunism: the policy or practice of exploiting opportunities without regard to ethical or moral principles.

Over; **P**lea-sure; **P**aradise; **O**verture; **R**ipple;
Togetherness; **U**ltimate ness; **N**ascence; **I**nvolvement;
Serenity, **s**implicity; **M**agic, **m**astery, **m**iracle; **m**omentum

Opportunity: an appropriate or favourable time, occasion or option. A situation or condition favourable for attainment of a goal. A good position, chance, or prospect for self-advancement.

Onset; **P**re-sent; **P**resent; **O**asis; **R**esilience;
Turn-point; **U**nity; **N**est; **I**ntegrity; **T**rust; **Y**ield

Oppression: the burdensome, unjust exercise of authority or power. The act or an instance of oppressing. The state of being oppressed. The feeling of being oppressed in mind or body.

Orchestra; **P**lentitude; **P**eace; **R**oad; **E**steem; **S**ignificance; **S**ight; **I**nnovation; **O**bservance; **N**ow

> E.S.T. Exercise - see: pp. 133
> Pre-sent present presents - see: pp. 134
> H.T.P. - see: pp. 134

Order: an authoritative communication by which a person addressed is directed to do something; command. A system or arrangement, classification, or coordination of persons or things, as by sequence or rank: alphabetical order.

O(h)range; **R**evelation; **D**elight; **E**xpertise; **R**ung

Ore: the tincture, or metal, gold: represented either by gold or by yellow.

Origin; **R**enaissance; **E**asy does it
Opportunity; **R**ampage; **E**cstasy
Option; **R**elief; **E**nthusiasm
Omnipresence; **R**ipple; **E**xultation

Out: something that is out, as a projecting corner. A means of escape, as from a place, punishment, retribution, responsibility, etc.

Orientation; **U**ttermost; **T**ranquillity, **t**ransparency

Out-rage - **Outrage**: an act of wanton violence; any gross violation of law or decency. Anything that outrages the feelings. Obs. Passionate or violent behaviour or language; fury or insolence.

Outstanding; **U**niverse; **T**enderness;
Relief; **A**ffection; **G**ratitude; **E**lation

E.S.T. Exercise - see: pp. 133

Key-phrases/words: *Preliminary rounds*: angry, anxious, filled with wrath, frustrated, furious, ill-tempered, out-raged, raging mad, raving, short-tempered, worried… *Positive affirmations rounds*: calm, ease, peace, relief, relaxation…

P

Pain: bodily suffering or distress, as due to injury or illness. A distressing sensation in a particular part of the body: a back pain. Mental or emotional suffering or torment.

Peace; **A**ffection; **I**ntuition; **N**urture
Presence; **A**lliance; **I**nnovation; **N**est

See: Ache, pp. 7
E.S.T. Exercise - see: pp. 133

Palpitation: an abnormal rapid or violent beating of the heart.

Phase; **A**ttunement; **L**ove; **P**ractice **p**eace; **I**nnermost;
Tranquillity; **A**wareness; **T**ransition; **I**nvitation; **O**ption; **N**ow

E.S.T. Exercise - see: pp. 133

Key-phrases/words: *Preliminary rounds*: anxiety, fear, at a loss, horrified, miserable, overwhelmed, panicked, poor, terrorized, shocked, stressed… *Positive affirmations rounds*: safe, safe to flow, out of danger, relaxed, protected, secured…

Balance exercise - see: pp. 21
Pre-sent present presents - see: pp. 134
H.P.T. - see: pp. 134

Pancreas: *Gk* pănkreas = sweetbread, pan = bread, kréas = flesh, meat. *Anat., Zool.* a gland, situated near the stomach, which secretes a digestive fluid into the intestine through one or more ducts and also secretes the hormone insulin. Pancreatic juice: a thick, colourless, very alkaline fluid secreted by the pancreas. Containing enzymes that break down protein, fat, and starch. Pancreatin: a substance containing the pancreatic enzymes, trypsin, amylase, and lipase.

Peace of heart and mind; **A**nchor; **N**est;
Concurrence; **R**elief; **E**nthusiasm; **A**ffection; **S**erenity

E.S.T. Exercise - see: pp. 133

Key-phrases/words: *Preliminary rounds*: bitter, cynical, deflated, depressed, desperate, detest, dropped out, failure; good for nothing; helplessness, hopeless, miser, miserable, poor, sorrowful, traumatized, vict-I'm... *Positive affirmations rounds*: competent, committed, empowered, hopeful, open hearted, open minded, motivated, safe, skilled, out of danger, relaxed, protected, secured, life is beautiful, miracles are sweet...

H.P.T. - see: pp. 134

Paradise: heaven, Eden, a place of extreme beauty, bliss, delight, happiness, joy, mirth. A state of supreme bliss, delight, happiness, joy, mirth. A belief, perception and a state of mind.

Plea-sure; **A** state of mind, **a**ttitude;
Reality; **A**spect; **D**elight; **I**ntuition; **S**implicity; **E**xistence.

Partner: a sharer or partaker; associate. *Law.* A person associated with another as a principal or contributor or capital in a business or a joint venture. Spouse. One's companion in a dance. A player on the same side or team as another.

Pal; **A**wareness; **R**apture; **T**enderness; **N**est; **E**ase; **R**elationship
Peace; **A**ffection; **R**ejuvenation;
Treasure; **N**ewness; **E**nergy; **R**ipple
Pleasure; **A**ttuneent; **R**eservoir; **T**rust; **N**ext; **E**xpansion; **R**elief

Partnership: participation; association; joint interest. The state or condition of being a partner. *Law.* The relation subsisting between partners. The contract creating this relation. An association of persons joined as partners in business.

Pass-i-on - Passion: any powerful or compelling e-motion or feeling. Strong affection: love. A strong or extravagant fondness,

enthusiasm, or desire for anything: a passion for music. Violent anger.

Paradise; Affection; Sensibility;
Sensuality; Innermost; Orchestra; Navigation

See: Reason and Passion, pp. 184

Peace: the normal condition of the world. A period during which such condition exists. A state of harmony. The freedom from disorder. Freedom of the mind from annoyance, distraction, etc. A state or condition conductive to, proceeding from, or characterized by tranquillity. Silence, stillness.

Pre-sent present presents; Education; Authenticity; Creation;
Expansion
Privilege; Ecstasy; Attitude; Current; Eden
Paradise; Endowment; Ascension; Concurrence; Elation
Party; Esoteric k-now-ledge; Acceptance; Courage; Evolution
Purity; Existence; Affluence; Cuddle; Esteem
Play; Excitement; Attentiveness; Caress; Ease
Pledge; Earth; Abundance; Culture; Essence

Peace is my default state of being

To recreate or revive your inner peace, practice Letting Go fun exercise, pp. 105 and E.S.T. exercise, pp. 133.
Clear and let go whenever you feel blocked energy anywhere in your body; muscle clenching in your throat, stomach, neck, nape, or chest. Stagnant energy lets you know it is time to let it go, let it out. Pressure is the inner-self telling you that it is now time to release every last ounce of that energy. Clenching/pressure let you know an e-motion asks to come out and is, instead, repressed, or shoved aside/under. We either let go or repress. Let go whenever you feel pressured, repressed energy, stress or tightness so that you are at ease, free, light, in peace.
How do I clear and let go?
I close my eyes, feel the clenching, engage in deep peaceful breathing, while feeling and/or watching the energy come out and leave.

Person: a human being, the actual self or individual personality of a human being. The body of a living human being, sometimes including the clothes being worn: he had no money on his person.

Presence; **E**ase; **R**esourcefulness;
Sovereignty; **O**mnipresence; **N**ewness

Phobia: an obsessive or irrational fear or anxiety. Syn. aversion, hatred, dread.

Present; **H**atred; **O**ver-ride; **B**last; **I**rritation; **A**buse
Past; **H**ell; **O**ut; **B**rutality; **I**nferiority; **A**bandonment
Post; **H**arassment; **O**ppression; **B**elt; **I**llness; **A**ggression
Peace, **p**resence; **H**ear no evil, see no evil,
speak no evil, **h**ere and now; **O**rigin; **B**reath; **I**n; **A**ffection

E.S.T. Exercise - see: pp. 133

Key-phrases/words: *Preliminary rounds*: addiction, anger, anxiety, fear, frustrated; harassed; hate; horrified, hysterical, miserable, overwhelmed, panicked, poor, shocked, stressed, terrified; terrorized... *Positive affirmations rounds*: calm, empowered, in-control, I now choose to hold the horse's reigns with both my hands; protected, relaxed, safe, safe to flow, out of danger, secured...

Pre-sent present presents - see: pp. 134
H.P.T. - see: pp. 134

Pit-y - **Pity**: sympathetic grief or sorrow excited by the suffering or misfortune of another, often leading one to show mercy.

Past; **I**nnocence; **T**ake; **Y**esterday;
Present; **I**ntegrity; **T**enderness; **Y**ield

Change pity to affection
Compass-i-on, empathy, mercy, or sympathy to love

Plea-sure

Pleasure: the state of feeling of being pleased. Enjoyment or satisfaction derived from what is to one's liking; gratification; delight. Worldly or frivolous enjoyment. A sensual gratification.

Presence; **L**ove; **E**njoyment; **A**ttitude;
Simplicity; **U**niformity; **R**elief; **E**nthusiasm

Poison

: a substance that has an inherent tendency to destroy life or impair health. Something that is harmful or pernicious, as to happiness or well-being.

Phase **O**ne **I**s **S**imply t**O** **N**ot

On October 29, 2014, an exterminator sprayed the apartment with pesticide in the afternoon. His instructions were to shut the place for three hours. He said that when the three hours are over I could go back in and about my daily routine. I came home after the three hours were over, opened the bathroom and bedroom windows, turned on the ventilator by my bedside and went to sleep. On Thursday I worked in my office, with window closed, believing the room was aired because the kitchen and guest room windows were left open all along. Shortly after I left my office for errands in Nahariya, I started feeling that my chest and breathing become constricted, my head felt heavy; I sensed dizzy spells and became nauseated and out of focus. I called up Nira Hartman to find out if these symptoms were homeopathy related and found they were signs of pesticide poisoning. I managed to make my way home from Nahariya, where I had a couple of minutes to change clothes before driving to Goren Spa and a possibility to find out if Nira's idea was false or true. While changing my clothes I worked with Larry Crane's youtube video clip www.youtube.com/watch?v=eeA5VlFRNxc to feel all symptoms leave within less than two minutes. Fifteen minutes later I drank a glass of milk at Goren Spa. While giving the massage I felt I had cleansed any remaining side effects and that I fully was healed.

Why did I not go or rush to the hospital?

A long the line of beliefs create reality, beliefs being

perceived as as evidence, matter, proof, reality or thing, a Temperature case (See: Temperature, pp. 226) and a Hematoma case (See: Hematoma, pp. 106) became proofs to "all begins and ends in my/your head", also known as "it is all in the head,". By November 2013 the proof from the Hematoma case became the basis to my publishing of the e-books series A Word Keeps The Doctor Away, on amazon. In September 2014 I heard that my GP broke a leg and left the healthcare institute I am a member of; then in came an e-mail with a 24 hours replay of a sales promotion session with Larry Crane, for The Abundance Course. I listened to this replay to hear my heart say "this is it, this is what you were waiting for from the day you embarked Health Way Creation in 1997". With new approaches and attitudes that I adopted since 1997, beliefs that became what we perceive to be proofs, knowing the true meaning of words (See: Sex, pp. 202), tapping and the release technique in my tool box "going or rushing to a hospital" did not come up to my conscious, did not cross[*] me nor crossed my mind. Also:

I had no proof to Nira's suggestion that these symptoms were from a pesticide poisoning. I had to arrive for a 20:00 hrs massage session in Goren Spa = now was not the right time to go to the hospital.

When proof came from the clearing with Larry Crane video clip and the glass of milk that I drank at Goren Spa there was no longer a place nor any sense to go to the hospital.

♦ Decay and poisoning are revealed in one's eyes, voice, words, to later show in appearance, look, smell, aches, agonizing pain, disease, illness or sickness.

Emotional, habitual, physical, sentimental, sensual, spiritual, verbal food poisoning cleansing

Make and take time to create; dance, drink fresh filtered water; laugh, learn your heart language, follow your heart, play, walk along a country road, lake, meadow, river or sea shore to connect with the air, breath, colours, earth, smells, sounds, the wild life surrounding you and within you.

Free yourself from nerve abusing or irritating activities such as: computer, gossip, internet, newspapers, news programmes, reality

---

[*] Cross: A frustration or thwarting. Any misfortune or trouble. *v.t.* to lie or be thwart. *Adj.* angry and annoyed, snappish. Petulant, irascible, cantankerous, cranky, ill tempered, irritable, testy. Cros, ILL-NATURED, PEEVISH, SULLEN, refer to being in a bad mood or ill temper. Cross means temporarily in an irritable or fretful state, and sometimes somewhat angry: a cross reply; cross and tired.

programmes, small-talk, action, documentary, drama, spy, tragedy or war films. Ear shattering music, screaming, talking, vocabulary and words. Artificial food additives or ingredients, clothes, fabrics or materials; factory or laboratory made or processed drinks, foods, hair dye-colour, fast food, junk food, processed foods, sugars or sweets.

E.S.T. Exercise - see: pp. 133
Pre-sent present presents - see: pp. 134
H.P.T. - see: pp. 134

Poison clearing letter

1. Find a time and a place where you feel comfortable, free and safe.
2. It is important to keep a free and intuitive flow, do not stop to correct or read what you write, else you stop to think, "What more do I want to let go and out of my system."
3. Take a pen and paper, sit down and start writing in the following format:

To (reason, person, situation)
free intuitive flow…
Signature
Date

4. Tear your letter to pieces.
   Burn the pieces (optional).
   Throw pieces and/or ash to waste bin.
5. Discard, when going out, into the trash can.
   Repeat this procedure three days in a row.
   On days 2 and/or 3, should nothing come out, write

To (reason, person, situation)
your signature and the date
   and follow steps 4, 5.

The Four Agreements[6]

1. Never assume, opine, postulate, suppose or take for granted.
   When in doubt, clear, inquire, investigate, verify. When unsure, ask, clarify, make clear and make sure. Assumptions, inferences and suppositions create fictitious films or scenarios.
2. Be true to your word, honour it, respect it, stand up to it and walk it.
   One's words are state of being and state of mind reflection and perception.
   Be truthful, sincere, honest, genuine, and authentic.
Honouring, respecting, standing up to and walking my/your word is honouring and respecting, standing up to my/yourself. Be coherent; mean and speak your idea, intention, opinion then act on it and walk it.

**A word is a belief energy that create e-motions and reality.
Declaration is an arrow to destination; A destiny creator.**

3.   Acknowledge and walk the truth: that at each and every moment you are doing the best; that in the doing new ideas can come up and that acting on these new ideas and following a new idea is a way to do better, excel and succeed.

4.   Maintain a non-participant observatory approach and attitude remembering to never take things personally. Words express and reflect their speaker's perception.

Possibility: the state or fact of being possible. Something that is possible.

Privilege; **O**bservance; **S**upport; **S**tream; **I**ntuition;
Betterment; **I**ntegrity; **L**ove; **I**'m possible; **T**reat; **Y**ield

Potency: power, authority. Efficacy; effectiveness; strength. Capacity to be, BE-come, or develop.

Pleasure; **O**utstanding; **T**rait; **E**steem; **N**ow; **C**ore; **Y**ield

Poverty: the state or condition of having little or no money, goods, or means of support; condition of being poor; indigence. Lack of something specified. Deficiency of desirable ingredients, qualities etc. scantiness; insufficiency.

Portion; **O**rder; **V**ariety; **E**volvement;
Replenishment; **T**ime; **Y**oung

E.S.T. Exercise - see: pp. 133

♦ At the root of every manifestation of lack, state of poverty or scarcity are fear and limiting beliefs, customs, habits, patterns, perceptions, prejudice, stance, stand points or view points.

Angela Treat Lyon[12] shared with me a financial model that got me to where I am today.

10 % Play
10 % Invest

5 % Give (contributions, donations, gifts, presents)
10 % Education
55 % Expenses
10 % Spend

100% PIGEES

Power: ability to do or act; capability of doing or accomplishing something. Great or marked ability to do or act; strength; might; force. The possession of control or command over others; authority; ascendancy: power over human being's mind. Legal ability, capacity, or authority. Delegated authority; authority granted to a person or persons. A person or thing that possesses or exercises authority or influence. A military force.

Presence; **O**wnership; **W**ellness,
will, **w**ill-power; **E**veryday; **R**eunion
Present; **O**ut-come; **W**ish; **E**volvement; **R**emedy
Pre-sent, **p**resent, **p**resents;
Omnipotence; **W**ealth; **E**ndowment; **R**eality, **r**ealization
Pact, **p**eace; **O**ption; **W**isdom;
Exploration, **e**-motion; **R**eflection, **r**evelation

Power Of The Word

Sometime after my mother gave us a copy of her will, in which my share is greater than the others', living hell started. She and her brother angered and did not want to attend her 90 Birthday celebration, and a few months later her aching and broken heart yielded a hospitalization. At some stage I began to firmly and steadfastly hold on to cold minded saying 'I have the best, the greatest, the most…'. At her burial service I began enjoying a loving, open and supportive relationships with one of my brothers, a few years later with my uncle (her brother) feeling more confident than before the same is now happening with my second brother.

In late autumn of 1995, while after effects of my trip to Prague still echoed and stormed, duty summoned my first meeting with Dorit Roizman. We talked for hours on life and love and in the last five minutes remembered to attend and conclude the matter for which our meeting was scheduled and set. On another meeting, approximately two years later, I heard her say, "You know, you will write a book…" I smiled and we continued chatting. Then she added, "You probably want to know when this will happen? It will be before you are 60 years of age." I started composing the Hebrew version of The Challenge, in my 51st year. In my 55th year the Hebrew version was published and reached Israel's chain bookstores shelves. In my 58th year the English version was published and a children's book is already in the making.

In early autumn of 1995, I travelled with a friend to Prague, where my bag with all my valuables was stolen on Rosh Hashana (New Year holiday). Among the valuables were: passport, a camera (I bought in 1976, making a dream come true), flight ticket, electronic address book and diary, credit cards, cash to pay for the room and expenses till the end of my holiday, and more. On our way to report the incident at the police-station, I said to my friend "The only item I care for is my passport." At the airport, while waiting with my friend, for our turn to check in, my eyes sighted a handsome man pass by and I heard "So what is happening with the visa to the U.S.A.?" "I suppose I shall apply for a new one," "I understand than that you do not want your passport back." I turned toward the voice and saw it belonged to the handsome man. "Yes I want it," I said. He handed it to me.

In January 1995, I heard, "… She says things she cannot tell how nor from where she knows them. I applied the reality test to them, and most of them proved to be true. You should have listened to her."

In autumn 1988 I came to a job interview. At the end of the interview I recall that I heard "The job is practically yours, yet please go to our personnel department to receive the address and details for a placement test." At the end of the placement test I asked "How long it will take for the results to reach the personnel department?" "Two weeks." A week or so after the placement test I accepted an offer to replace a secretary that went for three weeks holiday. I took that offer feeling this is a way to make a living for the meantime. A month or so, after the placement test, I called the lady that sent me to this job interview "May I know why I did not get the job?" "I am not at liberty to tell you," "I did not get the job and I am not going there, so please tell me what was the reason," "Your IQ is higher than 140." My temporary three weeks job ended being over nine years job, in which the idea 'if I can make this company so much more money, I can do it for myself' was born.

In 2011 came the insights that the seeds that were planted in 1988 and 1995 sprouted to bring my resignation from a well paying job and a past of sorrowful experiences and events to go do what I love; acknowledge my love, realize my passion; grow out and up to bear and manage my own business, become an author, creator, mentor and speaker enjoying and happily living more dreams come true.

In August 2014 amid blows of hot summer winds and bursts of cool autumn breezes, at the closure of Av (the month in which Jews lament the destruction of the temple) and before Elul (the following month in Jewish calendar), I heard myself state "No one shall ever again take my happiness away from me" and a few days later "I shall never again give away my happiness to anyone".

What made me come up with such resolutions and statements?

17 years of becoming aware, conscious and mindful of the bare truth in

A bad or a good (action, life) is a mere perception.

A change of a perception changes reality.

An individual is born with interest and will power to thrive.

No one knows what is in the other's person head, heart or mind; nor how he/she will act, answer, react or respond at any given moment.

Mind sets, i.e. words, bring up and well e-motions and reality, have the power to create state of being, are e-motion, perception, state of being and state of mind creators.

Reality is a reflection of a perception, be the perception conscious, subconscious or unconscious.

The Four agreements (See: pp. 169).

Sorrowful actions, behaviours, manners and words of M (a colleague) and G (a man I had a short affair with in my mid twenties) who returned - some 30 years later, said he wants to have what he had with me way back then for my heart to say no can be, can be a client.

What did these two do?

M turned his back to me, uplifted his arms to protect his head? as he walked as far back as he could to hide from me? having heard? seen? me walk in with a greeting and a smile. I bid farewell to his boss, walked out and went about my business. M came after me, called my name - to get the silence treatment from me. Later that day his boss and I met for him to explain M's behaviour and me to say: it's time M stops his foul-play with me. A week or so later as I walked from my car to where he works, he came out with a newspaper, sat on the threshold to read it. I turned back, walked straight back to the car, gave him the silence treatment again. He then sent me an sms "Where did you run away to?", some time later I answered it with "...you blocked the way, I walk along open ways only..." He then called and got the silence treatment again.

G became a client. During a massage he consulted with me on an intimate question. After the massage I asked him to wait a minute (for us to leave the house together). He asked what I was doing, having heard my answer he asked "To whom did you do that?", "For my self" I answered with body language. He repeated the question for me to answer it a 2nd time, this time with both out-spoken words and body language and hear "You are such a retard". I walked the 1st, 2nd and 4th agreements with him. I called him to get an answer to a question. He answered it to make me send him a sms "Please forgive me for all the times that I made you helpless". The following day I woke up to keep away from blasphemous people and who called? M called. I heard "You shall be coming at ... to pick me up ...", having heard my decision he moved from Hebrew to English speaking for me to hear "... stupid decision..." I then heard my inner self say "I did not ask for your opinion", felt a smile came up as my heart rejoiced at the way I managed to walk the 2nd and 4th agreements to stay away from what to me are acidity, hostility, sorrow and negativity full manners and words. A few days later I woke up to realize the 1st, 2nd and 4th agreements are a way to stay out of his and his likes foul-play and gossip talking.

These resolutions and statements brought along, within less than a week, a new course of growing gratitude. The brother that speaks with me, talked of stress to bring up stress free conduct and management, manifest his greatness and strength with me. At the end of this week, on his youngest daughter wedding, I saw that he did that with his loved ones and also danced his happiness and joy time and time again. During the wedding day and celebration more miracles happened: his wife shared with me sorrows with the daughter that was getting married, opened the way for me to back her up, stand behind her, see and watch her greatness and strength too, for me to feel fortunate and proud she changed her ways. Like my mother and others, she too, proved to me that love always wins and that old dogs learn new tricks too. I heard, saw and sensed that one of my nieces, that I asked to let the anger rest in the past, did that - she looked, seemed and sounded very happy. M and I met for me to see he kept the right distance to remain my happy space and zone.

1ˢᵗ September I was surprised to see G called. A week later G called again, this time to reveal to me that that time he came in for a massage he expected to come out with his wet dream come true and to ask me if I know that I did not fulfil his expectations. I am thankful G let his burning oil float over his troubled water. Would you have liked to have a client that said to you that he came for a product you sell, paid more than he was asked for, told you to keep the change then defamed you, revealed to you that he came for a product you do not sell and asked you if you know that you did not fulfil his expectation?

During these 17 years I started to believe in myself. I found out that

* A change of letters order is the difference between dog and God;
* Any human belief is changeable;
* Most people are unaware of prejudice, superstitions and words of folly that align in line and bring along acts of wrong doings and injustice;
* To change a letter is to change the world;
* Words are the real and true creators of e-motions perceived as evidence or reality, false/true, right/wrong.

The Power Of The Word and The Four Agreements became my new way, to manifest ever growing inner happiness and peace.

See: Heartache pp. 103
Stress, pp 218
Wisdom, pp. 250
Word, pp. 252

To claim your power and become a creator you are to take full responsibility. How to take full responsibility and claim your power? E.S.T. (see: pp. 133) and

Ho'oponopono[13]

I am sorry	(Recognition)
Please forgive me	(Data erasing)
I love you	(Connection to Holy Spirit)
Thank you	(Gratitude)

Reciting the above phrases one after the other, in any order, cleans/erases the data that created the energy form 'reality' you now wish to transform and allows new data to come up. Reciting before sleep allows the process to go on during sleep time. Being emotional/passionate when reciting these phrases makes the transformation more effective.

Presence: the state or fact of being present, as with others or in a place. Attendance or company. The ability to project a sense of ease, poise, or self-assurance.

Peace; **R**elief; **E**ssence;
Simplicity; **E**xpansion; **N**ew; **C**reation; **E**ra

Pre-sent Present Present

On May 8, 2007[14]

I received a flower from Arad, and from Eyar an envelope closed with a red headed pin - that pinned to the envelope - a paper heart she had cut and painted red. I opened the envelope and saw that Eyar had pencil sketched the reality that manifested then and there for me to marvel and rejoice.

Five principles to a pre-sent present presents
♦ Bless the present, be grateful for it, cherish, love, nurture and pamper it.
♦ Love creates happiness.

♦ Beliefs, ideas and thoughts are e-motions manifesting in matter.
♦ Trust yourself, truth is measured with success.
♦ Want, wish and visualize what for you is amazing, amusing, appropriate, best, heart-desire and passion, miraculous, perfect, suitable and wonderful. Dance, draw, paint, sketch, walk, write it.

See: Fake, pp. 84

Prison: Any place of confinement, imprisonment.

Parity; **R**esponsibility; **I**ntegrity;
Sufficiency; **O**pportunity; **N**ext; **n**est

In one of my sessions with Perla I shared a dream I could not make sense of nor understand. In the dream, I saw myself inside a cage. Its bars gradually moved sideways making way for a bright light to come in, fill the cage and show me an opening to come out through. Later this dream enlightened me to realize that

Prison is a belief, a perception, a stand point, a state of mind, a view-point. Changing one is a way to free yourself to enjoy freedom of choice making and decision taking to a new rung

Prosperity: the state or condition of flourishing or being successful, esp. financially.

Preference; **R**espect; **O**h; **S**tart; **P**assage;
Efficacy; **R**ung; **I**nspiration; **T**hanksgiving; **Y**outh

Punishment: a penalty being inflicted for an offense, fault, etc.

Purity; **U**ni-verse; **N**ature;
Intelligence; **S**implicity; **H**ear no evil, see no evil, speak no evil; **M**entality, **m**ind; **E**ducation; **N**urture; **T**ruth

> Punish and personify less
> to a guilt and punishment
> free conduct and life

To be and to become my natural amazingly authentic, brilliant, genuinely inspired self, truly blessed, excellent genius, gifted, great, loved, skilled, talented, wise and wonderful me is a birth right.

> See: Violence, pp. 241
>
> E.S.T. exercise - see: pp. 133

The Four Agreements[6]

1. Never assume, opine, postulate, suppose or take for granted.

   When in doubt, clear, inquire, investigate, verify. When unsure, ask, clarify, make clear and make sure. Assumptions, inferences and suppositions create fictitious films or scenarios.

2. Be true to your word, honour it, respect it, stand up to it and walk it.

   One's words are state of being and state of mind reflection and perception.

   Be truthful, sincere, honest, genuine, and authentic.

   Honouring, respecting, standing up to and walking my/your word is honouring and respecting, standing up to my/yourself. Be coherent; mean and speak your idea, intention, opinion then act on it and walk it.

   A word is a belief energy that create e-motions and reality.
   Declaration is an arrow to destination; A destiny creator.

3. Acknowledge and walk the truth: that at each and every moment you are doing the best; that in the doing new ideas can come up and that acting on these new ideas and following a new idea is a way to do better, excel and succeed.

4. Maintain a non-participant observatory approach and attitude remembering to never take things personally. Words express and reflect their speaker's perception.

Q

Qualification: a quality, accomplishment, etc., that fits a person for some function, office, or the like. A circumstance or condition required for exercising right, holding an office, or the like. Modification, limitation, or restriction.

Question; Use; Accomplishment; Lesson;
Innovation; Fun; Increase; Craftsmanship;
Alleviation; Tangibility; Innermost; Outstanding; Nirvana

Quality: a characteristic property, or attribute. Character or nature, as belonging to or distinguishing a thing. Character with respect to fineness or grade of excellence. High grade; great excellence. An accomplishment or attainment.

Quiet; Uniqueness; Affluence; Love; Identity; Trust; Yes

Quantity: a particular, infinite, or considerable amount of every thing. An exact or specified amount or measure. A considerable or great amount.

Quay; Universe; Adventure; Next;
Treasure; Intuition; Thanksgiving; Youth

R

Race: a contest of speed, as in running, driving, or sailing. Any competitive activity in which speed is important. Onward movement: an onward or regular course.

Reality; **A**dventure; **C**aress; **E**ase
Relief; **A**ffection; **C**reativity; **E**nthusiasm
Respect; **A**pproach; **C**ourse; **E**ndurance

Race: a group of persons related by common descent, blood, or hereditary. *Ethnol.* A subdivision of the human species, characterized by a more or less distinctive combination of physical traits that are transmitted in descent. The human race, mankind. *Zool.* a variety; a subspecies. A natural kind of living creature; the race of fishes.

Ripple; **A**ce; **C**omfort; **E**xpansion
Resilience; **A**ttitude; **C**ore; **E**volvement

Rage: anger, fury; violent anger. Fury or violence of wind, waves, fire, dis-ease, etc. violence of feeling, desire, or appetite. A violent desire or passion. Ardour, fervour, enthusiasm. A fad of craze. Obs. Insanity.

Reflection; **A**ccess; **G**ratitude; **E**xuberance
Revelation; **A**necdote; **G**ear; **E**quilibrium

Rrrrrrrrr age?

E.S.T. exercise
1.   Find a place and a time in which you feel comfortable, free and safe to practice emotional and spiritual transformation. You may practice while walking, sitting with your back straight, head up, both your feet firmly on the floor/ground, or lying down with your legs, back and head straight on a mattress, floor or ground (i.e. all body parts are within mattress frame, no bent knees, nape or neck). Use a pillow to ease stress and tension in knees, or rolled towel under the nape (head resting on mattress). You are here to experience change, be open to awareness, listen to your e-motions.

2.	Set the jug and glass within an easy to reach distance, the paper, pen or pencil on a desk or a firm surface on which you are comfortable to write. On the paper: draw a 10 - 0 e-motion scale, 10 = strongest e-motion, 0 = zero e-motion.

3.	Write down the words and/or phrases that came up while you were listening to your inner self. These words and phrases are your key-words and key-phrases to insert in the following sentences:

Although I...(*) I completely and deeply love myself.
Although I...(*) I whole heartedly honour myself.
I deeply and fully for-e-give and accept myself although...(*).

4.	Start gentle tapping with one hand's fingers tips on the outer-side of your other hand (The Karate chop point), or gently massaging - in a clockwise-direction - your sore-chest points (marked **S** in the chart). While gently tapping with your finger tips on the Karate chop point or massaging the sore-chest points start saying, out loud, the key-phrases and key-words you wrote down in stage 3 bove.

Let words flow freely and refrain from corrections.

Repeat this step until you feel ready to move to the next stage.

5.	Move to repeat, saying out loud, the key-phrases and/or key-words you wrote in stage 3 above while gently tapping with your finger tips, on the following points:

1 Top of the head (Chakra 7)
2 Depression above eyebrows/nose ridge (Chakra 6)
3 Eye brow inner side rim
4 Eye side rim
5 Eye lower rim
6 Under the nose (depression)
7 Chin (depression)
8 Clavicle bone (v shape - Chakra 5)
9 Under the armpit (man: nipple line, woman: bra strip line)
10 Ribs 7-8 (L: over spleen, R: over liver)

6.	Take a deep breath, close your eyes and listen to your emotional body. What level are you in now?

Write it down.

Repeat stages 4, 5, & 6 until you feel relieved or ZERO e-motion.

Should a new emotional wave well up, flow through stages 3, 4, 5, & 6 with the new key-phrases and key-words it brought up.

(*) fill with key-words, key-phrases

> Pre-sent present presents - see: pp. 134
> H.P.T. - see: pp. 134

Rage clearing letter

1. Find a time and a place where you feel comfortable, free and safe.
2. It is important to keep a free and intuitive flow, do not stop to correct or read what you write, else you stop to think, "What more do I want to let go of and out of my system."
3. Take a pen and paper, sit down and start writing in the following format:

To (reason, person, situation)
free intuitive flow...
Signature
Date

4. Tear your letter to pieces.
   Burn the pieces (optional).
   Throw pieces and/or ash to waste bin.
5. Discard, when going out, into the trash can.
   Repeat this procedure three days in a row.
   On days 2 and/or 3, should nothing come out, write

To (reason, person, situation)
your signature and the date
   and follow steps 4, 5.

Rape: an act of coercion, forcing an idea or will, seizing. Any act that is forced upon a another person. The act of physically forcing a man or awoman to have sexual intercourse.

Rage; **A**buse; **P**ro-vocation; **E**ra;
Resentment; **A**nger; **P**ast; **E**volvement
Recognition; **A**ge; **P**eace; **E**ase
Reset; **A**ffection; **P**hase; **E**ssence
Revival; **A**spect; **P**resence; **E**xpansion

> E.S.T. Exercise - see: pp. 180
> H.P.T. - see: pp. 134

Rash: Inflammation, irritation emotional or spiritual poisoning clearing manifestation, with or without itching or urge to scratch.

Rage; **A**ffliction; **S**our; **H**arm;
Remedy; **A**wareness; **S**hift; **H**urt;
Rejuvenation; **A**dventure; **S**urrender; **H**eaven on earth

See: Cream, pp. 57

E.S.T. exercise - see: pp. 180
H.P.T. - see: pp. 134
Letting Go fun exercise - see: pp. 105

Additional remedies

The skin belongs to our respiratory system, among it's services: to let us know when intake is perceived as dangerous, harmful, poisonous, clearing of e-motional and spiritual refuse, absorbing/ clearing fluids to balance body temperature and water level.
1. Drink plenty of freshly filtered, lukewarm water, take 2-3 sips at a time, every 10-15 minutes, attentively and intentionally chew and mix them with saliva, then swallow.
2. Take lukewarm showers to wash off refuse.
3. Dress with cannabis, cotton or linen clothes and socks; frequently change them with clean and fresh ones.
4. Locate external sources such as artificial foods, creams, deodorant, dish-washing soap, drinks, foods, odors, perfumes, processed foods, soap, shaving cream, synthetic fabrics, washing machine soap and softener, etc.
5. Refrain from applying creams, jells, oils, ointments or pastes. They contain ingredients that fill the skin pores, thus block and prevent the body vitally important detoxification, sweat secretions, ventilation and water absorption.

Reality: Resemblance to what is real, true. A real thing, or fact. *Philos*. Something that exists independently of all other concerning it. Something that exists independently of all other things and from which all other things derive.

Revelation; **E**volution; **A**bundance; **L**ove; **I**'m; **T**hank **Y**ou

Today's reality is the produce and result of yesterday's set of beliefs

To change reality one is to adopt and set a new belief

See: Fake, pp. 84
Law, pp. 136

Letter, pp. 138
Power Of The Word, pp. 171
Word, pp. 252

Realization: An instance or result of realizing.

Reality; **E**xistence; **A**ction; **L**eisure; **I**ntuition;
Zaibatsu; **A**scension; **T**reat; **I**nspiration; **O**utlet; **N**ow

New reality creation - see:
Dream, pp. 72
Fake, pp. 84
Memory, pp. 147
Presence, pp. 176
Remembrance, pp. 189

Reason: a basis or circumstance explaining some belief, action, fact or event. The mental powers concerned with forming conclusions, judgments, or inferences.

Restitution; **E**ase; **A**wareness; **S**ense; **O**rigin; **N**ature

Reason and Passion[15]

Your soul is oftentimes a battlefield, upon which your reason and your judgment wage war against your passion and your appetite. Would that I could be the peacemaker in your soul, that I might turn the discord and the rivalry of your elements into oneness and melody. But how shall I, unless you yourselves be also the peacemakers, nay, the lovers of all your elements?

Your reason and your passion are the rudder and the sails of your seafaring soul. If either your sails or your rudder be broken, you can but toss and drift, or else be held at a standstill in mid-seas. For reason, ruling alone, is a force confining; and passion, unattended, is a flame that burns to its own destruction. Therefore let your soul exalt your reason to the height of passion, that it may sing. And let it direct your passion with reason, that your passion may live through it's own daily resurrection, and like the phoenix rise above its own ashes.

I would have you consider your judgment and your appetite even as you would two loved guests in your house.

Surely you would not honour one guest above the other; for he who is more mindful of one loses the love and the faith of both.

Among the hills, when you sit in the cool shade of the white poplars, sharing the peace and serenity of distant fields and meadows - then let your heart say in silence, "God rests in reason." And when the storm comes, and the mighty wind shakes the forest, and thunder and lightning proclaim the majesty of the sky - then let your heart say in awe, "God moves in passion." And since you are a breath in God's sphere, and a leaf in God's forest, you too should rest in reason and move in passion.

Reception: the act of receiving. The state of being received. A manner of being received.

Rapture; **E**xpansion; **C**ertainty;
E-motion; **P**resent; **T**ime; **I**…, **O**pen; **N**ectar

See: Wisdom, pp. 250

Recognition: the perception of acknowledgement of something as true or valid. Appreciation of achievements, merit, services, etc. or an expression of this.

Revelation; **E**xcellence; **C**larity; **O**rder;
Gentleness; **N**est; **I**nspiration; **T**rust; **I** am; **O**h; **N**ewness

See: Wisdom, pp. 250
Zero, pp. 260

Re-cover-y - Recovery: the regaining of something lost or taken away. Restoration or return to health or normal condition, as after sickness or disaster.

Revival; **E**ase; **C**onstruction; **O**pen;
Vitality; **E**volvement; **R**ipeness; **Y**ield

E.S.T. Exercise - see: pp. 180
Pre-sent present presents - see: pp. 134

> H.P.T. - see: pp. 134

Reflection: a thought occurring in consideration or meditation. The return of heat, light, images, etc., by a reflecting surface.

Readiness; **E**volution; **F**low; **L**ife; **E**ducation;
Confidence; **T**rait; **I**nnovation; **O**mnipresence; **N**ice

Regret: a sense of loss, dis-appointment, dis-satisfaction, etc. a feeling of sorrow or remorse for a fault, act, loss, etc.

Refinery; **E**quilibrium; **G**ratitude;
Refreshment; **E**nthusiasm; **T**ime

> E.S.T. exercise - see: pp. 180
> Pre-sent present presents - see: pp. 134
> H.P.T. - see: pp. 134
> Letting Go fun exersie - see: pp. 105

Rejection: a refuse to accept (a person); rebuff. A refuse to grant (a request, demand, etc.). A refuse to have, take, act upon, etc.

Revival; **E**xcellence; **J**ubilation;
Energy; **C**reativity; **T**ime; ; **I**; **O**rder, **N**ewness

A friend of mine saw in her dreams that she will mother a daughter and one more son. She made these dreams come true against her man's will. By doing so she forced her will on her man, raped her man to bear children he did not want. She one day woke up to realize that holding on to her job created a reality in which the son was cared for by the father, that did not want him. That that son grows up feeling and sensing the father's way about and in life and living, recycles the father's rejection, resentment, sorrow and ways. She left her job to make amendments with this son, fill her son with her joy and love. Her man's and son's anger, frustration, guilt, and hostility erupt daily making their home and life hell, justifying her being right, and being the Queen Mother.

A young woman sorrowful with suffering her mother's abuse, humiliations and rejection shared with me that after she lived hell on earth she came to her parents and spoke her truth out. I heard that her mother then let all hell break out, poured more salt to the open wounds = threw her out and disinherited her. "Mother always hurl... for mother everything is about money." When I asked what did the father do then? I heard that he stood up for the daughter and that the daughter is aching and in despair because she asks him to come over to her and he does not do it. In our talks I heard the daughter has painful memories from her infancy: mother to daughter: "You are a boy, not a girl, no girl does what you do;" when the father stood up for the daughter and asked the mother to stop forcing her will to a point that made the daughter move away from the pain and start crying the mother shouted: "You stay out of this." Infancy and childhood: time and time again the daughter came to her father asked for attention and comfort and heard: "Go out and see that I am outside" = I have no energy, room nor time for you. Childhood: **mother**: "You knew 7 words out of 9 words in your test... so you are not going to grandma... do you want to go to the beach with me and dad?" **Daughter**: "No to grandma yes to the beach?" left the mother wordless. Teenage: "Mother started coming to my basketball games a few years after I started playing and after the team gained success." In my last talk with the daughter I heard that the mother invited her for lunch in which the daughter said "All my life you went against me to no avail, stop being so eccentric" and the mother said "I cannot accept ... I knew it all along..., I lost a friend, and it's my entire fault..."

In fact the daughter's truth was a desperate cry for help. She rebelled against a lifetime abuse, hurls, and punishments for her mother failed to accept her and she failed to live and stand up to her mother's dream and fantasy world.

In reality the daughter walked the mother's way, recycled - abuse, despair, insecurity, and rejection, reproach sorrowful actions and behaviour.

The daughter's truth added oil into the mother's insecurity and righteous fire and in the vicious cycle the mother hurled the daughter into the arms and influence of outsiders instead of showing the daughter she can embrace her, take her into her arms and bosom, wholeheartedly comfort her aching soul and soothe her open wounds, show the daughter that she can give love, loves her as she is and for what and who she is, nurture and support her.

> "Kindness and love
> are the root of the matter"
> - Dekel Efron

> See: Ache, pp. 7
> Memory, pp. 147
> Right, pp. 195
> Violence, pp. 241
> Wisdom, pp. 250

What is your call and choice now?

To go on being and thinking I am right, thinking I know better = recycle poor me, Vict-I'm me OR to become Vict-**OR**ious me through learning from the situation I am in what it is here to teach me?

To rise above anger, despair, frustration, feelings of rejection and self-pity to dare find in my heart and self to ask for forgiveness, to share my inner sorrow and truth, to keep an open mind, be, make and speak right with my self and my loved ones?

To dare abort aching, poisoned self?

To nerve cleanse and clear the poison for all concerned and involved to heal?

Or let fear and insecurity manage, recycle and run ill affairs and sick relationships with myself, my loved ones and others?

What matters is what action I freely chose and decides to take, not what was done to me, and how I am feeling it, perceiving it, seeing it, and thinking about it.

Doing now the right thing and what is right to all concerned and involved is a mature way for self love to grow out of anger, degradation, despair, hostility, rejection and sorrow, to end youthfull rebellion, and to transform a living hell into heaven on earth.

To openly admit and recognize a wrong doing, outcome, or saying with your child is a way to change, come out, ease pain and sorrow from all; to forgive and to be forgiven; reveal authenticity, humane greatness and responsibility that can save you and your child from pain killers, psychology and other therapies sessions.

Awareness, acknowledgement, centring and focusing on self happiness, health, love and respect, aborting abuse, disconnecting from aches, negating negative approach and negativity vibrations, by asking my heart/self: how does it feel? Bad = I stop right here and now, Good = I follow, is a way to change and heal.

> E.S.T. exercise - see: pp. 180
> Pre-sent present presents - see: pp. 134
> H.P.T. - see: pp. 134

> Letting Go fun exersie - see: pp. 105

Relationship: a connection, association, or involvement.
Connection between persons by blood or marriage. An emotional or other connection between people.

Realm; Expansion; Love; Alliance; Talent; Intuition; Option;
Net; Safety; Heart; Innermost; Peace;
Radiance; Ecstasy; Leisure; Acceptance; Treasure; treat; truth;
trust; Innocence; Oneness; opportunity; Nest; nurture;
Security; shelter; ship; Happiness; health; heaven on earth;
Integrity; intelligence; Pleasure; practice

Relief: ease or deliverance through the removal of pain, distress, anxiety, etc. something that provides a pleasing change, as from monotony.

Realm; Energy-motion; Love; Interest; Exultation; Freedom

> E.S.T. Exercise - see: pp. 180

Key-phrases/words: I am ease, inspiration, relief, peace, I give myself permission to feel relief, I feel relief…

Relish: liking or enjoyment of the taste of something. Pleasurable appreciation of anything; liking.

Revelation; Ecstasy; Leisure; I am; Serenity; Heart

Remembrance: a retained mental impression; memory.

Reservoir; Evolvement; Make; Era; Mirth;
Bestowment; Reference; Awareness; Next; Creativity; Essence

> See: Memory, pp. 147

E.S.T. exercises

Exercise 1⁽¹⁰⁾:

Find a place and a time where you shall feel at ease, and at peace.
1. Sit with your back, chin and head straight up.
2. Hold together all five fingers of your right hand and gently tap along half a circle (from your temple, above your right side ear until the depression behind your right side ear) while saying or singing out loud: "I feel grateful I remember essential and important details; I am grateful I always remember what I need and should remember at each and every given moment."
You may repeat this exercise again in half an hour and every half an hour.

Exercise 2:
Ingredients:
A crystal glass
Fresh filtered water, at room temperature or lukewarm
Procedure:
1. Fill the crystal glass with the fresh filtered water before you retire to your good night's sleep, take it to your bedroom and put it on the nightstand, a dresser or a shelf near you.
2. Take three deep breaths (inhaling through your nostrils, exhaling gently and peacefully through your mouth).
3. Say or sing out loud: "I am grateful my memory is crystal clear, good and sharp."
4. Take a sip or two of water, chew and mix attentively and intentionally with saliva, and gently swallow.
Repeat stages 3-4 three times.

Remorse: deep and painful regret for wrongdoing; compunction. Obs. Pity; compassion.

Revival; **E**ase; **M**omentum; **O**pportunity;
Remedy; **S**erenity, **s**incerity; **s**implicity; **E**xpansion

E.S.T. Exercise - see: pp. 180

Key-phrases/words: *Preliminary rounds*: admonition, agony, compassion, compunction, fear stricken, morbid, mortified, regret, remorse, reproach, self-correction, self-criticism, self-guilt, self-pity, self-punishment, self-torment, suffering… *Positive affirmations rounds*: calm, confident, peaceful, relaxed, safe…

Pre-sent present presents - see: pp. 134
H.P.T. - See: pp. 134
Letting Go fun exersie - see: pp. 105

kidney stones

Clove bud infusion (See: Gum infection, pp. 97), drink one glass per day.

Small and tiny kidney stones

Replace artificial drinks, coffee, soda, tea with fresh filtered water. Take 2-3 small sips at a time, chew and mix water attentively and intentionally with saliva, then swallow. Drink one glass during an hour from wake up time to sleep time and bring yourself as quickly as you can to an experienced and skilled reflexology practitioner or a body-masseur. When urinating, pay attention to urine colour and smell. Listen to the sound of the stone hitting the toilet's wall.

Repeat the procedure the following day together with a reflexology or a body-massage session should you feel unsure or if the pain's frequency and strength seem similar to the ones on the previous day. It is recommended to drink filtered fresh water for good and for healthy kidney function.

Medium and large kidney stones

Replace artificial drinks, coffee, soda, tea with fresh filtered water. Take 2-3 small sips at a time, chew and mix water attentively and intentionally with saliva, then swallow.

Prepare and drink, every day until you feel pain-free for 7 days and nights, fresh Indian corn hair infusion[*]. Take 2-3 small sips at a time, chew and mix infusion attentively and intentionally with saliva, then swallow. Drink one glass during an hour. 2-3 glasses a day.

Re(ap)proach
- **Reproach**: blame or censure conveyed in disapproval. An expression of upbraiding, censure, or reproof. Disgrace, discredit, or blame. A cause or occasion of disgrace or discredit. An object of scorn or contempt.

Rebirth; **E**steem; **P**ossibility;
Reach; **O**ut; **A**ffection; **C**ome; **H**ere
Right; **E**ntity; **P**act; **R**emedy;
On-ward; **A**ccess; **C**aress; **H**eaven on earth

---

[*] Indian corn hair infusion: put a heaping teaspoon of Indian corn hair in a crystal glass, fill with boiling water, cover with a glass saucer and allow to soak (infuse) for 10 minutes and more. Do not sweeten. Drink to health.

New angle, Re-approach

> to a new porch
> E.S.T. Exercise - see: pp. 180
> H.P.T. - see: pp. 134
> Letting Go fun exersie - see: pp. 105

Re-sent-ment - Resentment: the feeling of dis-pleasure or indignation at some act, remark, person, etc. regarded as causing injury or insult.

Relief; **E**ssence; **S**ensation; **E**njoyment; **N**ature;
Thank you; **M**iracle **m**omentum; **E**ntertainment; **N**est; **T**reat

> See: Rejection, pp. 186
> Terror, pp. 229
> Violence, pp. 241

> E.S.T. Exercise - see: pp. 180
> Letting Go fun exersie - see: pp. 105

Resilience: the ability or power to return to the original form or position after being bent, compressed, or stretched; elasticity. Ability to recover from illness, depression, adversity, or the like; buoyancy.

Rampage; **E**nthusiasm; **S**erenity; **I**'m, **L**ove;
Intuition; **E**xpansion; **N**ext; **C**reation; **E**xuberance

Resistance: opposition offered by one thing, force, etc. to another. *Psychiatry*. Opposition to an attempt to bring repressed thoughts or feelings into consciousness.

Relief; **E**soteric knowledge; **S**isterhood; **I**ntegrity;
Sustenance; **T**alent; **A**ffection; **N**urture; **C**reativity; **E**den

> E.S.T. Exercise - see: pp. 180
> Letting Go fun exersie - see: pp. 105

Respect: a particular, detail, or point (usually prec. by in): to differ in some respect. Relation or reference: inquiries with respect to a route. Admiration for or a sense of the worth or excellence of a person, a personal quality or trait, or something considered as a manifestation of a personal quality or trait. The condition of being esteemed or honoured.

Rectitude; Excellence; Spirit;
Peace; Endowment; Creation; Transparency

The Four Agreements[6]

1. Never assume, opine, postulate, suppose or take for granted.
When in doubt, clear, inquire, investigate, verify. When unsure, ask, clarify, make clear and make sure. Assumptions, inferences and suppositions create fictitious films or scenarios.
2. Be true to your word, honour it, respect it, stand up to it and walk it.
One's words are state of being and state of mind reflection and perception.
Be truthful, sincere, honest, genuine, and authentic.
Honouring, respecting, standing up to and walking my/your word is honouring and respecting, standing up to my/yourself. Be coherent; mean and speak your idea, intention, opinion then act on it and walk it.
A word is a belief energy that create e-motions and reality.
Declaration is an arrow to destination; A destiny creator.
3. Acknowledge and walk the truth: that at each and every moment you are doing the best; that in the doing new ideas can come up and that acting on these new ideas and following a new idea is a way to do better, excel and succeed.
4. Maintain a non-participant observatory approach and attitude remembering to never take things personally. Words express and reflect their speaker's perception.

Response: an answer or reply, as in words or in some action; rejoinder. *Biol.* Any behaviour of a living organism that results from stimulation.

Rest assured; Ease; Support; Peace;
Opportunity; Nest; Sustenance; Elevation;

See: Wisdom, pp. 250

> E.S.T. Exercise - see: pp. 180
> Pre-sent present presents - see: pp. 134
> H.P.T. - see: pp. 134

Responsibility: a particular burden or obligation upon a person who is responsible. Something for which a person is responsible. Reliability or dependability, esp. in meeting debts or payment.

Reliability; **E**ducation; **S**elf; **P**otency; **O**h, **N**ice; **S**uper; **I**ndividuality; **B**est; **I**ntellect; **L**ove; **I**nsight; **T**hank **Y**ou

> See: Wisdom, pp. 250

Retardation: slowness or limitation in intellectual understanding and awareness, emotional development, academic progress, etc.

Revival; **E**xpansion; **T**reat; **A**ffection; **R**emedy; **D**evotion; **A**cceptance; **T**rait; **I**ntuition; **O**mnipotence; **N**urture

> E.S.T. Exercise - see: pp. 180
> H.P.T. - see: pp. 134

Riches: abundant and valuable possessions; wealth.

Ride; **I**nspiration; **C**reativity; **H**eart; **E**ndearment; **S**tance

Ride: to be born along on or in a vehicle. To move along in any way; be carried or supported. To move up from the proper place or position. To continue without interruption or interference.

Rhyme; **I**s; **D**evelopment; **E**nterprise
Realm, **I**llustration; **D**irection; **E**ntertainment

Right: a just claim or title, whether legal, prescriptive, or moral. That which is morally, legally, or ethically proper. The side that is normally opposite to that where the heart is; the direction toward that side.

Reality; **I**ntuition; **G**rowth;
Hear no evil, see no evil, speak no evil **h**eaven on earth; **T**ime

See: Rejection, pp. 186
Terror, pp. 229
Wisdom, pp. 250

E.S.T. Exercise - see: pp. 180
Pre-sent present presents - see: pp. 134
H.P.T. - see: pp. 134

Root: a part of the body of a plant that develops, typically, from the radicle and grows downwards into the soil, fixing the plant and absorbing nutrients and moisture. Something resembling or suggesting the root of a plant in position or function. The fundamental or essential part: the root of the matter. The source or origin of a thing.

Road; **O**nward; **O**h; **T**hanks

Root Canal: Dentistry, the root portion of the pulp cavity.

Repression; **O**rder; **O**ut you go; **T**ime
Creativity; **A**ttunement; **N**ewness; **A**ssessment; **L**ove

I now attend to a root of a matter;
clean, cleanse, clear, let go of
a root of a matter
to live happily thereafter

♦ Please do not rush to lose your tooth nerve and root. The dentist killing it and the crown construction will not heal your nerve, nor will they calm down your burning desire, boil, flame, passion, rage, sadness, simmer or sorrow.

See: Gum, pp. 96
In-flam(e)-mation, pp. 121
Tooth, pp. 234
E.S.T. Exercise - see: pp. 180

Key-phrases/words: *Preliminary rounds*: anger, fear stricken; inflamed; painstaking phase/step…; sadness; sorrow… *positive rounds*: confidence; freely flow; heal; I have the nerve to get to the bottom, to the heart, to the root of the matter; I dare expand and explore, I choose to educate myself, I give myself permission to reprogramme myself...

♦ To induce and support gum healing add Co Q-10 soft gels, Zinc lozenges or liquid drops, gum massage, salty sea water compress; sea-water rinse. When pain is relieved gradually lower the number of Zinc lozenges or drops taken. Clean gums and teeth with circle or from the inside out gentle movements rather than brush them.

Rout-in-e - Routine: a customary or regular course of procedure.
Regular, unvarying, habitual, or unimaginative procedure.

Right; **O**ff course now; **U**niqueness; **T**rust; **I**magination, **i**nspiration, **i**ntuition; **N**urture; **E**xuberance **e**xcellence

Ruin: A fallen and wrecked or decayed condition. The downfall, decay, or destruction of anything. The complete loss of health, hope, means, position, or the like.

Renovation; **U**nity; **I**nsight; **N**avigation

E.S.T. Exercise - see: pp. 180
Letting Go fun exersie - see: pp. 105

Rush: a rapid, impetuous, or violent onward movement. A hostile attack. An eager rushing of to some region to be occupied or exploited. A sudden appearance or access. Hurried activity; busy haste. A hurried state, as from pressure of affairs. Press of business, traffic, etc.

Rage; **U**ncertainty; **S**hed, **s**orrow; **H**ostility
Remedy; **U**nion; **S**heer; **H**appiness;
hear no evil, see no evil, speak no evil; **h**ealth

Remedies

♦ Parent, often a time the child is your mirror and reflection for what you are unaware or unconscious of and to bring you a possibility to change, heal and learn your lessons. Thus you may wish to consider practicing E.S.T. exercise (See: pp. 180), for yourself, your baby or with your child.
Baby: follow E.S.T. exercise bearing your baby and yourself in your mind while tapping on yourself, or your baby.
Child: encourage the child to practice it alone. Should child avoid or resist, encourage the child to follow you and repeat after you. Be easy about it, make it a fun, humour-full, and play-full process, do not convince or force the child to do it. Along the way you may discover that tapping alone - on your issues with your child - will heal you and your child.

E.S.T. Exercise - see: pp. 180

Key-phrases/words: *Preliminary rounds*: afraid, anxious, burning with desire, eager to, in a hurry, rushing to, he/she (child's name) is making me be and feel... *Positive affirmations rounds*: calm, confident, I choose to make progress taking one step at a time, I love when things come my way easily, effortlessly, and naturally, all is in divine and perfect orchestration and order, I love learning the lessons my child brings...

Pre-sent present presents - see: pp. 134
Letting Go fun exersie - see: pp. 105

S

Sadism: *Psychiatry*: sexual gratification gained through causing physical pain or humiliation. Any enjoyment in being cruel.

Self-**s**abotage; **A**bnormality;
Deformation; **I**nferiority; **S**ymbol; **M**echanism
Sorrow; **A**we; **D**estitution; **I** am; **S**hift; **M**anifestation moment

E.S.T. Exercise - see: pp. 180

Key-phrases/words: *Preliminary rounds*: abuse, anger, fear, good for nothing, helpless, hopeless, humiliated, harm, hurt, offence, revenge, pain, pay back, sadness, sorrow, torment, torture, unworthy, weak… *Positive affirmations rounds*: I choose and decide to heal, I give my self permission to… I am deserving of love, worthy of love, peace, safe…

Pre-sent present presents - see: pp. 134

Self-love; **A**ttendance,
Decision; **I**sland; **S**anity; **M**easurement **m**omentum;
Solemn; **s**erenity; **A**wareness;
Dedication, **d**evotion; **I**ntention; **S**incerity; **M**astery

Sadness: the quality or state of being sad, unhappy, or melancholy.

Sail; **A**ffection; **D**elight; **N**urture; **E**ase; **S**implicity; **S**ureness

E.S.T. Exercise - see: pp. 180
Pre-sent present presents - see: pp. 134
Letting Go fun exersie - see: pp. 105

E.S.T. exercise

♦ Sadness and so(ar)-row(ing) evoke nervousness and induce sure-less-ness. Acknowledge, experience, own and respect these e-motions with crying, dancing, playing, roaring, screaming, shouting, sleeping, taping, writing, and every way you can come up with.

♦ Laughter stimulates the brain to clear aches, pains, sadness and sorrow with natural self-made tranquilizers (endorphins, for one). Force yourself into artificial laughter. Within seconds your feeling and mood will change; ease and clear the sadness and stress. Begin with artificially forced laughter to enjoy good, natural, whole hearted joyful laughter (See: Laugh, pp. 136).

Internet surfers: a warm recommendation to join Willie Skratter[9] laughing baby video clip.

Satisfaction: the cause or means of being satisfied, confident acceptance of something as satisfactory, dependable, true, etc. the act of satisfying, the state of being satisfied.

Song; Attitude; Trait; Intuition; Safety;
Freedom; Acceptance; Concurrence; Treat; I'm; Open; Now

Scar: the mark left by a healed wound, sore, or burn. Any lasting after-effect of trouble.

Seed; Creation; Amendment; Revival

E.S.T. Exercise - see: pp. 180

Scarcity: insufficiency or smallness of supply; dearth. Rarity, infrequency.

Satisfaction; Compliment; Abundance;
Refinement; Consistence; Innovation; Thank; You

See: Poverty, pp. 170

E.S.T. Exercise - see: pp. 180
Letting Go fun exersie - see: pp. 105

Scare: to suddenly fill with fear or terror.

Security; Common-sense
confidence; Awakening; Revelation; Eye

> E.S.T. Exercise - see: pp. 180
> Letting Go fun exersie - see: pp. 105

Sea: the salt waters that cover the greater part of the earth's surface. Ocean. A widely extended, copious, or overwhelming quantity. Sea of love.

Spirit; **E**xpansion; **A**ward
Soul; **E**lation, **A**wareness
Ship; **E**ase; **A**dventure
Sixth sense; **E**ntertainment; **A**rt
Sex; **E**nergy; **A**bundance
Sensuality; **E**scapade; **A**ttunement
Sensibility; **E**-motion; **A**scension
Self; **E**nrichment; **A**pproach
Sanity; **E**nthusiasm, **A**ttraction
Sail, **E**cstasy; **A**ffection

Self: a person or thing considered with respect to complete individuality or separate identity. A person's nature, character, etc.

Sincerity; **L**ove; **E**xuberance; **F**estivity

> Ani = אני = ego, self
> Ain = אין = there is no, without

When there is no ego there is not an abyss to fall into.
When I am without (ego-free) I am in a state of liberty to make a choice, take a stand that shall uplift me to the next step.
When I allow and give myself the liberty and permission to be without I am in zero. From 0 there is no loosing, nor lower place to fall to yet there is a higher place to long for and reach.

A way to reach both zero and higher places is E.S.T. Exercise - see: pp. 180

> Self-destruction, self-murder
> See: Child, pp. 42
> Fear, pp. 85

Foul play, pp. 88
Rejection, pp 186
Terror, pp. 229
Young, pp. 258
Self-love - see: Love, pp. 143
Tongue, pp. 233
Wisdom, pp. 250

Sensation: the operation or function of the senses. A mental condition or physical feeling resulting from stimulation of a sense organ or internal bodily changes. *Physiol.* The faculty of perception of stimuli. A general feeling not directly attributable to any given stimulus, as discomfort, anxiety or doubt. Mental excitement, esp. a state of excited feeling in an individual.

Season; **E**nthusiasm; **N**est; **S**atisfaction;
Adventure; **T**aste; **I**ntegrity; **O**pportunity; **N**ascence

Sense: any of the faculties as sight, hearing, smell, taste, or touch, by which man and animals perceive stimuli originating from outside or inside the body. A feeling or perception produced through the organs of touch, taste; etc. or resulting from a particular condition of some part of the body. A faculty or function of the mind analogous to sensation.

Smile; **E**ndowment; **N**ew; **S**implicity; **E**nthusiasm

Sensibility: capacity for sensation or feeling. Acuteness of appreciation. Sensibilities, emotional capacities; sometimes, ability to feel hurt or offend; often, capacity for intellectual and aesthetic distinctions, feeling, taste, etc.

Sixth **s**ense; **E**xultation; **N**ew; **S**eason; **I**nformation;
Balance, **b**eauty; **I**ntimacy; **L**oyalty; **I**nspiration; **T**hank; **Y**ou

Sensitivity: the quality or state of being sensitive. *Physiol.* The ability of an organism or part of an organism to react to stimuli; irritability; degree of susceptibility to stimulation. Sensitive: endowed with sensation. Readily or excessively affected by external agencies or influences. Having acute mental or emotional sensibility. Easily affected, pained, annoyed, etc.

Secret; **E**xcitement; **N**urture; **S**incerity; **I**ntuition;
Time; **I**nnovation; **V**ibrancy; **I**dentity; **T**ruth; **Y**ippee

> Sense, sensibility and sensitivity are divine blessings and gifts. Honour, nourish, nurture and own them with gratitude and love to your advancement and advantage
>
> E.S.T. Exercise - see: pp. 180
> Pre-sent present presents - see: pp. 134
> Letting Go fun exersie - see: pp. 105

Sensualism: sensuality. Aesthetics. Emphasis on sensuousness as the most important element in the beautiful.

Sensation; **E**cstasy; **N**ascence; **S**oul;
Unity; **A**dvancement; **L**ife; **I**ndividuality; **S**upply; **M**irth
Sensibility; **E**levation, **N**ew; **S**pirit;
Ultimate ness; **A**dventure; **L**ove; **I**nspiration; **S**ustenance; **M**iracle

Serenity: the state or quality of being serene, calm, or tranquil.

Sequence; **E**ase; **R**ipple; **E**steem; **N**earness; **I**n; **T**ruth; **Y**outh

Sex: either the female or male division of a species, esp. as differentiated with reference to the reproductive functions. The sum of the structural and functional differences by which the female and male are distinguished, or phenomena or behaviour dependent on these differences. The instinct or attraction drawing one sex toward another or it's manifestation in life and conduct. Coitus.

Sensuality; **E**xpansion; **X**ebec
Sport; **E**nergy; **X**-ray
Shift, **E**xpression, **X**erography

Anal intercourse is act of aggression, revealing false perception of what is moral or immoral, right or wrong, misconception of sex.

Anal intercourse is against nature's law
Did you ever see any other animal do it in the name of love? I did not. What life's university showed me and taught me was that a female in heat is a female ready to become pregnant and have

offsprings. Her being in heat was a call to the male. The male did all within his abilities and power to please the female so that she will let him have sexual intercourse with her. When the male missed the female's vagina and entered her rectum she let him know so that he could correct himself and get it right. Any act of aggression is humiliating and sheer hostility and offence to a living creature's intelligence; be the living creature an aardwolf, eagle, fish, gazer, human being, or reptile.

Oral intercourse is a naturally born communication channel, in which we give and receive, express and reveal our e-motions, state of being and state of mind.

Living creatures (a human being is an animal called human being) have oral intercourse with each material and every matter to connect with their own e-motions, to find out about, have knowledge, learn. Do you remember having seen babies take all things straight into their mouth and their parent reaction coming from false perceptions, fear or worry? If you don't, why not take time to watch babies? Find out how they find satisfaction and solutions; know to enjoy and have fun in each move and every step along their way, with simple things too; how happy they are with what they have, and how wise they are. Learn from them. They are the best and most loving teachers one can have.

Sexual harassment: bullying or coercion of a sexual nature, or the unwelcome or inappropriate promise of reward in exchange for sexual favours.

Sexual intercourse: genital contact, esp. the insertion of the penis into the vagina followed by ejaculation.

Sexual intercourse is not an anal intercourse nor is it an oral intercourse.
Sexual intercourse is a primitive way to reproduce. An erection comes for a penis to enter a vagina, ejaculation is for sperms to make their way into a vagina.
Did you ever get the penis to enter the vagina without having a hard on?
Did you ever have an ejaculation without erection?
I was a witness to men becoming frustrated and getting upset from not getting a hard on; and men being satisfied from having ejaculation with no erection. Having a hard on is no proof to manhood same as dryness is no proof to wom(b)manhood. Being a man and a wom(b)man is more than just reproducing.

Having Sex

With men and women having different sizes of sex organs, sexual intercourse can bring anger and anguish; pleasure and satisfaction when combined with making love. Love making takes creativity, hands, fingers, love, mindfulness, mouth, senses, sensitivity, sensualism and sensuality.

Adding fear of human beings[*] and failure, lack of confidence, lack of experience and practice, misconceptions of making love, sexual intercourse, what is and who is a man as well as a woman; poor self-esteem and want and you are into deep troubled waters, a full with good intentions and meaning straight road to hell; a lose lose situation.

See: Love, pp. 143

Sexuality: sexual character; possession of the structural and functional differentia of sex. Recognition of or emphasis upon sexual matters. Involvement in sexual activity. An organism's readiness to engage in sexual activity.

In the summer holiday between 2nd and 3rd primary school grades (1962) to pour more oil into my already burning fire of abuse, aggression and humiliation dis-eases and upsets, the local paedophile had his way with me, (See: Freeze, pp. 70). At age eight and a half I did not have the knowledge and the skills to deal with a sex offender violating my dignity, honour and respect. I also did not have a person I could trust enough to turn to with my degradation and heartache. I buried it deep, down under in my black box.

In the 1st week of the month before my 43rd year (January 1997) at a time of frustration, I met with Dorit (See: In early autumn..., pp. 172). She: "What is missing in your life?" Me: "Learning." She: "What will you learn Law or Medicine?" Me: "17 years in the branch (with lawyers) were more than enough. In my heart: 7 years medicine studies, are you out of your mind? Out loud: perhaps reflexology? Can I still learn?" (At age 27, I asked myself: "What will happen when I grow old, at the age of 43-44?" I then opened several savings accounts, so that when I am old, at a time of need I shall be able to open one at a time to come out of a lack). She handed me a flyer and I recall she said: "Why don't you go find out?" I laughed with all my heart and said: "With my luck this seminar will be when Irgunit staff will be on holiday to Jordan." And? So it was. In the seminar the

---
[*] human beings kill for territory, animals do not. They are the most dangerous, violent and vicious animals on earth.

memory of the paedophile actions came out and up into my consciousness, I broke down with violent crying. The seminar's teacher's farewell gift to me was Billy Joel's song, Honesty. Nine months later I started learning Reflexology to embark on Health Way Creation.

17 years later, 1st week in January 2015, I gave a 90 minutes massage to a man. The following story is my recall from that session. Shortly after the massage started, He: "Do you know that there is god?" Me: "I don't know." My reply made him philosophize (his word). I perceived his philosophizing as an attack on my stand-point, I felt my blood pressure go up sky high. I heard him accuse me for being a philosophizer and kept quiet. When I massaged his arms I found out that I was giving a massage to a man with blocked energies. I heard that he would rather have his hands massaged with no oil. Me "Would you like me to dry the oil?" He: "No, I am saying this just because you asked me to let you know when something is too much." He: "What do you see in my body?" My interpretation was what is my body telling and having not a single good word to say kept me silent. When I massaged his legs, the dialogue from his hands massage repeated itself. When I massaged his thigh in deep tissue massage, He: "Do you know that it sexually arises me?" Me: "I don't know. My hands do not feel what your body feels." I looked up to see no erection. I left the thigh to massage the shins and feet. His remark made me share with him a July 2014 experience in which a man that came to a massage made me an offer of 600 N.I.S. to masturbate his penis. My "no, thank you" answer made that man come up with offers from 200 N.I.S. to 20,000 N.I.S. for a blow job to hear my same answer. A few minutes before the end of the session he asked to double the 45 minutes massage, the Spa manager approved so I gave him a 2x45 minutes massage. Before he left the massage room he told me that he will have me give him another 2x45 minutes massage. Two days later we met again, I gave him the 2x45 minutes massage to see that he did not let go of his manipulative way with me, and that when he walked out he had a deep sadness in his eyes. I asked myself if his behaviour and sadness were because his parents bought him? Could it be that he has to buy his wife to make love with him?

Following my sharing, I heard the man on the massage table say that he does not believe me; that he believes that every person has her/his price. He made me an offer of 1,000,000 dollars. I dared him to come up with the money to find out what my answer will then be, for a blocked person knows only belligerence and lose lose situations. He moved on to sexual insinuations and told me that every time he comes to the village of his childhood days, he plays with his family children. With those that are 3 - 12 years old, he also lies down on his back for three hours in which each one of them touches different parts of his body for about 5 minutes. At the end of the session he opened his arms as he said: Come here. I turned around and walked out of the room.

I sat in the waiting hall to realize that I did not respond to any of this man's sexual insinuations nor to his outspoken call for sex at the end of the session.

He came out of the massage room and asked my colleague where was his wife. The "Do you know that there is god?" scene repeated itself with the difference that this time it was with my colleague and all about where his wife was. When his wife came out of the massage room they sat down with my colleague and I. His talking opened the way for his wife to ask me what did his body tell me. This time I let all present hear my impression, that he is a blocked person and the true meaning of being one, to hear his wife approve and have a good laugh. In this forum he told me that my impression of him being a lies teller was true. This later made me wonder if telling me the story of his way with the 3 - 12 years old children was a self-incriminating evidence or his wet dream.

After the couple left my colleague, who knows them in person, asked me if I remember the case in which a... was charged for sexual harassment of women? I answered that I do not remember. I heard her tell me that the man I gave a massage to was that man; that one of the women he sexually abused was his secretary and that his sister-in-law shared with her that when he gave a lift to her and his brother's teen-age daughter he sexually abused their daughter. I asked my colleague, "And what did the family do with this?" "They shoved it under the carpet, they do not talk about it, they fucked up the teen-age daughter life," was her reply.

A few hours later, on my way home from the Spa, it came to me that this man came into my life for me to see that I am no longer falling for sex offenders. My heart filled with gratitude and relief, circle closed.

By midnight my blood pressure went down to 142. I went to bed knowing in my heart that this was the end of two weeks with high blood pressure. In the following days, my blood pressure continued to go down, and by the 3rd day it was down to 122/78 (See: Stress, pp. 218).

We came to this universe with sex organs to reproduce human beings through sexual intercourse. Reproduction of human beings, any other living creature or thing, can be wildly enjoyable, graceful, respectful and satisfying with love making, or painful.

I can have gratitude and pleasure of giving and receiving unadulterated and unconditional love; be honourable, wildly loved, loving, respected and respectful when I ask my other and use my senses (See: Sense, pp. 201) to find out what makes her or him be wildly happy, pain free and satisfied, instead of I have a hard on, I have to, I need; imposing my will, mazo/sado or porno sex education.

Please remember that life is to be enjoyed by all concerned and involved and so is love making, reproduction with sexual intercourse and sexual intercourse for enjoyment, love and satisfaction of both my other and myself.

What is your call, choice and decision now?
A battle field in which I fight for bread?
A peace filled with knowledge to enjoy life's delicious cakes, cookies and sweets?

Unadulterated and unconditional love making or war making?

See: Love, pp. 143
War. pp. 244

Shame and **shyness**:
Shame: the painful feeling arising from the consciousness of something dishonourable, improper, ridiculous, etc., done by oneself or another. Susceptibility to this feeling. Disgrace; ignominy. A fact or circumstance that is a cause for regret.

Simplicity; **H**eart; **A**ffection; **M**astery; **E**xuberance

Shyness: bashfulness, draw back, recoil, retirement, suspiciousness, distrust, reluctance, short of a full amount or number. A sudden start aside, as in fear.

Surpass; **H**ead-on; **Y**oung-me;
Next; **E**levation; **S**ureness; **S**pectacle

E.S.T. Exercise - see: pp. 180

Key-phrases/words: *Preliminary rounds*: afraid, bashful, frightened, shy, timid, unconfident; unsure... *Positive affirmations rounds*: calm, confident, empowered, inspired, peaceful, strong...

Dare enjoy and experience life's offering and presents
Shame or shy not

See: Dare, pp. 64
Examination, pp. 80

Shock: a sudden and violent blow or impact; collision. A sudden and violent disturbance of the mind, e-motions, or sensibilities. *Pathol.* A collapse of circulatory function, caused by severe injury, blood loss, or dis-ease, and characterized by pallor, sweating, weak pulse, and very low blood pressure. The physiological effect produced by the passage of an electric current through the body.

Sense; **H**eart; **O**rientation; **C**hoice; **K**nowledge

E.S.T. Exercise - see: pp. 180
Pre-sent present presents - see: pp. 134

Short: having little length; not long. Having little height; not tall. Extending or reaching only a little way. Brief duration, not extensive in time. Brief or concise, as writing. Rudely brief; abrupt. Low in amount; scanty.

Song; **H**eaven; **O**peration; **R**esourcefulness; **T**une
Stretch; **H**eight; **O**pportunity; **o**ption; **R**esilience; **T**reat

E.S.T. Exercise - see: pp. 180

Key-phrases/words: *Preliminary rounds*: insufficient, little, not enough, short... *Positive affirmations rounds*: enough, long, plenty, sufficient, tall...

Additional remedies
Replace 'little', 'short', 'small' with 'young' 'lots of opportunities and ways to grow-up', 'plenty of time to gain experience', 'I chose and want to be as tall as...', 'I can be as tall as', 'I am as tall as...', 'I love being tall and growing up to be tall', 'I have all the time in the world to grow tall and up'...

For a child whose height potential is greater than manifested
Measure the child's height, write it down before you begin the following exercise and keep this data where you shall be able to find it a year later.
Once a day, every day, for a whole year, tap on the child's chest centre with your hand, fingers or fist for 3-5 minutes.
When the year has ended take that data out, measure again, calculate height growth.
Encourage the child to do it alone. The tapping stimulates the Thymus gland⁽*⁾, diaphragm muscle, heart and lungs thus clearing stress, restoring ease and elasticity, allowing free flow and growth.
This exercise also develops and strengthens the immune system, replaces anxiety, extreme desire, eagerness, enthusiasm, passion, or sensitivity symptoms with ease; short-temper with common-sense and tranquillity, short-breath with calm (peaceful) breath.

Should-er - Shoulder:
The most mobile joint in the human body, at each side of the body in a man, at the top of the trunk, extending from each side of the base of the neck to the region where the arm articulates with the trunk.
A reserved area by the verge of a road or motorway.

Support; **H**ead; **O**ption; **U**plift; **L**oyalty; **D**elight; **E**ase; **R**eason **S**equence; **H**eart; **O**pportunity;

Unity; **L**egacy, **D**edication; **E**lasticity; **R**elief
Sustenance; **H**eaven on earth; **O**rientation;
Ubiquity; **L**ove; **D**evotion; **E**quilibrium; **R**esort

Should: duty; expediency, must, ought, propriety.
Self; **H**umour; **O**ption; **U**nity; **L**ife; **D**rive

To give a shoulder: to reach an arm, to reach out, to hand out support.

See: Wisdom, pp. 250

⁽*⁾ The thymus is a specialized organ in the immune system. The functions of the thymus are the production of T-lymphocytes (T cells), which are critical cells of the adaptive immune system, and the production and secretion of thymosins, hormones which control T-lymphocyte activities and various other aspects of the immune system. One of its most important roles is the induction of central tolerance.

Shoulder pain, frozen/stiff shoulder remedies

♦ Reflexology massage with emphasis on area from toes roots to diaphragm reflection line (pad bridge line), sides of the ankles. Deep Tissue massage and neck stretching. Also, see: Ache, pp. 7.

♦ Roll a towel, place it on the bed, lie with your spine or shoulder belt on it, thus letting your arms and neck naturally stretch and rest on the mattress.

♦ Place a tennis ball on the bed, lie on it, roll your body over it from one aching/cramped muscle to the next, let aching muscle rest on the tennis ball, while you focus on peaceful breath, until relief is felt.

♦ Clip laundry clips to the tissue between each finger, in the hand that is on the same side as your frozen/stiff shoulder, nose ridge and eyebrows - move step after step from inner side towards the outer side of the eyebrows. It is highly recommend to cry, dance, jump, scream, or shout out loud to clear the agony and pain. Remove the clips should pain increase or after you feel relief.

In case of pain increase: take a deep breath and rest before you once again clip the laundry clips to the aching tissue.

Repeat until neck/shoulder feel pain free.

Exercise 1:

♦ Stand or sit, lift your chin up, with your back and head straight.

♦ Bend one of your elbows, placing finger tips on shoulder joint cavity of this arm.

♦ Turn your face towards this arm. Focus your attention on that elbow's edge.

♦ Begin to turn your arm and shoulder joint **forward** while:

1. Your look is fixed at that elbow's edge to your best ability.
2. Your attention, awareness, intention and focus are on creating as flowing a movement as you can while drawing as large a circle with your elbow as possible.

Feel and listen to your shoulder and neck muscles e-motion and story.

Repeat this exercise three times before you proceed to do it with your other arm.

Now begin turning your arm and shoulder joint **backwards** while repeating steps 1 and 2 above.

Repeat this exercise three times before you proceed to do it with your other arm.

Exercise 2:

♦ With your chin and head up straight, look straight forward attentively and intentionally. Turn your head to one side, slowly, as far as you possibly can, pain, strain or tension free, feeling and sensing every muscle in your chest, shoulder belt and neck.

Remain in this position for a peaceful count of 1-2-3.

Begin gentle and slow turning of your head, with same attention and focus, until you look straight ahead.

Repeat three times in each direction, alternately, and proceed to the next step, should you feel stress build up or muscles cramp in your neck and/or shoulder belt muscles.

♦ Stretch your neck to form as round an arch as you possibly can, attentively and intentionally bend your head **forward** until your chin touches your chest.

Remain in this position for a peaceful count of 1-2-3.

Begin to gently and very slowly lift your head up, keeping your head and neck as stretched as you possibly can, until you are looking straight ahead.

Take a deep breath (inhaling through your nostrils, exhaling through your mouth).

Repeat three times.

♦ Stretch your neck to form as round an arch as you possibly can, attentively and intentionally bending your head **backward** until your chin points to the sky.

Remain in this position for a peaceful count of 1-2-3.

Begin to gently and very slowly lift your head up, lower your chin down, keeping your head and neck as stretched in as round arch like shape as you possibly can, until you are looking straight ahead.

Take a deep breath (inhaling through your nostrils, exhaling through your mouth).

Repeat three times.

Exercise 3:

♦ Exercise 1 above, with arm straight (instead of bent).

Exercise 4:

♦ Repeat this exercise three times, first with one arm and then the other.

♦ Sit or stand with your back straight, looking forward at an imaginary or real point. Jerk and shake your arms and shoulders to clear all tension, letting them hang free and loose by your side.

♦ With a free and loose shoulder, arm gently touching your side, fingers pointing towards the floor, raise your elbow up (like an 'L'), fingers pointing forward. Attentively and intentionally rotate the forearm sideways, fingers pointing to the side away from body. Once you reach the limit of your ability, open and straighten the elbow, fingers pointing to the floor, (keeping your upper arm gently touching the side of your body) feeling and sensing the arms and upper back muscles strain and stretch sensations.

Side: one of the surfaces forming the outside of or bounding a thing. An aspect or phase: *to consider all sides of...* region, direction, or position with reference to a central line, space, or point. A slope, as of a hill. One of two or more contesting teams, groups, parties, etc. the position, course, or part of a person or group opposing another: *I am on your side of this...* Part or half of a family with reference to the line descent through a parent. The space immediately adjacent to something or someone indicated.

Succession; Initiative; Direction; Elasticity

Sight: the power or faculty of seeing; vision. The act, fact, or instance of seeing. One's range of vision on some specific occasion: land is in sight. A view: glimpse. Mental perception or regard; judgment. Something seen or worth seeing; spectacle. Something shocking or distressing to see.

Surprise; I am; Gratitude; Heaven on earth; Treat

Silence: an absence of any sound; stillness. The state of being forgotten; oblivion. Concealment; secrecy.

Side; In; Love; Essence; Now; Choice; Era

Simplicity: freedom from complexity or the possibility of confusing. Absence of luxury, pretentiousness, etc.; plainness. Freedom from deceit or guile; sincerity. Lack of mental acuteness or shrewdness.

Serenity; Intuition; Make; Plea-sure;
Life; Is; Creativity; Innermost; Truth; Yard

See: Child, pp. 42
Know, pp. 131

Sincerity: freedom from deceit, hypocrisy, or falseness; earnestness.

Sweet; Innocence;

New; **C**ompetence;
Evolvement; **R**edemption;
Influence; **T**enderness; **Y**es

Skill: the ability to do something well, arising from talent, training, or practice. Competent excellence in performance.

Self; **K**indness; **I**nspired action; **L**eadership; **L**eisure

Slavery: severe toil; drudgery. Ownership of a person or persons by another or others. The condition of a slave.

Sail; **L**everage; **A**wareness; **V**ision; **E**xpansion; **R**emedy; **Y**ield

E.S.T. Exercise - see: pp. 180

Key-phrases/words: *Preliminary rounds*: addicted to…, multi-tasking, prisoner, slave, workaholic… *Positive affirmations rounds*: choice, decision, faith, free, one step at a time, I act on inspiration…

Small: of limited size; of comparatively restricted dimensions; not big; little. Slender, thin, or narrow: a small waist. Not great in amount, degree, number, duration, value, etc. of low numerical value; denoted by a low number. Having but little land, capital, power, influence, etc., or carrying on business or some activity on a limited scale. Of minor importance. Humble, modest, or unpretentious. Of little force or strength; slight. Mean or petty.

Smile; **M**omentum; **A**bility; **L**ove; **L**egacy

See: Short, pp. 208

Smell: the sense of smell; faculty of smelling. Odor; scent.

Sense; **M**astery; **E**ssence; **L**esson; **L**earning

Smile: a facial expression usually indicating plea-sure, favour, or amusement, but sometimes derision or scorn, characterized by an upturning of the corners of the mouth and usually accompanied, esp. in indicating pleasure, by brightening of the face and eyes. To regard with favour: luck smiled on us in that instance.

Surprise; **M**ake, **m**iracle, **m**omentum; **I**sland; **L**ove; **E**xpansion

Did you know that a child smiles over 400 times a day?
How many times a day do you smile?

Sobriety: the state or quality of being sober. Temperance or moderation, esp. in the use of alcoholic beverages. Seriousness, gravity, or solemnity.

Stream; **O**pportunity; **B**alance;
Ripple; **I**nspiration; **E**xit; **T**hank; **Y**ou

E.S.T. Exercise - see: pp. 180

Key-phrases/words: *Preliminary rounds*: afraid, annoyed, drowning, sad, sorry... *positive affirmations rounds*: awaken, calm, focused, peaceful...

E.S.T. exercise

Imagine there is a river to cross and ask yourself whom and which of the three attitudes is my companion on this journey:
Stupid, who will go in, get wet, turn back and come out on the same side?
Or...
Sober, who will walk in, get wet and somehow come out on the other side?
Perhaps...
Wise, who will reach the other side bright, dry, fresh, happy, glowing, shiny and smiling?

Sorrow: distress caused by loss, affliction, disappointment, etc.; grief or regret, as an affliction, a misfortune, or trouble. The expression of grief, sadness, disappointment, or the like.

Simplicity; Opportunity; Relief;
Rise; Onward, on word; Wellness

E.S.T. Exercise - see: pp. 180

Key-phrases/words: *Preliminary rounds*: angry, disappointed, frustrated, grieving, sad, sorry... *Positive affirmations rounds*: forgive, new opportunity; peace, relief...

See: Violence, pp. 241

Spite: a malicious desire to harm, annoy, or humiliate another person. A particular instance of such attitude or action; grudge. Obs. Something that causes vexation; annoyance.

Song of songs; Peace; Inspiration; Tenderness; Ease

E.S.T. Exercise - see: pp. 180

Key-phrases/words: *Preliminary rounds*: angry, annoyed, frustrated, hurt... *Positive affirmations rounds*: calm, confident, love, protected, safe...

Status: the position of an individual in relation to another or others. A state or condition of affairs.

Safety; Trust; Authenticity; Treat; Unity; Self

Step: a movement made by lifting the foot and setting it down again in a new position, accompanied by a shifting of the body in the direction of the new position.

Sound; Talent; Era; Plea-sure, pleasure, peace, present

Stone: the hard substance, formed from mineral and earth material, of which rocks consist. Any small, hard seed, as of a date; pit. *Bot*. the hard endocarp of a drupe, as of a peach. *Med*. A calculus concretion in the body, as in the gall bladder. A dis-ease arising from such a concretion. A gravestone, a tombstone, a grindstone, a milestone, a hailstone.

Spring, **s**ong, **s**tream; **T**une; **O**pportunity; **N**ew; **E**volvement

> E.S.T. Exercise - see: pp. 180

Key-phrases/words: *Preliminary rounds*: admonition, agony, bitter, self-correction, fear stricken, frozen, morbid, mortified, regret, remorse, reproach, self-criticism, self-guilt, self-punishment, self-torment, sore, suffering... *Positive affirmations rounds*: calm, change, confident, flow freely, forgive, open, peaceful, relaxed...

Gall bladder and liver cleansing
Frequent anger, bitterness, sourness remedy

Ingredients:
Citrus juice squeezer
Crystal glass
Fresh, mellow, ripe yellow lemon
Olive Oil (cold pressed, acidity value up to 1.8)

21 days procedure:
Women in fertility cycle are to begin procedure on cycle's 7th day.
Every day, half an hour before your first drink or meal, squeeze fresh lemon juice and mix it with olive oil into a homogenous mixture, drink to health.
    Begin with 1 table spoon each; proceed to 2 table spoons each.

Gall bladder stones, severe constipation

Ingredients:
Citrus juice squeezer
Crystal glass
Fresh, mellow, ripe yellow lemons
Large size strainer
Olive Oil (cold pressed, acidity value up to 1.8)

3 days procedure:
Women in fertility cycle are to follow this procedure between cycle's 7th-28th day.
Place strainer near the toilet seat.
Every night, two and a half hours after your last drink or meal, before you lie down, squeeze fresh lemon juice. Fill half of the crystal glass with the freshly squeezed lemon juice and half with the olive oil. Mix the lemon juice and olive oil to a homogenous mixture, drink to health and lie down. Mentally prepare yourself to liquidity feces. When time comes, place the strainer under your rump, and when done, look for the stones in it.

kidney stones

Clove bud infusion (See: Gum infection, pp. 97), drink one glass per day.

Small and tiny kidney stones

Replace artificial drinks, coffee, soda, tea with fresh filtered water, take 2-3 small sips at a time, chew and mix water attentively and intentionally with saliva, then swallow. Drink one glass during an hour from wake up time to sleep time and bring yourself as quickly as you can to an experienced and skilled reflexology practitioner or a body-masseur. When urinating, pay attention to urine colour and smell, listen to the sound of the stone hitting the toilet's wall.

Repeat this procedure the following day together with a reflexology or a body-massage session should you feel unsure or if pain's frequency and strength seem similar to the pains on the previous day. It is recommended to drink filtered fresh water for vibrant health and kidney health.

Medium and large kidney stones

Replace artificial drinks, coffee, soda , tea with fresh filtered water, take 2-3 small sips at a time, chew and mix water attentively and intentionally with saliva, then swallow.
Prepare and drink, every day until you feel pain-free for 7 days and nights, fresh Indian corn hair infusion(*). Take 2-3 small sips at a time, chew and mix infusion attentively and intentionally with saliva, then swallow. Drink one glass during an hour. 2-3 glasses a day.

Storm: a violent outbreak of expression. A violent disturbance of affairs, as in an inner commotion. A disturbance of the normal condition of the atmosphere, manifesting itself by winds of unusual force or direction often accompanied by rain, snow, hail, etc.; a heavy fall of rain, snow, or hail, or a violent outbreak of lightening

and thunder unaccompanied by strong winds.
v.i.: to rage or complain violently; to rush to an assault or attack; to rush angrily.

Sign; **T**ime; **O**rder; **R**e-feel, **r**elief; **M**astery, **m**omentum

E.S.T. Exercise - see: pp. 180

(*) Indian corn hair infusion: put a heaping teaspoon of Indian corn hair in a crystal glass, fill with boiling water, cover with glass saucer and allow to soak (infuse) for 10 minutes and more. Do not sweeten. Drink to health.

Key-phrases/words: *Preliminary rounds*: agony, e-motional explosion, fear stricken, self-guilt, self-punishment, self-torment, suffering…*Positive affirmations rounds*: calm, change, confident, flow freely, forgive, open, peaceful, resilient, relaxed…

Strength: bodily or muscular power; vigour. Mental power, force, vigour. Moral power, firmness, or courage. Power of reason of influence, authority, resources, numbers, etc. vigour of action, language, feeling, etc. amount, quantity; proportion. Intensity.
Someone or something that is a source of power or encouragement

Source; **T**enderness; **R**esilience; **E**-motion; **N**ew; **G**ratitude; **T**reasure; **H**ear no evil, see no evil, speak no evil; **h**ere and now

Stress: importance or significance attached to a thing; emphasis. *Mech. Physics.* **a.** the action on a body of any system of balanced forces whereby strain or deformation results. **b.** the internal resistance or reaction of an elastic body to the external forces applied to it. *Physiol.* Any stimulus, as fear or pain, that disturbs or interferes with the normal physiological equilibrium of an organism. Physical, mental, or emotional strain or tension.

Sigh; **T**ime; **R**elaxation; **E**steem; **S**elf; **S**hift

I am stress free when I fret not and fuss not

In July 2014 I moved to another apartment. The Internet and Telephone cable supplier's - Hot Telecom - employees breached our verbal agreements time and time again, thus engaging in actions of deceit, exploitation, fraud, robbery and theft in broad daylight. On August 25th, 2014 following a telephone conversation to settle a money return dispute, in which I was asked to give my cellular telephone number and gave it; it's system sent me a sales promotion sms. In return I sent a sms to 2323 (the number to send a sms to remove a telephone number from the Hot distribution list). Instead of writing "No" I wrote a request - see pp. 219. A message with the word "failed" showed up on the screen. This sms was another breach of a verbal agreement. A few days later I recalled that in this case I have the right to sue Hot for a breach of 2008 spam law.

The law suit that I filed on September 10, 2014 was

registered as T"K 27604-09-14. A couple of months later Hot's offer to settle the dispute included a gag order clause. I asked that this clause be removed, for what is the sense in having such order else the hat on the thief's head is on fire?

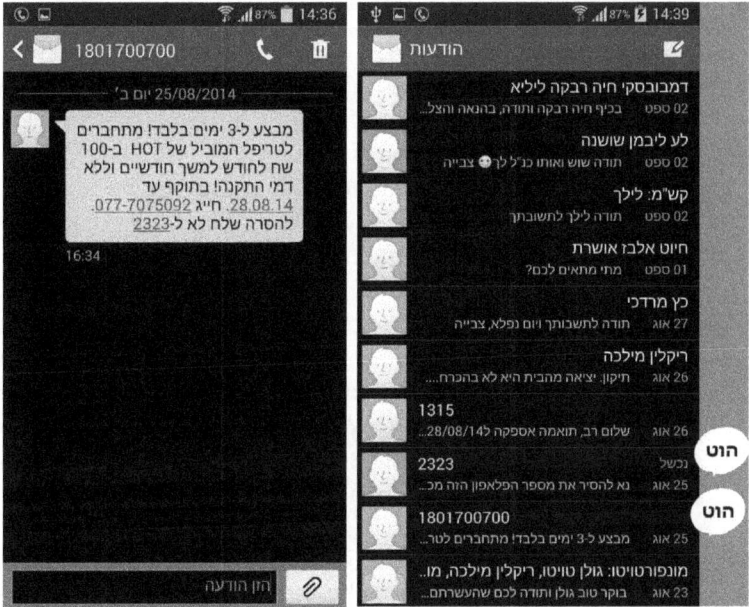

When I heard the Hot employee deny my request I said to him that going to court will give me this demand. On December 23 I received Hot's statement of defense, I felt my heart and neck contract with paralyzing fear. The following day I found out that my blood pressure went up to 140/65. To bring it to my usual 120-100/70-60 pressure I cleared and let go by tapping with Brad Yates "Feeling Like You Are Failing", "Guilt Free Gratitude", "Deciding and Committing" video clips on youtube; and followed Lester Levenson (b.h.m.) and Larry Crane's "Release Technique." Within a couple of minutes, I felt the contraction make way to inner-peace, stress free e-motion. I measured the blood pressure to see it was down to 100/55. I then could move on to prepare myself for the court session on January 7th, 2015. Since then every day has begun with blood pressure measuring 140-150. Thus I started tapping and letting go with the release technique every day before sleep and after waking up, as well as every time I felt stress in my chest, nape, neck or throat. By Sunday, January 5th, 2015 the idea of going to court (without a single proof) no longer felt stressful. On January 7, 2015 I woke up to a day with blue sky and shining sun. My original plan was to leave at 07:30, yet I decided to attend to another affair and take time to call the court information service to find out that all is aligned in line and in order. Having heard that it is so I left home between 08:35-08:40, to see the roads were free of traffic jam (see: Jam, pp. 127) (**proof** to fear being baseless and groundless). Arriving at each traffic light I saw it change from red to green (**reassurance** to being aligned in line on the right track). On the way to a parking lot I saw two lawyers standing in the way. We exchanged smiles and enlightening sentences, then they moved out of the way for me to see that every parking place was occupied. One of the two lawyers came up to me and said that if I would wait for him to drive away I can have his car's parking place, thus enjoying free parking (proof to having become more positive, no longer giving away my power to men or being vict-I'm). When I came out of the car I saw the sky covered with dark and heavy clouds, and before I entered the court building a drizzle started. In court I heard all systems were down, just-ice justice failing and failure at it's best (smile please) (see: Just-ice, pp. 128). Order was an outcome of fighting and pushing lawyer. How did I come with this idea? My lawsuit was to be the 1st, a stressful and thwarted lawyer pushed his case to be the 1st. The judge's way and words proved me to have a case. The judge over ruled the law (because I had a case, not a proof), and got the Hot representative to accept a compromise agreement - in my favour AND gag order clause free. A couple of days before the court session the idea that I can become victorious crossed my mind, I tapped on it. Along the way I also tapped on fearing love, to be loved and loving.

To add sugars and sweets to that day's course:

On my way home I parked in double parking. When I came out of the car I heard a man repeat the lawyer's words in the court's parking. I waited for him to drive away and then parked in his car's parking space.

I gave my smart-phone to the technician for repair. The technician worked for over 2 hours, during which I enjoyed fun and good company with the staff. I was presented with a bill for 50 N.I.S., instead of 70 N.I.S. because I was a returning customer. During these hours the storm - that was expected to come the following day - started.

When I came to the car the wind blew my sunglasses off my head straight into the street. I saw them fly right under a passing by car. I walked over to pick them up, saw the car did not run over them and that nothing had happened to them

(**Proof** to have been in my power, i.e. I did not give my power to everybody and everything. **Proof** to my letting go of fear, wanting control or to be safe; being guilt and punishment free. **Proof** that the belief and truth that I am out of any danger; protected, safe and secure anywhere and anytime became my being and reality). L.Z., from the telephone shop, watched the scene and came over to me to share his surprise at what had just happened right before his very own eyes.

At the close of the day, sometime after 22:00 hrs, with the temperature feeling like -2 degrees centigrade the road from Goren was ice free.

I heard that restaurants would be closed because of the storm. I called one and heard it was open now, but closing soon. So I drove home to remember that there is a Sandwich Bar in Shlomi that could be open. It was open, the two employees were sitting at a table. A hail storm broke a few minutes after I walked in. During the meal I had a lovely talk with one employee. He came up to me and asked if I have someone to donate bread loaves to, I answered that I know not anyone. He then brought a bag with bread loaves to my table, and I recall he said, "take them home and put them in the freezer for your enjoyment, because we do not use yesterday's bread".

The outcomes and services that I received that day are fruits that fell into my lap from daily clearing my old personal behaviours customs of accuse, blame, fear, guilt; habits of false being, right/wrong, fault finding vict-I'm-hood. Vict-I'm has excuses, who to accuse, blame, fear and find to be guilty, right and wrong. Thus giving her/his power to everybody and everything, letting the other state of being and state of mind be her/his conductors and rulers; hold and place her/himself in false-play poor me, vict-I'm. Being in vict-OR mode and phase is becoming and being the creator of my reality. Being in my power; omnipotent, holding on to my power, and taking full responsibility for each action and every decision created that day's course of events and reality.

It is my and yours call and choice to become the creator of my/your life and reality, experience and live a negativity stressful life or a positivity; stand up to my/your birth right to become victorious life; enjoy ask and it is given, have a life I/you truly can have and deserve.

Where did I begin?

        I began with E.S.T. Exercises.

How did I do it?

I did it by clearing and letting go. "The Release Technique" served to delete old programmes, make love and positivity become clear and greater. Tapping also served to programme new ideas and ways.

E.S.T. Exercise - see: pp. 180

Key-phrases/words: *Preliminary rounds*: ache, afraid, agony, angry, annoyed, anxiety, defied, deflated, depressed, frustrated, tormented... *Positive affirmations rounds*: calm, flow freely, open, protected, safe, supported...

See: Growth, sleep, pp. 95

Larry Crane, The Release Technique video clips on youtbue
https://www.youtube.com/watch?v=XJ1hP2ucO8k
https://www.youtube.com/watch?v=eeA5VlFRNxc
https://www.youtube.com/watch?v=iicbY0--C2A

Calm, chill down, chill out, clear, let go, let out, love all, relax, rest rather than stress

Study: application of the mind to the acquisition of knowledge, as by reading, investigation, or reflection.

Significance; **T**urn; **U**nity; **D**evotion; **Y**outh

Stupidity: a stupid act, notion, speech. The state, quality or fact of being stupid.

Sincerity; **T**alent; **U**sefulness; **P**resence;
Intuition; **D**elight; **I**nspiration; **T**hank; **Y**ou

Success: the favorable or prosperous termination of action, performance; achievement, outcome.

Serenity, **s**implicity; **U**nity; **C**redence;
Creativity; **E**ase; **S**incerity, **s**tamina; **S**urprise

See: "Zvia come", pp. 44

> Examination, pp. 80
> Fake, pp. 84
> Law, pp. 136
> Loyalty, pp. 145
> Miracle, pp. 150
> Terror, pp. 229
> Wisdom, pp. 250
> Young, pp. 258

Sugar: a sweet, crystalline substance, obtained chiefly from the juice of the sugar cane and the sugar beet, and present in sorghum, maple sap, etc.

Sorrow; **U**rgency; **G**ravity; **A**ddiction, **a**vidity; **R**avenous
Self; **U**niverse; **G**ladness; **A**ppreciation; **R**estitution

♦ Processed sugar (white sugar) irritates the nervous system, drains out of the body calcium, magnesium - thus causes muscles cramps, reduces immune system efficiency, acts as glue in the intestine and raises acidity. You may want to gradually give it up, replacing it with Stevia fresh leaves or liquid drops, settle for 1-2 fruit portions a day.
♦ To lower sugar level prepare fresh Fenugreek seeds infusion everyday and drink 1-3 glasses, daily.

> E.S.T. Exercise - see: pp. 180

Key-phrases/words: *Preliminary rounds*: afraid, angry, annoyed, craving, eager, sad, sorry, sour... *Positive affirmations rounds*: balanced, calm, confident, equilibrium, in control, open, safe...

Survival: of or pertaining to the food, clothing, equipment, etc. necessary to or aiding in a person's survival in adverse circumstances.

Sun; **U**tility; **R**ay; **V**itality;
Infra-structure; **V**ariety; **A**wareness; **L**ift

Sweet: a sweet flavour, smell, or sound; sweetness. Something that is sweet or causes or gives a sweet flavour, smell or sound. A

beloved person, darling, sweetheart.

Simplicity; **W**ellbeing; **E**ntity; **E**ssence; **T**reat

Sympathy: a quality of mutual relations between people or things whereby what ever affects one also affects the other. The ability to share the feeling of another, esp. in sorrow or trouble; compassion or commiseration. Harmony of or agreement in feeling, as between persons or on the part of one person with respect to another.

Selectivity; **Y**ard; **M**astery;
Peace; **A**ffection; **T**ie; **H**appiness; **Y**ield

♦ Being in a state of sympathy is feeling the other's pain and sorrow oftentimes resulting in my/your dis-comfort or dis-ease.

Sympathy out
Compassion out

♦ Being in a state of love allows one to extend aid, help and protect one's health from dis-comfort or dis-ease and their manifestations.

Love in

T

Target: a goal or end to be attained. An object, as one marked with centric circles, to be aimed at in shooting practice or in competition. Any thing to be struck with missiles. An object of abuse, scorn, derision, etc.; butt. Any of various markers intended to be visible at considerable distances.

Tap; Aspiration; Revelation; Gladness; Evolvement; Tenderness

Taste: the sense by which the flavours of things are perceived when they are brought into contact with the tongue. The quality perceived by this sense; flavour. A small quantity tasted; a morsel, bit, or sip. A personal inclination to enjoy or appreciate certain things (often followed by for). The sense of what is fitting, harmonious, or beautiful. The attitude of a place or period as to what is beautiful or harmonious. An artistic or decorative manner or style reflecting this attitude. The sense of what may be done or said without giving offense or committing an impropriety. A slight experience of pleasure, sorrow etc., or a source of these. Obs. A test or trial.

Tact; Affection; Study; Treat; Essence

Tear: a drop of the saline, watery fluid continually secreted by the lacrimal glands between the surface of the eye and the eyelid, serving to moisten and lubricate these parts and keep them clear of foreign particles. This fluid appearing in or flowing from the eye as a result of e-motion, esp. grief.

Treasure; Eye; Art; Ripple

> Letting Go fun exercise - see: pp. 105

Temper: a particular state of mind or feelings. Habit of mind, esp. with respect to irritability or patience; disposition. Heat of mind or passion, shown in outbursts of anger, resentment, etc. Calm disposition or state of mind; to be out of temper.

Take it; **E**asy; **M**agic; **P**eace; **E**den here and now; **R**evival

> E.S.T. Exercise - see: pp. 180
> Letting Go fun exercise - see: pp. 105

Temperature
: a measure of the warmth or coldness of an object or substance with reference to some standard value. *Physiol.*, *Pathol.*: the degree of a heat in a living body, esp. the human body. The excess of this heat above the normal.

Truth **t**ime; **E**ase; **M**iracle, **m**omentum; **P**rivilege; **E**ra; **R**emedy; **A**ffection; **T**ouch; **U**nity; **R**ealm; **E**xpansion

♦ Temperature rise indicates immune system activity to ensure health; a need and a time to change a routine or way of living.
♦ Our body is wise and well equipped with amazing healing abilities and techniques.
♦ When your body temperature rises immediately treat yourself to plenty of rest, sleep and to drinking of fresh filtered water, lukewarm or warm. During the first three days ask yourself, "What is my lesson? What am I to learn?" Check, observe, reflect and study what's changing or happening in your life. Seek medical advice If your temperature remains unchanged or rises.

On February 1996 during my formal office hours I felt exhausted. I drove home feeling obscured and powerless. I hung the purse on the first chair I came to and walked into the bedroom. I found a thermometer, put it under the lower side of my tongue, waited a minute or two, and took it out. My temperature was 43.5°C (110°F).
43.5°C how is that possible? All my life I had heard that at 42°C one dies. I looked again - yes, my eyes did not deceive me. I thought the thermometer was out of order and went to sleep.
I slept straight into the following day. When I woke up I took my temperature. It was 39.8°C (104°F).
I called the managing director and informed him that, as of
yesterday, I have high temperature thus I am staying at home.
The temperature of 39.8°C (104°F) remained for 10 days or

so, in which all that I had the power to do was drink, sleep and shower. I went to the GP who was surprised when I arrived with such a temperature for, "… This is all about the flu," he said.

"Flu?" I wondered.

Flu lasts 7 days with grandma's penicillin (home made chicken soup), a week with GP prescribed medicines, between a few minutes to a few hours for those that clear and let go of each dis-comfort and every dis-ease. Parallel to my return to office I went to the gynecologist to get the Intrauterine device out and followed his advice to consult a virus specialist. The specialist gave me several tests to negate various possibilities, from aids through cancer, and other creepy creatures such as Tuberculosis (TB). At the end of April, the TB test returned positive, although the answers to all the TB specialist questions were "No." It was explained to me that the preliminary treatment to prevent or stop TB requires six months of antibiotics and a follow up every second week. In the first follow up, my perception guided me to think that the data I had supplied to the TB specialist on our first and subsequent meetings had somehow undermined the test result, yet I was asked to undergo an invasive test. In my hysterical hi-story I feared to death invasive tests and only in August, four months after the antibiotic treatment began, and several implorations from the TB specialist did I agree to call the Sheba Medical Centre. The test was set for October. It conclusively revealed - clear lungs.

In 2002 I met with Zipi Schloss. She applied the IPEC test and asked me if I have or had Mononucleosis. I learnt from her that exhaustion is a symptom of Mononucleosis. I recalled the high temperature from February 1996 and asked her how I could verify this diagnosis. She told me that a simple blood test is all I need to do. The following day I did this blood test, and it showed my blood contained the Mononucleosis antibody.

Thanks to tapping and Homeopathic spiritual counseling with Nira Hartman in 2006 my cheerfulness and life-power started coming back to me.

High temperature remedies

♦ Gentle and gradual temperature decrease is your aim and the name of the game.

♦ A sudden drop of 1° or to a higher degree may result in a shock.

♦ With babies and children be alert, aware and cautious.

♦ Temperature remains unchanged? Increases? Seek medical aid.

Bathtub: Fill the bathtub with lukewarm water, add one kg of salt. Immerse your body, step by step. Duration: 15-20 minutes.

You may want to drop on the dry salt 6-8 drops (in total) of pure essential oils such as: Eucalyptus (globules), Lavender, Lemon, Melissa, Pine, Rosemary, Siberian pine and then mix it with the water.

With temperature exceeding 39°C (102°F) it is recommended to fill half the bathtub and drop Black pepper pure essential oil on the dry salt. Add the salt with the Black pepper drops to the water and mix together.

Black pepper pure essential oil dosage: **baby** (1-3 months): 2 drops on one spoon of dry salt, **child**: 3-5 drops, **adult**: 10 drops.

Black pepper pure essential oil stimulates perspiration and circulation and is also a remedy for inflamed joints, organs and tissues.

Take temperature 10-15 minutes after coming out of the bathtub and drying your body. If temperature remains unchanged, or increases, seek medical aid.

Shower: stand under a water stream for as long as you feel like it.

Apple Vinegar compress:
Materials:
A glass bowl
Cannabis/Cotton/Linen cloth or towel
Cannabis/Cotton/Linen socks
5% Austrian, British, German or Swiss made Apple vinegar
Thermometer
Water, at room temperature or lukewarm
Dosage:
Babies: ¼ glass 5% Apple vinegar + ¾ glass water.
Children: ⅓ glass 5% Apple vinegar + ⅔ glass water.
Teens: ½ glass 5% Apple vinegar + ½ glass water.
Adults: pure 5% Apple vinegar.
Procedure:
Pour the vinegar and water into a bowl; mix them into a solution; soak cloth and/or socks in this solution and administer the soaked cloth on forehead and/or dress feet with the soaked socks.

When cloth/socks feel dry or hot replace it/them with a newly soaked one.

Temperature is gently and gradually decreasing? Repeat until it is under 38°C/100°F. Temperature remains unchanged? Increases? Seek medical aid.

Drink a shot of **Gin/Vodka**[16] with a pinch of black pepper powder and a pinch of salt in it, then lie in bed to rest or sleep.

Continue to heal, rest and take it easy until you feel 'as good as new'. Return to a new routine or way of living, after you feel 'brand new' for three straight days.

Tender: soft or delicate in substance; not hard or tough. Weak or delicate in constitution; not strong or hardy. Young or immature. Delicate, soft, or gentle. Easily moved; kind, tender heart. Affectionate or loving. Acutely or painfully sensitive. Easily distressed.
To present formally for acceptance.

Touch; **E**ndowment; **N**avigation; **D**elight; **E**xistence; **R**ichness

Pre-sent Present Presents - see: pp. 134

Tension: mental or emotional strain; suspense, anxiety, or excitement. A strained relationship between individuals, nations, etc., pressure, esp. of vapour. *Mech.* The longitudinal deformation of an elastic body that results in its elongation. The force producing such deformation. *Mach.* A device for stretching or pulling something.

Thought; **E**xperience; **N**ascence;
Sight; **I**ntake; **O**pportunity; **N**ew-born

E.S.T. Exercise - see: pp. 180

Key-phrases/words: *Preliminary rounds*: afraid, angry, anxious, insecure, nervous, stressed, strained, tensed... *Positive affirmations rounds*: calm, relax, safe, anything is possible, I am taking it easy, I can take it easy, miracles are happening here and now...

See: Growth, sleep, pp. 95

Pre-sent Present Presents - see: pp. 134

Terror: intense, sharp, overmastering fear. A feeling, instance, or cause of intense fear.

Tenderness; **E**volvement; **R**eassurance;

Resourcefulness; Openness; Re-formation

One afternoon I joined the 13 year old sitting at the dining table, eating I don't remember what, and I recall that I heard "Did you see my end of the year certificate?" "No, I did not, where is it?" "It's right under your arm." I looked down at the table, moved my arm and saw the certificate was indeed right under it. I picked it up, read it, saw that his marks in Arabic and English were higher than 7 and 8 respectively, and that there were no below 7 marks. I looked him straight in the face and said, "If you were my son this is the best certificate you could have brought me." I saw he turned his head down and sideway. His eyes filled with tears, and then he said, "How can you say that? I don't have an A in all the subjects,". "I said it because I remember our talks in which I heard what you went through with your Arabic and English teachers." The house rules for him were such that before an exam it was prohibited that he get what one needs most to successfully pass an exam (a clear head, peaceful mind and plenty of rest). No meeting, playing or talking with family members or friends, no rest or sleep, no TV. He was to sit and study from the moment he came home from school until he went to bed at night on the day before an exam. On the day of the test he was to get up at 05:00 hrs to study until school time. These rules terrorized the child to the point of exhaustion. He had to beg and cry for rest from the most sympathetic parent. He was then given a permission for a half an hour rest and was forced to promise that he would walk his word.

"Did my giving him the time he needed to rest or sleep, telling him I shall stand up for him when the parent comes home and hears the truth, bring about his gestures of gratitude (sparkling bright eyes, cheerful greeting and a polite "Hi, how do you do, what's going on?") in the following years when he saw me - with others' children - at the country club or in the street?

See: Dread, pp. 69

Dread, fear, fight, flight, freeze, fright, scare, terror
fare(in)well
Ability, capability, comfort, confidence, control
Wel(l)-come home

E.S.T. Exercise - see: pp. 180

Key-phrases/words: *Preliminary rounds*: afraid, angry, anxious, insecure, nervous, stressed, strained, stuck, tensed, terrorized... *Positive affirmations rounds*: all is aligned and is in line, all is well, calm, protected, safe...

> Letting Go fun exercise - see: pp. 105
> Pre-sent Present Presents - see: pp. 134

Test: the means by which the presence, quality, or genuineness of anything is determined; a means of trial. A trial of that quality of something: to put to the test. A particular process or method for trying or assessing. A form of examination for evaluating the performance, capabilities, traits, or achievements of an individual.

Truth; **E**ntity; **S**hift; **T**rust
Treat; **E**xpansion; **S**ong; **T**ime

> See: Examination, pp. 80
> Power Of The Word, pp. 171

> Dare test ability, belief, faith in-stance, mind-set, perception, stand and view-points to delve into new fascinating horizons

> E.S.T. Exercise - see: pp. 180

Key-phrases/words: *Preliminary rounds*: anxious, eager, excited, failure pattern, fear of failure, fear-stricken... *Positive affirmation rounds*: calm, I am doing my best, I have all that it takes, I can pass it, test is a way for me to measure my knowledge, to realize what I know, to choose and to decide what to focus on, learn and study next...

> Letting Go fun exercise - see: pp. 105

Thread: Something having the fineness or slenderness of a filament. That which runs through the whole course of something, connecting successive parts.

Trip; **H**eart; **R**elief; **E**levation; **A**dventure; **D**elight

Throat: the passage from the mouth to the stomach or to the lungs, including the fauces, pharynx, esophagus, larynx, and trachea. Some analogical or similar narrowed part or passage. The front of the neck below the chin and above the collarbone.

Thank you; **H**eart; **R**evelation; **O**ption; **A**dventure; **T**aste
♦ Throat dis-ease is the body's red traffic-light, asking you to stop, take time to ask questions such as: "What is so painful for me to swallow?" "What is so painful for me to go through?" "What do I want to express, say or spit out that is too painful for me to do?" Listen to your heart's message. Is it ego? Fear? Shame? Sorrow? that block and hurt? Follow your heart's desire (See: Tongue, pp. 233).

Remedies
E.S.T. Exercise - see: pp. 180
Key-phrases/words: *Preliminary rounds*: angry, annoyed, ashamed, burdened; conflict, disgrace, distressed, eager, frustrated, fear-stricken, frozen; grief; impatient, insecure, nervous, sad, sorry, stressed, strained, tensed, unsure, worked-up… *Positive affirmations rounds*: calm, confident, ease, safe, it is safe to voice my heart, I am protected when I follow my heart, I am safe and no longer need to hold on to my armoured shield…

♦ Satureja Montana, Thyme (dry or fresh) infusion: put 3-5 branches in a crystal glass, fill with boiling hot water, cover with a glass saucer and allow to soak (infuse) for 10 minutes and more. Do not sweeten. Drink to health.

♦ Synergy Master Blend pure essential oil: drip 1-2 drops on your palm, rub your palms with each other, then lovingly massage the baby's neck. Adults and children that can open their throat and let the middle finger reach deep inside the throat: drip 1 drop on the middle finger's pad and with the pad reach as deep inside the throat as you can, touch the wall, take the middle finger out and inhale deeply.

♦ Drink some water with 3 drops of Eucalyptus globules pure essential oil [16] or Lavender pure essential oil.

Tie: string, cord or wire used for fastening. Device for holding components together. Long narrow piece of cloth worn around the neck and tied in a special knot in front, (pl.). Something that unites. Equality of score or votes. Structural member resisting tension forces along the grain. Heavy piece of wood or ferroconcrete supporting a railroad track. Low shoe fastened with a lace. Curved line connecting two musical notes of the same pitch and indicating that they are to be played without a break.

Thrive; Implementation; Ecstasy

Timidity: lack of self-assurance or courage, shyness, characterized by or indicating fear.

Time; I; Master; Irrevocable; Dare drive;
Innovation, inspiration, intuition; Truth; Yield

E.S.T. Exercise - see: pp. 180

Key-phrases/words: *Preliminary rounds*: ashamed, bashful, embarrassed, fear-stricken, shy, terrorized, timid... *Positive affirmations rounds*: calm, confident, ease, self-assured, it is safe to be authentic, I am protected when I am naturally truly me.

Tongue: the usually movable organ in the floor of the mouth in man and most vertebrates, functioning in eating, in tasting, and, in man in speaking. The strongest muscle in the body. The human tongue as the organ of speech. The faculty or power of speech. The language or dialect of a particular people, region, or nation.

Tune; Offering; New; Genius; Uniformity; Ensemble

Tongue cramps and/or temporary paralysis sensations may result from changes, deformations, or sclerosis in cervical spine, artery, muscle, or nerve. The cramps and/or paralysis come to shed a light on being negative, stuck in the past, undeserving, unloving, a need to ask my inner-self a question, make a change, and take inspired action; homeopathy, pestecides, spiritual poisoning.

E.S.T. Exercise - see: pp. 180

Key-phrases/words: *Preliminary rounds*: these cramps, this paralysis, pain, fear, distress... *Positive affirmations rounds*: I allow myself to re-form, straighten out and up, I give myself permission and let myself move on with ease and grace, express myself freely and naturally, I let go and let out, I open and welcome change with love and peace...

In January 2010 I shared my dream, to live near the sea shore. In mid March, when laying in bed, I put my hand on my heart then asked: "If I weren't afraid, what is the one thing I would most love to do now?" "To give her a slap."

The following day I remembered that on my last talk with my C.P.A. he suggested I call her and let her know. I picked up the telephone, called her and I remember I said, "I am calling because there is news. I am to sign a contract this evening and I ask to have Wednesday free to go up north to find my home." "How do you want to do it?" she asked. "With ease" I answered. A few hours later I answered the phone and heard blazing hell eruption "… are you resigning? Giving me notice? When?" - "Yes, easy is one month (notice), yet I would love and prefer two weeks…" I answered.

On Wednesday, on the train from Hod Hasharon to Nahariya, I wondered who will accompany and inspire me in Nahariya: Shay Agnon (author, Literature Noble prize winner) or Haim Nahman Bialik (author and poet, Israel prize winner)?

I walked into the apartment in Agnon street and felt overwhelmed. I walked into the one in Bialik Street and felt my heart filled with joy and started singing for reality outdid the real estate agent description and my imagination (the western windows view is sea, trees, and flowers). The moving company then offered a 35% discount for moving my belongings on Pesach (Passover) evening, and so two weeks after I dared slap her (resign) the truck drove my belongings to Nahariya.

> Dreams and heart wished wishes come true and create a reality surpassing vivid and wild imagination

Tooth: one of the hard bodies or processes usually attached in a row to each jaw, serving for the prehension and mastication of food, as weapons, etc. and in mammals typically composed chiefly of dentin surrounding a sensitive pulp and covered on the crown with enamel. A reflection and testimony of one's health.

Talent; **O**n-ward; **O**n-word; **T**ruth; **H**ealing
Treasure; **O**h; **O**rder; **T**reat; **H**ealth

Take; Option; Opportunity; Thrive; Happiness

♦ In the Roman Empire the merchant opened the slave's mouth for the prospective client to see the slave's state of health.

One autumn, a dentist diagnosed a cavity in a left wisdom tooth in the lower jaw. The dentist recommended to pull it out, "...extensive scientific research shows wisdom teeth are troublemakers and useless... there is a laser treatment, it costs 2,000 NIS, why waste money... ?" he said.
I went for a 2nd opinion and heard that a root canal can save this tooth and will cost less. I met the root canal specialist. She started digging and excavating, stopped, walked out of the room and returned with the dentist who suggested the root canal procedure. He took a close look at the tooth and I heard "It looks like an ordinary filling is all that is needed, what would you like us to do? Continue with the root canal or a conservative procedure of ordinary filling?" I chose the conservative procedure, paid 300 NIS to later realize that when the dentist recommends to pull out a tooth it's not her/his tooth that will be pulled out, it's not her/his body, energy motion, soul, spirit that this procedure will invalidate, traumatize and violate. In the wisdom tooth case, it's not the dentist's wisdom that is abused and is pulled out. Please honour, nurture and treasure your body, it's your highest and most valuable masterpiece creation. Do not haste or rush to agree with the 1st opinion a dentist or an MD expresses. Your body (and teeth in this case) play roles that their essence, implications and importance exceed and surpass the human ability to comprehend, imagine, see or visualize. (See: Inflam(e)-mation, pp. 121)

Trait: a distinguishing characteristic or quality, esp. of one's personal nature.

Truth; Revelation; Admittance; Inspiration, intuition; Trust

Tranquillity: quality or state of being tranquil; calmness; peacefulness; quiet; serenity.

Treasure; Relief; Awareness; Nascence; Quality;

Unity; **I**nnermost; **L**ife; **L**ove; **I**ntuition; **T**ouch; **Y**outh

Trauma: the condition resulting from an injury. *Pathol.* A. a body injury produced by violence or any thermal, chemical, or other extrinsic agent. *Psychiatry*: a startling experience that has a lasting effect on mental life; shock.

Touch; **R**emedy; **A**ffection; **U**biquity; **M**iracle; **A**wareness
Tenderness; **R**esilience; **A**ttitude; **U**nity; **M**irth; **A**lleviation
Trust; **R**est; **A**cceptance; **U**niqueness; **M**astery; **A**vailability

E.S.T. Exercise - see: pp. 180
H.P.T. - see: pp. 134
Letting Go fun exercise - see: pp. 105

Treat: an entertainment of amusement, drink, food, etc., given by way of compliment or as an expression of friendly regard.

Track; **R**adiance; **E**xuberance; **A**ffection; **T**aste

Trial: Law. The examination before a judicial tribunal of the facts put in issue in a cause, often including issues of law as well as of fact. The determination of a person's guilt or innocence by due process of law. The act of trying, testing, or putting to the proof. A tentative or experimental action in order to ascertain results; experiment. The state or position of a person or thing being tried or tested; probation. Subjection to suffering or grievous experiences; a distressed or painful state: comfort in the hour of trial. An affliction or trouble. A trying, distressing, or annoying thing or person.

Truth; **R**elief; **I**ncrement; **A**ssembly; **L**ove

E.S.T. Exercise - see: pp. 180

Key-phrases/words: *Preliminary rounds*: annoyed, distressed, insecure, nervous, stressed, strained, tensed, unsure, worked-up… *Positive affirmations rounds*: birth right, calm, confident, deserving, successful, truthful, valued, worthy…

Trust: belief in and reliance on the ability, integrity, strength, surety, etc., of a person or thing. Confident expectation of something; hope. Charge; custody; care. Reliability.

Truth; **R**ealm; **U**niqueness; **S**ong; **T**une

Truth: true or actual state of a matter: the truth about one's health. Conformity with fact or reality: verity: the truth of a statement. A verified or indisputable fact, proposition, principle, or the like: mathematical truth. State or character of being true. Actually or actual existence, ideal or fundamental reality apart from and transcending perceived experience: the truth of the universe. Agreement with a standard or original. Honesty, integrity, truthfulness.

Treasure; **R**elief; **U**biquity; **T**reat;
Hear no evil, see no evil, speak no evil, **h**eart, **h**eaven

In one of my visits at my mother's, in Ma'anit, she asked me to clean the kitchen closet. Exploited vict-I'm me angrily answered her that this is the duty of... and added, "I am not your maid." This time I saw she filled with hurt and sorrow. In the days that passed between this visit and the next one, I realized that in her asking me to do that task, she actually and factually revealed to me, 'In you I trust and on you I rely'. Thus, I decided that from now on, every word she says is sheer truth and I will accept it as such. Furthermore, every time I visited her, I brought with me an approach and an attitude of good will. When she asked me to do something, I did it gladly and lovingly, having kept her best interests in mind, rather than regarding it as a chore or duty. Gradually I created the new habit with Perla's encouragement and support and let go of the habit to regard her from a dutiful stand-point. My relationship with my mother so turned from hell to heaven on earth.

Use good feeling and will to right
hell into heaven on earth

The Four Agreements[6]

1. Never assume, opine, postulate, suppose or take for granted.

When in doubt, clear, inquire, investigate, verify. When unsure, ask, clarify, make clear and make sure. Assumptions, inferences and suppositions create fictitious films or scenarios.

2. Be true to your word, honour it, respect it, stand up to it and walk it.

One's words are state of being and state of mind reflection and perception.

Be truthful, sincere, honest, genuine, and authentic.

Honouring, respecting, standing up to and walking my/your word is honouring and respecting, standing up to my/yourself. Be coherent; mean and speak your idea, intention, opinion then act on it and walk it.

A word is a belief energy that create e-motions and reality.
Declaration is an arrow to destination; A destiny creator.

3. Acknowledge and walk the truth: that at each and every moment you are doing the best; that in the doing new ideas can come up and that acting on these new ideas and following a new idea is a way to do better, excel and succeed.

4. Maintain a non-participant observatory approach and attitude remembering to never take things personally. Words express and reflect their speaker's perception.

See: Wisdom, pp. 250

Turn: a movement of partial or total rotation: a slight turn of the handle. Act of changing or reversing position or posture as by rotary movement: a turn of the head. A time or opportunity for action that comes in due rotation or order: It's my turn to do this. Act of changing or reversing the course or direction: to make a turn to the right. Direction, drift, or trend. Any change, as in nature, circumstances, etc.

Twist; **U**nity; **R**ange; **N**ow ness

U

Ugly: mean, hostile or quarrelsome.

Usher; Gladness; glamour; Love; Yes

E.S.T. Practice - see: Beauty, pp. 21

E.S.T. Exercise - see: pp. 180

Key-phrases/words: *Preliminary rounds*: angry; annoyed, miserable, sulking, swollen, unattractive, unpleasant… *Positive affirmations rounds*: beautiful, calm, enthusiastic, empowered, peaceful, radiant, tranquil, vibrant…

Under: below, beneath and covered by.

Up I move; New; Delight; Exuberance; Rise

Up: an upward movement; ascent. A rise of fortune, mood, etc. an upward course or rise. On the up and up, informal: frank, honest, sincere.

Uniqueness; Party
Unity, Peace

V

Vacancy: emptiness. A gap; opening; breach. Lack of thought or intelligence; vacuity. Obs. Leisure or unoccupied time.

Vitality; **A**dvancement; **C**asualness;
Adventure; **N**est; **C**uriosity; **Y**outh

Value: attributed or relative worth, merit, or usefulness.

Virtue; **A**wareness; **L**ove; **U**niformity; **E**xpression

Veil: a piece of opaque or transparent material worn over the face. Something that covers, separates, screens, or conceals.

Validation; **E**ntity; **I**ntegrity; **L**esson

E.S.T. Exercise - see: pp. 180

Key-phrases/words: *Preliminary rounds*: afraid, deceived, false, hypocrite, keeping up appearances, mask, unsure… *Positive affirmations rounds*: authentic, calm, confident, frank, honest; self-assured, sincere; solemn, it is safe to be authentic, I am protected when I am genuine me, I am success…

Vibration: An emanation that is sensed by or revealed to those attuned to the occult. *Physics*: **a**. the oscillating, reciprocating, or other periodic motion of a rigid or elastic body or medium forced from a position or state of equilibrium. **b**. the analogous motion of the particles of a mass of air or the like, whose state of equilibrium has been disturbed, as in transmitting sound.

Virtue; **I**ntegrity; **B**rilliance;
Resort; **A**ttendance; **T**rust;
Inspiration; **O**pportunity; **N**ative

Vict-I'm - Victim: a person who suffers from a destructive or injurious action or agency.

Vice; **I**mmaturity; **C**redence; **T**ime; **I**ntelligence; **M**astery
Vict-OR; **I**rrevocable; **C**redibility; **T**ruth; **I**nnocence; **M**iracle

> E.S.T. Exercise - see: pp. 180
> Letting Go fun exercise - see: pp. 105

Vigour/Vigor: active force or strength. Healthy physical or mental energy or power; vitality. Healthy growth in any living matter or organism, as a plant. Effective force, esp. as having legal validity.

Validity; **I**ntuition; **G**reatness; **O**ngoing; **U**niqueness; **R**evelation

Villain: a cruelly malicious person; scoundrel.

Vision; **I**nfluence; **L**esson; **L**ove; **A**ttitude; **I**ntention; **N**ow

Violence: rough or injurious action, or treatment. Rough or immoderate vehemence, as of feeling or language. Injury, as from distortion of meaning. A swift and intense force. An unjust or unwarranted exertion of force or power.

Vanity; **I**njury; **O**utlet; **L**ife; **E**ssence;
Necessity; **C**o-existence; **E**nthusiasm
Vengeance; **I**nsult; **O**ut you go; **L**ove;
Existence; **N**ew; **C**reation; **E**volution

> E.S.T. Exercise - see: pp. 180
> Letting Go fun exercise - see: pp. 105

We are not born violent, nor is violence a character, genetics, 2nd nature. Violence is a pattern implanted, well programmed and deeply rooted in human history and tradition. An act of violence comes from a sense of danger, fear, threat; following and walking a way of a model figure child me/you considers and takes as example, perceives as an authority - knowing no better; living up to a word's true meaning = truth. Among it's expressions are actions such as: a forceful, harsh or strength-full hold, a 'gentle' bite, or blow, an enraged look, a murderous look, a roaming silence, a supposedly caring dab, nip, pat, pinch, slap, touch, and phrases such as: brat, Satan, you little criminal/devil/rascal; "When will you do/learn?" "You are good for nothing you know that?" and more. **Violence causes brain and nervous system damage**, resulting in deformations, disorders, amongst is A.D.D., A.D.H.D., anorexia, bulimia, compulsive and/or obsessive manners, hyper-action, hyper-tension, insomnia, retardation and more.

> Life and living can be colourful, joyful, just and respectful when I let violence go; embrace, let in and welcome honour, love and respect

> Between a firm idea and respectable approach, attitude or manner are 64 scales and shades of blue, green, orange, pink, purple, red, and yellow

    My neighbour used to share her sorrows with me; among her sorrows was one from her early twenties, when she took her young family (a sick husband and two sick infant sons) out from a community that demanded she commit them to mental institutions, throughout Israel.
    Thanks to her commitment and love her husband lived to 80, her eldest son lived to become a grandfather, and died at 56.
    More sorrows she lived were having her eldest grandson live in a mental institution. Knowing her eldest granddaughter is being financially supported by the welfare authority since her twin-daughters were born; finding out this granddaughter raises a family with a man who goes in and out of jail.
    In retrospective sick them brought and raised sick offspring's, who in their turn brought to our world and raise sick children.
    After my neighbour died, one of her friends, who saw she used to come to me for an advice to help him out, started coming over.
    What they had in common were children suffering sorrowful and violence deformations = dis-ease = disorder. In one of our meetings he brought a medical report he received from his son's last commitment to a mental ward, following a

paranoia and schizophrenia diagnosis made in his son's early twenties.

With this in mind, when one Friday his son knocked on the door of my flat, I asked him if he wants to heal and is willing to heal. He said he is and does. We tapped on fear, scare and terror until his body language revealed dis-comfort. A couple of days later the father called me and told me that over the weekend he saw that his son's frequent going to get a drink of water and to the toilet decreased. In one of our later meetings I brought that experience up and told him what I did with his son. The two of them came over and the father joined his son's tapping. A year after I moved to Nahariya, the father told me that his change of ways with his son to more accepting, loving, and respectful ones allowed and enabled his son to make a seven years progress.

See: Child, pp. 42
Foul play, pp. 88
Growth, pp. 95
Heartache, pp. 103
Rejection, pp. 186
Wisdom, pp. 250

Vocation:
particular occupation, business, or profession; calling. A strong impulse or inclination to follow a particular activity or career. A function or station in life to which a person is called by Holy Spirit.

Vividness; **O**pportunity; **C**reativity; **A**dventure; **T**ruth; **I**nnermost; **O**mnipresence, **o**mnipotence; **N**ature; **n**urture

W

War: any conflict or competition suggesting active hostility. A battle. To be in conflict or in a state of strong opposition.

Ward; **A**ggression, **a**nguish; **R**ejection
Waste; **A**ffliction, **a**larm; **R**emorse, **r**eproach
Wrong; **A**buse, **a**gitation; **R**esentment, **r**evenge
Wilderness; **A**nger; **R**esistance

A mother made a placard with the home and house rules and hanged it on the refrigerator door. This placard did not contain the answer to the question "When can I eat sweets?" I called up the mother and heard: "My mother told me I can eat sweets after lunch. Tell her that she can eat sweets after lunch". In the first lunch the question came up after the 7 years old ate her lunch; on the second lunch she played with the food in her plate, said she does not feel like eating her lunch and asked if she can now eat her sweets; on the third lunch I heard "Can I have my sweets now?" as she sat down for lunch.

Such a rule became a war declaration between two seemingly interested parties. The daughter who is doing all that it takes to get her way = win, and the mother who - in this particular case ended walking her ancestors' way "The fathers have eaten sour grapes, and children's teeth are set on edge," (Ezekiel 18:2).

The rule for sweets eating is: sweets eating is an independent meal - for sweets - as all other foods - contain nutrients. It is an equal to a food with high sugar level, such as fruit, and thus should be considered as a light meal rather than a prize to win.

War?

In the raW?

In the raw: in the natural or unrefined state; nature in the raw. *Slang.* In the nude; naked.

Rampage **A**ffluence; **W**isdom

Remedy; **A**ffection; **W**ide, **W**ild, **W**orld
Revelation; **A**wareness; **W**hole hearted peace

How do I change war to raw?
I embrace, let in and welcome love and peace, approach, attitude, spirit, way and wind.

> Love and peace is my default state of being and mind

Waste: useless consumption or expenditure. Neglect, instead of use: waste of opportunities. Gradual destruction, impairment, or decay. Devastation or ruin, as from war, fire, etc. anything unused, unproductive, or not properly utilized.

Win-**w**in; **A**rt;
State of being and mind; **T**aste; **E**xcellence

> E.S.T. Exercise - see: pp. 180

Water: a transparent, odorless liquid, a compound of hydrogen and oxygen, H_2O, freezing at 32°F or 0°C and boiling at 212°F or 100°C, which in a more or less impure state constitutes rain, oceans, lakes, rivers, etc.

Way; **A**bundance; **T**ribute; **E**xpertise; **R**elief

Way: manner, mode, or fashion. Characteristic or habitual manner. A method, plan, or means for attaining a goal. A direction. A vicinity. Passage or progress to a definite goal. Distance. A path or course to a place. A means of passage or movement. Course or mode of procedure that one chooses or wills. The method or manner of acting that one advocates: we'll do it your way. A person's intended path or course of action.

Whole hearted **w**ave; **A**ssembly; **Y**ield

Wealth
: a plentiful amount. All goods that have a monetary or exchange value. Anything that has utility and is capable of being appropriated or exchanged. A great quantity or store of money or property of value. Rich or valuable contents or produce. The state of being rich; prosperity; affluence. Happiness.

Whole hearted **W**ill-power;
Exuberance; **A**spect; **L**ine; **T**ouch;
Hear no evil, see no evil, speak no evil

> See: Fake, pp. 84
> Foul play, pp. 88
> Law, pp. 136
> Loyalty, pp. 145
> Poverty, pp. 170
> PIGEES, pp. 170
> Wisdom, pp. 250

Weapon
: any instrument or device for attack or defense in a dispute or fight. Anything used against an adversary, opponent, or vict-I'm.

Wound, **E**ruption; **A**buse; **P**oison; **O**ut; **N**ext **n**est **n**ow peace

> See: Curse, pp. 60
> Power, pp. 171
> Tongue, pp. 233
> Violence, pp. 241
> War, pp. 244
> Wisdom, pp. 250

> Mind your word it is a destiny,
> energy-motion, faith, fate
> and reality creator

> A word creates heaven or hell,
> Makes a heart sing or sob,
> break, bleed, freeze or paralyze to death

The Four Agreements[6]

1. Never assume, opine, postulate, suppose or take for granted. When in doubt, clear, inquire, investigate, verify. When

unsure, ask, clarify, make clear and make sure. Assumptions, inferences and suppositions create fictitious films or scenarios.

2. Be true to your word, honour it, respect it, stand up to it and walk it.

One's words are state of being and state of mind reflection and perception.

Be truthful, sincere, honest, genuine, and authentic.

Honouring, respecting, standing up to and walking my/your word is honouring and respecting, standing up to my/yourself. Be coherent; mean and speak your idea, intention, opinion then act on it and walk it.

A word is a belief energy that create e-motions and reality.
Declaration is an arrow to destination; A destiny creator.

3. Acknowledge and walk the truth: that at each and every moment you are doing the best; that in the doing new ideas can come up and that acting on these new ideas and following a new idea is a way to do better, excel and succeed.

4. Maintain a non-participant observatory approach and attitude remembering to never take things personally. Words express and reflect their speaker's perception.

Weep: weeping, or a fit of weeping, exudation of water or liquid.

Wild; **E**ntity; **E**xpansion; **P**resence

E.S.T. Exercise - see: pp. 180
Letting Go fun exercise - see: pp. 105

Well: well-being, good, fortune, success. A hole drilled or bored into earth, as to obtain water, petroleum, natural gas, brine, or sulfur. A spring or natural source of water.

Wisdom; **E**ase; **L**ife; **L**ove

Whip: an instrument for striking, as in driving animals or in punishing, typically consisting of a long flexible lash with a rigid handle. A whipping or lashing stroke or motion.

Wonder; **H**eart; **I**ntuition; **P**rosperity

Whip-lash: the lash of a whip. Also called whip-lash injury, a neck injury caused by a sudden jerking backward and forward of the head as during an automobile accident.

Window; **H**eart; **I**ntuition; **P**rospect
Let; **A**spiration; **S**implicity; **H**eaven

E.S.T. Exercise - see: pp. 180

Key-phrases/words: *Preliminary rounds*: arrogant, hard-headed, immodest, presumptuous, stubborn, stuck... *Positive affirmations rounds*: authentic, flowing, humble, modest, safe...

Letting Go fun exercise - see: pp. 105

Whole
: all the amount or every part of something. A thing complete in itself, or comprising all its parts or elements. An assemblage of parts associated or viewed together as one thing; a unitary system.

World; **H**eaven on earth; **O**pportunity; **L**eisure; **E**steem

Wife
: a woman joined in marriage to a man.

Woman; **I**nnocence; **F**low; **E**ase
Well-being; **I**ntuition; **F**reedom; **E**xuberance
Wellness; **I**nnovation; **F**ree-will; **E**ntity
Wild; **I**ntegrity; **F**ruit; **E**xpansion
Wisdom; **I**sland; **F**oundation; **E**ssence
Wing; **I**ntelligence; **F**aith; **E**nergy
World; **I**nnermost; **F**rankness, **f**estivity;
Enthusiasm, **e**nergy-motion

Wild
: uncultivated, uninhibited. Wilderness.

Wholeness; **I**ntegrity; **L**ove; **D**ivinity

E.S.T. exercise
1. Find a place and a time where you feel at ease, protected and

safe to freely express, honour and let wild you be and live.
2. Begin to cry, dance, hit, jerk, jump, kick, run, scream, shake, shout, sing, yell, wiggle as fancy's your heart, pleases your soul and pleasures your spirit.
3. Invite observers and watchers, passing by or stopping in awe, amazement, embarrassment, or puzzlement to come join you, celebrate wild you, surpassing embarrassment, fear of criticism or shame.

Will: the faculty of conscious and particularly of deliberate action; the power of control the mind has over its own actions: the freedom of will. Power of choosing one's own actions: to have a strong will. The act or process of using or asserting one's choice; volition: My hands are obedient to my will. Wish or desire. Purpose or determination, often hearty or stubborn determination; wilfulness. Disposition, whether good or ill, toward another.

Wonder; Integrity; Life; Legitimacy

Will and Have
Will, want, need, must, have to, desire, are expressions and states of being and states of mind of lack, not having, not being. Their practice came to me from hearing others use them, not knowing The Law of Attraction (See pp. 137); what they bring my way, create, truly reflect and stand for. Freedom of choice at each instant and every moment and step of the way is a right given to me at birth. Forgetting it is no excuse for being miserable, a vict-I'm, feeling sorry for oneself, having worried filled, self absorbed and self-centred life. To come out of negativity modus automatus, to disconnect from being reactive, requires ability, choice-making, decision-taking, Hutz-pah (dare/nerve), practice and time-taking to be authentic, loyal and true to my choice, decision; fully responsible for my actions, each thing and everything that happens in my life and with me, for myself and wellbeing.
I dare you by all means to want and have the will power, so that you can have the life you desire. I encourage you to come out of reacting and recycling lack and negativity so that you can create, demonstrate and manifest your ideas, thoughts and words, the life you truly can have and deserve.
How do I do it?
I do it by making a choice, taking a decision and time to let go of accuse, blame, fault finding, giving my power to the other, doing to the other what I hate done to me, guilt full me, holding the other for

being responsible, playing poor poor me. Please stop to ask, consider, mind and weigh each word that comes to mind and then out of the mouth; and then **replace**:

* **I want** to have a better / good / respectful relationship with my bank account, boss, child, credit card, significant other, etc. **with** I choose to have...
* **I need** more bread... **with** please give me more/some...
* **I must** go on / go to **with** I love being on time or going on... is easy and fun... gives me plenty of opportunities to find out that the universe loves me more than I love myself.
* **I have to** deposit money... **with** I have money to deposit.
* **I desire**... **with** I am deserving of, I can do it, I choose to have, I have what it takes, I love having..., I love it/that/this.

Bear in mind that all is energy, we are all energy. Beliefs are only believed to materialize into physical existence. They are not materials, nor are they physical beings, real. A desire to get, have to, need to, want to, will to will get you what you have always gotten. Your subconscious is a closed prison, full with words creating e-motions (energy motions), demonstrating events and manifesting situations and things. It works like a computer. Like a computer it has and knows only what was burnt and what was programmed. The subconscious require a confirmation/order to delete; erase a belief, have a new habit/programme.

Remember
Things are only thoughts.
Words make a difference.
Your subconscious and the universe take them at face-value - literally. Each thing and everything starts with a belief, and whatever you believe, feel, radiate, reflect and put out comes back to you.

E.S.T. Exercise - see: pp. 180
Letting Go fun exercise - see: pp. 105

Wind: air in natural motion, as along the earth's surfaces. A gale; storm; hurricane. Any stream of air, as that produced by a bellows, fan, etc.

Wave; **I**ndustry; **N**est; **D**ivinity

Wisdom: the quality or state of being wise; knowledge of what is true or right coupled with good judgment. Scholarly knowledge or learning. Wise sayings or teaching.

World; **I**ntuition; **S**ynchrony; **D**elight; **O**verture; **M**omentum

When proof reading The Challenge I heard GIVE TO RECEIVE. I turned my head and saw an Arab Christian come my way. After a complimentary and introductory talk he told me these two hi-stories and a couple more, from his life.

♦ When my daughter decided to marry we met with the future groom's family and the two families agreed to unite the young couple in marriage. A couple of weeks later the future groom's parents called me and I heard that he is too young to get married. After I heard from the young couple that they are adamant to unite in marriage, I told the young man's parents that the wedding shall take place, the young couple shall live in my home, I shall pay for all involved and that they are invited to the engagement and wedding celebrations and ceremonies. I walked my word.

If you wonder what since happened with the parents of my son in law; many many years after the wedding they started coming over to his home with my daughter to visit him and my daughter.

♦ When one of my sons decided to marry the year he finished high school I gave my home to him and moved out from my home and village to live in a rented place on a Kibbutz. Sometime after I moved to the Kibbutz, my income doubled. Three years after my move to the kibbutz I saw that my son had started to build a new home on our land. When he finished building this home my wife and I moved in and to this date we all continue to live together on the family land. I am very proud of my children's ways, and am grateful that my giving, honour and respect to my children has been returned today through their giving, honour and respect to me.

Wish: a distinct mental inclination toward the doing, obtaining, attaining, etc., of something; a desire felt or expressed: to disregard the wishes of others. An expression of a wish, often one of a kindly or courteous nature: to send one's best wishes. That which is wished: he got his wish, a new car.

Wing; **I**nnovation; **S**eed; **H**armony

Woe: grievous distress, affliction, or trouble. An affliction: she suffered a fall, among her other woes. An exclamation of grief, distress, or lamentation.

Wild; **O**ne; **E**xpression

E.S.T. Exercise - see: pp. 180
Letting Go fun exercise - see: pp. 105

Word: a unit or ward, consisting of one or more graphic representations or their spoken sounds, which functions as a principle carrier of spirit. A belief energy (vibration), MANIFESTING in graphic shape that is perceived as 'fact', 'self evidence', 'reality' or 'physical shape'.

Way; **O**asis **o**rder; **R**eflection; **D**emonstration

Change a word to change your world

See: Heartache, pp. 103
Power, pp. 171
Tongue, pp. 233
War, pp. 244
Weapon, pp. 246

My/your reality is created by energy forms = power waves = words that come out and come up from inspiration, inner-self, and conscious mind. To change an energy form 'reality' - weigh, sense, reflect, mind, consider, check, change a word then honour it, respect it and walk it. To change reality you are welcome to practice E.S.T. (see: pp. 180) and Ho'oponopono.

Ho'oponopono[13]

I am sorry	(Recognition)
Please forgive me	(Data erasing)
I love you	(Connection to Holy Spirit)
Thank you	(Gratitude)

Reciting the above phrases one after the other, in any order, cleans/erases the data that created the energy form 'reality' you now wish to transform and allows new data to come up. Reciting before sleep allows the process to go on during sleep time. Being emotional/passionate when reciting these phrases makes the transformation more effective.

Work: exertion or effort directed to produce or accomplish something; labour; toil. Employment, as in some form of industry, esp. as a means of earning one's livelihood: to look for work. Materials, things, etc., on which one is working or is to work. The result of exertion, labour, or activity; a deed or performance.

Ward; **O**ppression; **R**esistance; **K**ite
Worthiness; **O**rder; **R**evival; **K**aleidoscope

E.S.T. Exercise - see: pp. 180

Worry: disturbing thought; uneasiness, anxiety, a worried condition, feeling, state of mind. A cause of uneasiness, anxiety; torment with annoyance, anxiety, trouble, etc.

Waste; **O**f; **R**elaxation; **R**esource; **Y**awn;
Wrong; **O**ut; **R**ejuvenation; **R**emedy; **Y**es
Water; **O**pportunity; **R**evival; **Y**outh

E.S.T. Exercise - see: pp. 180

Key-phrases/words: *Preliminary rounds*: annoyed; all this worry; anxious; all this anxiety; constricted breathing; uneasy; all this uneasiness; discomfort, dis-ease, fear, panic, terror, worried...
Positive affirmations rounds: I now choose to feel calm, comfortable, confident, I allow myself to be calm, easy going, to feel comfortable, confident and content, to take it easy, relax, I give myself permission to breath freely and whole heartedly, to feel whole hearted peace, to act on inspiration, to have a clear mind, lucid perception, I know that deep inside me I can find whole hearted peace, I know that when I act on inspiration I am protected,
safe, and supported; I am protected, safe and supported when I enjoy, exhibit, radiate and project amazing, brilliant, excellence, genuine, genius, great, skilled, talented and wonderful me, I am able and can calm down, take it easy and relax...

Letting Go fun exercise - see: pp. 105

Wound: an injury to an organism, usually one involving division of tissue or rupture of the integument or mucous membrane, due to external violence or some mechanical agency rather than disease. An injury or hurt to feelings, sensibilities, reputation, etc.

Word; **O**ption; **U**niverse; **N**eatness; **D**evelopment

E.S.T. Exercise - see: pp. 180

Wrath: strong, stern, or fierce anger; deeply resentful indignation; ire. Vengeance or punishment motivated by anger.

Waterfall; **R**ay; **A**ffection; **T**reasure;
Hear no evil, see no evil, speak no evil

E.S.T. Exercise - see: pp. 180

Key-phrases/words: *Preliminary rounds*: angry, annoyed, eager, hurt, indignant, offended, resentful... *Positive affirmations rounds*: clear, cleanse, forgive, heal, love...

Wreck: a person's ruined health; someone in bad shape physically or mentally: the strain of his work left him a complete wreck. Any structure or object reduced to a state of ruin. Wreckage, goods, etc., remaining above water after a shipwreck, esp. when cast ashore. The ruin or destruction of a vessel in the course of navigation. The ruin or destruction of anything.

Wings to fly in a heaven on earth reality;
Respect; **E**ase; **C**omfort; **K**ite

E.S.T. Exercise - see: pp. 180

Wretch: a deplorably unfortunate or unhappy person. A person of despicable or base character.

Wonder; **R**emedy; **E**steem; **T**ouch; **C**aress; **H**eart

E.S.T. Exercise - see: pp. 180

Wrong: something that is unjust. Whatever would be incorrect or immoral to do, choose, or act upon.

Wisdom; **R**eference; **O**ption; **N**ewness; **G**rowth

E.S.T. Exercise - see: pp. 180
Letting Go fun exercise - see: pp. 105

X

Xerography: a copying process in which areas on a sheet of plain paper corresponding to those on the original that are to be reproduced are sensitized by static electricity and then sprinkled with coloured resin that adheres and is fused permanently to the paper.

Xylophone; **E**nergy; **R**eef; **O**rganization;
Gate; **R**emembrance; **A**ction; **P**arty; **H**ello; **Y**ield

X-ray: a form of electromagnetic radiation, similar to light but of shorter wavelength and capable of penetrating solids and of ionizing gases. A radiograph made by x-rays.

Xeroderma; **R**esemblance; **A**ffliction; **Y**ard

X-ray exhibits shadows. When X-ray is recommended, ask if Ultrasound is an option. Consider all factors including the variance in accuracy of both, then decide which of the two serves you best.

The one health empowered and empowering radiance I know is one's inner self beauty, brightness, brilliance, genuine integrity, love and peace glow.

Y

Yawn: an involuntary opening of the mouth with a prolonged, deep inhalation of air, as from drowsiness or weariness. An opening; open space, chasm.

Yes; **A**wareness; **W**ind of heaven; **N**ow

Yearning: deep longing, esp. when accompanied by tenderness or sadness.

Yarn; **E**valuation; **A**ffection; **R**ing;
New; **I**nterest; **N**avigation; **G**ladness

Yell: a cry uttered by yelling.

Yield; **E**xperience; **L**ife; **L**ight

E.S.T. Exercise - see: pp. 180
Letting Go fun exercise - see: pp. 105

When I cry - I raise fear.
When I jaw - do I destroy?
When I shout - I raise anger, annoyance and fear.
When I tell - I raise rejection and resistance.
When I yell - I raise hell on earth.

Where as

When I say - I can be attended to.
When I speak - I can be heard.
When I talk - I can be listened to.

Yelp: a quick, sharp bark or cry.

Youth; **E**xcitement; **L**ove; **P**eace

Yes: an affirmative reply.

Youngness; **y**outhfulness
Essence; **e**steem, **e**nthusiasm; **e**xcellence, **e**xpression,
Safety; **s**anity; **s**erenity; **s**implicity, **s**incerity, **s**uccess

Yield: produce or give forth by a natural process or by cultivation. Rendering, as homage or thanks.

Yodeling; **I**ntuition; **E**nthusiasm; **L**ove; **D**elight

Young: an early or first stage of life or growth. Having the appearance, freshness, vigour, or other qualities of youth.

Youth; **O**ption; **U**nity; **N**ascence; **G**reatness

When I nurtured children, I heard and saw the young follow their raw-model figures in calling/describing/perceiving themselves as small. One of them corrected me when he heard me call him 'young'. He hung onto 'small', rejected and resisted by saying to me, "I am small" and sending an angry, perhaps an offended/offensive look my way. I asked him, "Do you know what the meaning of young is?" "No," he replied. "Do you know what small means?" "No." He did not know that either. We then discussed each, the differences, using examples from that child's universe. Our discussion ended with whole-hearted laughter as my question "Now you tell me, are you small or young?" was answered with the child's "I am young" saying.

Following this discussion I was a witness to the following: while walking into the kitchen his father called him "small…" He came to the kitchen and said, "I am not small, I am young." The father turned around, and lovingly - with an enlightened expression and a smile on his face - caressed his head while saying "True, you are young." The child's face lit up and his whole self radiated with sheer happiness.

The 2nd Agreement[(6)]

Be true to your word, honour it, respect it, stand up to it and walk it.

One's words are state of being and state of mind reflection and perception.

Be truthful, sincere, honest, genuine, and authentic.

Honouring, respecting, standing up to and walking my/your words is honouring and respecting, standing up to my/yourself. Be coherent; mean and speak your idea, intention, opinion then act on it and walk it.

A word is a belief energy that create e-motions and reality.
Declaration is an arrow to destination; A destiny creator.

You may want to find and take time to reconsider 'little one', 'small', 'young', ask yourself how do you do right by yourself and with your children calling/describing/perceiving yourself, them or others as "little one" or "small", remembering that a young has ambitions, experiences, history too; each and every person, at all times and in each age, is gifted with authenticity, grandeur and uniqueness; calling or describing a person "little one" or "small" is condescending self praise, belittling, degradation and humiliation. Did I truly intend to degrade? Did I truly mean to humiliate? Who is the true degraded or humiliated one? Me? What way do I choose and decide now to walk? The one I was walking till now - condescending self praise, belittling, degradation and humiliation? or a truthful one in which blessings and praising the others' virtues betters and upgrades all concerned and involved - me?

> See: Child, pp. 42
> Curse, pp. 60
> Fear, pp. 85
> Small, pp. 213

Youth: the vitality characteristics of the young. The time of being young; early life. The early or first period of anything.

Yet; **O**pportunity; **U**ttermost; **T**rust; **H**earing
no evil, knowing no evil, seeing no evil, speaking no evil, **h**ealth

Z

Zap: to kill or shoot. To attack, damage, or destroy. To bombard with x-rays, laser beams, etc. force, energy, or drive. A bolt or charge, as of electricity.

Zero; **A**ncient; **P**attern

> E.S.T. exercise - see Rage, pp. 180
> Letting Go fun exercise - see: pp. 105

Zeal: fervour for a person, cause, or object; eager desire or endeavor; enthusiastic diligence.

Zest; **E**xistence; **A**ffluence; **L**ove

Zenith: the point on the celestial sphere vertically above a given position or observer. Highest point or state; culmination.

Zany; **E**levator; **N**iche; **I**nsight; **T**hank you; **H**eart

Zephyr: a gentle, mild wind.

Zeal; **E**xpansion; **P**ersonality; **H**eaven; **Y**outh; **R**elief

Zero: the figure or symbol 0, which in the Arabic notation is a number that stands for the absence of quantity; cipher. The origin of any kind of measurement, positive or negative, on a scale. A mathematical value intermediate between positive and negative values. Naught; nothing. The lowest point or degree.

Zing; **E**ase; **R**elish; **O**ption

> Zero and one are values

The difference between values is not one but one hundred percents. In one hundred percents there are thousands of steps to reach the top, while enjoying the process, making best of the ride and the most in the various stations on the way from zero to one heaven on earth. From one to zero there are thousand good will steps to crash on on the straight way to a sure hell. From zero there is no abyss to fall into.

Adopting, adjusting and aligning in line with zero one approach, attitude, mode, perception, position and status is a sure way to ego-free habits, letting go of dis-appointment and failure patterns, to open up to recognize and spot opportunities, then taking them one by one.

A hell free, safe, simple and straight way to abundant happiness, imperturbability and wealth stardom is made of 0 and 1 staircase.

Zest: keen relish; hearty enjoyment; gusto. An agreeable or piquant flavour imparted to something. Piquancy; interest; charm.

Zephyr; **E**njoyment; **S**uccess; **T**reat

Zigzag: a line, course, or progression characterized by sharp turns first to one side and then to the other.

Zoom; **I**ntegration; **G**ame; **Z**ing; **A**wareness; **G**ladness

Zing: vitality; animation. A sharp, singing or whining sound, as of a bullet passing through the air. To move or proceed with a sharp, singing or whining sound.

Zone; **I**ntuition; **N**ewness; **G**reatness

Zombie: the body of a dead person given the semblance of a life by a supernatural force. A person who is extremely unperceptive, unresponsive, and apathetic.

Zest; **O**ption; **M**irth; **B**alance; **I**nspiration; **E**quilibrium

E.S.T. exercise - see pp. 180
Letting Go fun exercise - see: pp. 105

Epilogue

I thank you for coming, joining, riding, surfing or travelling Health Way Creations, if for a brief and light moment.

Health Way Creations allows and challenges me/you, at all times and at every age and stage, time after time, to unravel and realize brilliance, dreams, excellence, genuine, genius, gifts, power of a letter and a word, greatness, love, passions, skills, talents through experiences rich with authenticity, bliss, creativity, enthusiasm, fun, happiness, honesty, joy, jubilation, laughter, simplicity, sincerity, use-full-ness and youth-full-ness a child knows, enjoying and rejoicing comfort, confidence, creativity, ease, faith, gratitude, history, intelligence, intuition, satisfaction, success and transformation of impossible to I'm-possible mature wisdom.

Enlightenments and ideas are blessed and welcomed. Please feel free to send and share them with me.

Zvia Frankfurt
Health Way Creations

To book lessons and for information please

Call: + 972 - 77 - 88 55 216 (land line)
+ 972 - 50 - 52 15 999 (cellular line)

Write to: info@zvia-est.com

Visit: www.zvia-est.com

E & O.E.

www.ingramcontent.com/pod-product-compliance
Lightning Source LLC
Chambersburg PA
CBHW062152080426
42734CB00010B/1661